# Respect and Loathing in American Democracy

# Chicago Studies in American Politics

A series edited by Susan Herbst, Lawrence R. Jacobs, Adam J. Berinsky, and Frances Lee; Benjamin I. Page, editor emeritus

ALSO IN THE SERIES:

*Countermobilization: Policy Feedback and Backlash in a Polarized Age*
by Eric M. Patashnik

*Race, Rights, and Rifles: The Origins of the NRA and Contemporary Gun Culture*
by Alexandra Filindra

*Accountability in State Legislatures*
by Steven Rogers

*Dynamic Democracy: Public Opinion, Elections, and Policymaking in the American States*
by Devin Caughey and Christopher Warshaw

*Persuasion in Parallel: How Information Changes Minds about Politics*
by Alexander Coppock

*Radical American Partisanship: Mapping Violent Hostility, Its Causes, and the Consequences for Democracy*
by Nathan P. Kalmoe and Lilliana Mason

*The Obligation Mosaic: Race and Social Norms in US Political Participation*
by Allison P. Anoll

*A Troubled Birth: The 1930s and American Public Opinion*
by Susan Herbst

*Power Shifts: Congress and Presidential Representation*
by John A. Dearborn

*Prisms of the People: Power and Organizing in Twenty-First-Century America*
by Hahrie Han, Elizabeth McKenna, and Michelle Oyakawa

*Democracy Declined: The Failed Politics of Consumer Financial Protection*
by Mallory E. SoRelle

*Race to the Bottom: How Racial Appeals Work in American Politics*
by LaFleur Stephens-Dougan

*Additional series titles follow index.*

# Respect and Loathing in American Democracy

## Polarization, Moralization, and the Undermining of Equality

JEFF SPINNER-HALEV AND
ELIZABETH THEISS-MORSE

The University of Chicago Press
Chicago and London

The University of Chicago Press, Chicago 60637
The University of Chicago Press, Ltd., London
© 2024 by The University of Chicago
Published 2024
Printed in the United States of America

33 32 31 30 29 28 27 26 25 24     1 2 3 4 5

ISBN-13: 978-0-226-83171-8 (cloth)
ISBN-13: 978-0-226-83173-2 (paper)
ISBN-13: 978-0-226-83172-5 (e-book)
DOI: https://doi.org/10.7208/chicago/9780226831725.001.0001

Library of Congress Cataloging-in-Publication Data

Names: Spinner-Halev, Jeff, author. | Theiss-Morse, Elizabeth, author.
Title: Respect and loathing in American democracy : polarization, moralization, and
    the undermining of equality / Jeff Spinner-Halev and Elizabeth Theiss-Morse.
Other titles: Polarization, moralization, and the undermining of equality |
    Chicago studies in American politics.
Description: Chicago : The University of Chicago Press, 2024. | Series: Chicago
    studies in American politics | Includes bibliographical references and index.
Identifiers: LCCN 2023037209 | ISBN 9780226831718 (cloth) | ISBN 9780226831732 (paperback) |
    ISBN 9780226831725 (ebook)
Subjects: LCSH: Respect—Political aspects. | Polarization (Social sciences) |
    Democracy—United States. | United States—Politics and government—21st century.
Classification: LCC E893 .S65 2024 | DDC 320.473—dc23/eng/20230823
LC record available at https://lccn.loc.gov/2023037209

♾ This paper meets the requirements of ANSI/NISO Z39.48-1992 (Permanence of Paper).

*We dedicate this book to Elyza Halev and Randy Morse,*
*for their love, support, and insistence that*
*we not spend every waking hour on this book.*

# Contents

# Preface

After the election of Donald Trump to the US presidency in 2016, there was a rush by many liberals to understand how such a thing could happen. As it happened, three books published in 2016 helped them to do just that: *Strangers in Their Own Land* (Hochschild 2016), *The Politics of Resentment* (Cramer 2016), and *Hillbilly Elegy* (Vance 2016) all looked at rural white people and tried to explain why they had turned away from the Democratic Party. These books were widely read and reviewed. Written by a sociologist, a political scientist, and an attorney, their central question was almost anthropological: Why did this strange group of people support the angry, populist politics promoted by some conservative politicians, including Donald Trump? What are these people like? What motivates them? And why do they resent others so much?

What struck us of the first two books mentioned above was the authorial stance that was repeated by many of their readers whom we knew: *we* liberals need to understand *them* because these others behave—and vote—in ways that are foreign to us. It felt to us like a quest that assumed that liberals are the rational ones, the ones who do not need explaining because our beliefs are relatively easy to understand and coherent. *We* do not need anthropologists to help translate our belief systems into something that others can understand, only these other people—these strange rural white people—need to be understood and explained.

Our book was born to challenge what we consider to be the anthropological assumption, that we liberals are the rational ones who do not need explaining. We do not claim that liberals and conservatives are equally rational or irrational. That we think that the tensions and contradictions within liberal citizens must be studied just like they are among conservative citizens does not mean we think that there are equivalences between the two groups in every way. Indeed, that a significant number of conservatives refuse to accept the 2020 presidential election results as fair or refuse to believe that there really was a COVID-19 pandemic is quite worrisome, with little equivalent from liberals. Our claim is not one of equivalency, but more modest: that while conservative citizens struggle with tensions and contradictions in their ideas, liberals do as well. This does not mean, however, that the struggles are similar in scope or dimension.

Our book began as an examination of whether American citizens respect each other, with an emphasis on what we call the liberal respect paradox. The exact moment that began the book was when one of us had lunch with a friend after the election, who declared: "I believe in equality and the importance of respecting my fellow citizens, but I cannot respect anyone who voted for Donald Trump." From that line, the liberal respect paradox that we study here was born. To believe in equality yet insist that 45 percent or so of your fellow Americans cannot be respected is a remarkable statement and, we thought, one worthy of study.

Of course, this was just one person who declared his inability to respect, and so we set out to study more liberals and their views about respect and equality. And it turns out that this person was far from the only one who could not respect Trump supporters and conservatives in general. Why was there this tension between respect and equality? How central is respect to equality? We decided to pursue these questions and then other related questions as well. While the liberal respect paradox is no longer as central to the book as we first conceived it to be, the ideas of equality, democracy, and respect are what motivate our book. We do not set out to study why people vote the way they do, nor do we focus on the politics of resentment. Rather, our focus is on the attitudes of citizens toward one another. The idea of respect is taken for granted by many democratic theorists, yet it is rarely explored in depth. Empirically, political scientists have studied toleration for quite some time, but few have studied respect.

Yet respect is central to democratic citizenship. As we began work on this book, we decided that we needed to take a broad view. This work is a collaboration between a political theorist and a political psychologist, and our interests lie in the way people think about respect and equality, and how they manage to work through the tensions in their beliefs. This book is about attitudes and ideas. To accomplish this, we needed to do more than talk to citizens, though this surely is important, and Arlie Hochschild and Katherine Cramer both do it incredibly well (indeed, our own attempts to speak to conservatives were met with suspicion and obstacles, so we are in awe of their ability to speak to so many conservative citizens). But our methodology is different from theirs (and J. D. Vance's). We did speak to many liberal and conservative citizens through a series of focus groups, but we also conducted three national surveys between 2018 and 2020. Focus groups and individual conversations can tell us a lot, and they provide a depth of thinking that a survey cannot convey. Yet focus groups can also lead us astray, and so our national surveys sometimes serve to validate our focus group findings, but sometimes they do the opposite (and sometimes our surveys move beyond the focus groups).

This book began as an examination of the attitudes of liberal citizens about respect and equality, but it evolved over time to include conservative citizens as well, as we realized that a comparative focus would allow us to further investigate the liberal respect paradox—and while this paradox plays an important role in the following pages, our book moves beyond this paradox. Our focus remains liberal citizens, but we often examine the views of conservative citizens as well. We also examine the attitudes of liberal citizens about respect and equality under the framework of what we call (following others) egalitarian political theory. The tensions we find in the ideas of liberal citizens have a parallel in normative arguments of egalitarian political theory that few theorists have faced. As we detail in the following pages, both liberals and conservatives struggle with respecting others, and both sets of citizens have tensions within their core beliefs. But the respect paradox is particularly liberal, since liberals believe in more robust versions of equality than do conservatives, and they are more likely to believe in the importance of respect.

This is in many ways a tragic book. In our focus groups we heard tales of lost friendships and families fractured over political views. We often heard, to our dismay, citizens unknowingly mischaracterizing the views of others. We heard people assume the worst of others, not the best. We heard anger, frustration, and dismissal. But we also heard understanding and sympathy. Some of our participants and some of our survey respondents do live up to democratic ideals. If democracy is going to remain strong in the United States, we need more of these citizens.

# PART I

# Respect: The Challenge of Democracy and Equality

# Democratic Equality and the Importance of Respect

I will now share with you my shallowness and my amorality, I can't get past it. . . . So I walk a lot in my neighborhood and to this day I know which houses had the Trump [signs] and I look at those people as I'm walking by and I am judging them. (Focus group participant, when asked if she respects Trump supporters after the 2016 election; NC Liberals 3, Woman 3)

Respect is in trouble. Many citizens in the United States know they should respect their fellow citizens. Some can give this respect, even when they heartily disagree with others. Most citizens, though, either struggle to respect opposing partisans or they simply find it impossible to do so. It is especially citizens who identify as liberal and typically vote Democratic who recognize that they ought to be respectful when it comes to opposing partisans but often find it hard, if not impossible, to grant respect. It is this struggle—what we call the liberal respect paradox—that motivates this book.

Respecting other citizens across political divisions is something many take for granted as important for democracy. Respect is central to democratic discussion and democratic equality. Democratic discussions are marked by speaking *and* listening; if we respect one another, we are more likely to listen to those with whom we disagree. We rarely listen carefully and considerately to those we do not respect, making it less likely that we will negotiate and compromise with them. Similarly, democratic equality means that we take the concerns of our fellow citizens seriously. We don't look down upon them with scorn or contempt. We accept their participation in the political process as legitimate. If we don't respect our fellow citizens, we are more likely to treat them with suspicion and to ascribe base motives to their actions than we would if we granted them respect. Even if we value compromise (Wolak 2020), we will view it with distrust, as almost a betrayal, if we do not respect our opponents. People with very different viewpoints must work together in democratic settings; a lack of respect makes that work much harder to accomplish.

That many believe in the importance of respect among citizens in liberal democracies is unsurprising since it is a basic part of civics classes. Citizens,

particularly those who believe in robust versions of equality, believe that respect is an important part of that equality and that listening respectfully to
others is simply part of what it means to be a democratic citizen. Perhaps
unsurprisingly, democratic theorists sing paeans about and widely accept the
importance of respect: "This fundamental idea of equal respect for all persons and of the equal worth or equal dignity of all human beings is widely
accepted" (Gosepath 2021). Democratic theorists assume respect as a cardinal
virtue, though they say little about the conditions that make respect possible
or the trade-offs between respect and other values. As Emily McTernan (2013,
95) says, "Equal respect among citizens . . . is an often-cited, but poorly defined egalitarian value."

While democratic theorists and most democratic citizens (as we show in
later chapters) assume the importance of respect, political scientists rarely
study the concept. There is, of course, a large empirical literature on political
tolerance, but as we explain below, toleration is not the same as respect. Moreover, political scientists don't often study how democratic citizens actually view
each other *as fellow citizens*, which is at the center of democratic respect. This
book defines democratic respect, studies it empirically, and then examines the
normative challenges that respect poses for egalitarian political theory.

Our book is a collaboration between a political theorist and a political
psychologist. Our goal is both to illuminate the theoretical idea of respect
commonly accepted among egalitarian theorists and to examine respect empirically. We break new ground on both fronts. Egalitarian theorists commonly accept the need for respect but rarely define it carefully or note the
challenges to the idea of respect. The main concern for theorists who discuss respect is that those with low status (related to such things as income,
race, and gender) will not receive the same respect as other citizens. These
arguments are not empirically grounded, nor is the domain of respect clearly
demarcated.[1]

Rather than focus on traditional markers of status, we place our examination of respect in the context of partisanship, which is clearly one of the
major cleavages of our day. We take what many theorists consider a democratic virtue, respect, and ask if citizens live up to this ideal in a polarized
environment. Notably, we do not look at respect by itself, but in tandem with
other values. It is easy to say that democratic citizenship demands respect,
but when we think of respect *and* justice or respect *and* solidarity, we can see
trade-offs that respect may ask of us. Maintaining respect may mean altering
how we view justice. The tensions we find among liberal citizens—those who
identify on the political left and usually with the Democratic Party—between
respect and justice are mirrored but rarely noticed in the egalitarian theory

literature. The normative goals of our book therefore include providing a better definition of respect than many theorists provide, while explaining how hard it is to grant respect and why this is the case. We also examine how respect and pluralism are intertwined and why the views of justice that many egalitarian theorists *and* many liberal citizens have restrict pluralism. By pluralism, we mean an acceptance that there are multiple worthwhile values that people will have and prioritize differently. We note, too, the challenges that conservative citizens have with respect, though their belief in respect is not as strong as it is for liberal citizens.

We take our cue in our combined normative and empirical analysis from one of the most important proponents of a respect-based democratic egalitarian theory, Elizabeth Anderson (2012, 55), who argues that "political philosophers need to become sociologically more sophisticated. Because the object of egalitarian concern consists of systems of social relations, we need to understand how these systems work to have any hope of arriving at normatively adequate ideas" (see also Lippert-Rasmussen 2018, 156). While we are not sociologists, we think that the normative idea of respect needs to have empirical grounding, whether in sociology or political science.

Throughout this book we draw parallels between the ideas of political theorists and ordinary citizens when possible. While it is common to think of academic theorizing as a stand-alone activity, here we show the connections between liberal citizens and egalitarian theorists, and between conservative citizens and conservative theorists. We find the connections on the liberal/egalitarian side more robust than on the conservative side. The larger gap between conservative citizens and theorists is one of the reasons why our arguments about liberals and their views of justice and respect are more far-reaching than our arguments about conservatives. Another reason is that the tensions within the ideas of contemporary liberalism are more intriguing. Conservatives are less committed to respect, justice, and equality, and so the tensions we find among egalitarians are not present among conservatives. Comparing liberals and conservative citizens throughout the book reveals important challenges for respect, even as our results show a more challenging dilemma for liberal citizens and egalitarian theorists than for conservatives. Indeed, while contemporary American conservatism has many and sometimes very worrisome challenges, few of them are the focus of our book.

Our book is the first major empirical examination of respect by political scientists. We study respect through a series of twenty-seven focus groups of college-educated liberal and conservative citizens, three surveys, and two experiments. (We explain in appendix A our focus on the college educated, and we explain below why we use liberals and Democrats interchangeably, and the same for conservatives and Republicans.) Our book is unusual as it weaves empirical arguments about respect with a conceptual analysis of the idea of respect and a normative analysis of egalitarian and democratic theory.

There are additional empirical innovations in our book beyond studying respect. Some scholars study political values like equality and egalitarianism, but not in the comprehensive way we approach them. We frame key liberal and conservative values as *worldviews* that affect how people respond to and interact with those with whom they disagree, which leads to another innovation. Our book has a large focus on how citizens perceive one another, particularly those with whom there is disagreement. The affective polarization literature examines how much people dislike opposing partisans and how people want to avoid opposing partisans (see, e.g., Iyengar and Westwood 2015; Iyengar et al. 2019), but this literature does not focus on people's perceptions of what motivates the other side, like we do here. Similarly, few scholars examine how people judge others based on their vote choice. People vote for many different reasons, yet we find here that partisans simplify the reasons for their opponents' vote and then moralize that vote choice: to vote for the wrong side is to vote for something that is bad and perhaps worse than bad.

Part of our book studies structural injustice and social justice, which we do in a novel way. Researchers have extensively studied procedural justice, distributive justice, and retributive justice, but there is little empirical work connecting social justice to the idea of equality and respect. Of course, there is considerable scholarly work on people's racial attitudes, but unlike others, we focus on attitudes about racial justice and people's understandings of historical progress as it relates to race and views of justice. These topics have been the focus of many journalistic discussions, but few scholarly works look at these issues empirically and from the view of normative political theory and link them to worldviews as we do here. Finally, scholars have studied critical and constructive patriotism versus uncritical and blind patriotism, which shows that conservatives tend to oppose criticism of their country (Huddy and Khatib 2007; Schatz, Staub, and Lavine 1999). Here, though, we connect these ideas to how conservatives evaluate or judge liberals.

Our book breaks new ground in many ways, but it is not a happy book. We heard sad stories from many of our focus group participants, like these two:

> Yeah, I think the emotion piece is very big with me because I've had many conservative friends, very close friends that go back to my birth that have meant so much to me throughout my life. Granted, we're not in community with them, most of them are back in Western New York where I grew up. But I was in community with them of a social media type of fashion and occasional

trips. Something changed when they voted for Trump. I mean because I did respect them before that, I didn't agree with them, and something happened when they all out, full out supported Trump. And even one, the most thoughtful of all of them, said to me the day before she was going to vote "This is such a hard decision" and I tried to point out a few things, and "well, [name], it's just hard." So, the difference for me was, if you asked if I respect them, I'd have to say "not now" because I look at my actions was that I just cut them off, after—I'm sixty-six years old—after all those years, that was too much. I could not. (Chicago Liberals 2, Woman 3)

Outside, at one of the tables sitting in a chair is my bride who got into a conversation with her sister about a year ago, and her sister during the course of conversation, and by the way, she's a retired professor from some university, her sister, and she just said "If you could vote for him, you're a hater." And I believe, and the last year, I don't think they've spoken twice, and they used to speak weekly. I mean, it's that bad, it's terrible. (NC Conservatives 2, Man 3)

There was also considerable vitriol from many of our focus group participants, with little understanding of or empathy toward opposing partisans.

The only thing I can come up with about people voting for Hillary Clinton is they have absolutely no understanding of what's happened in this world. The woman has been a liar, a thief. She has done more damage to the political parties in this country than anyone, you know, Donald Trump, I didn't particularly like him, still don't particularly like him, but one thing he can say, he stands up front and says "This is what I'm going to do" and that's what he tries to do. And, but Hillary, she left people to die in Benghazi, she defended Bill while she's standing there on the other side going "Me Too, Me Too," you know, how much lying do you need? And if you're gonna vote for that, either you don't listen, you don't watch the news, you don't believe any of it, or you're an idiot. So I go with the idiot most of the time. (NC Conservatives 2, Man 4)

I don't know what I'd do, because I'm a dick. Because I want to be that person that's like, "great, we have different, let's hear about, let's hear what you have to say and maybe we can come to a," No, I hung up on my great-aunt after she said to me it's a ban against terrorists, not a ban against Muslims, because she, but for the grace of the United States, came to this country during the Second World War, her own first cousin, my grandmother was turned away in the United States and she was like "No, no, it's, it's a ban against terrorists." And I was like "Yeah, I have to hang up the phone now because, go fuck yourself, because 'never again' apparently only applies to Jews." (Chicago Liberals 5, Woman 1)

To think that half of your fellow citizens are idiots or mentally disabled is astounding and depressing to hear—particularly because thoughtful people made these comments. On a less personal level, our book shows how hard it is for opposing partisans to respect one another. Democratic respect is very hard to grant, at least in these polarized times; empathy and understanding are in short supply, and belief in a reasonable pluralism is truncated.

Of course, some citizens do respect one another and understand opposing partisans, and some of our focus group participants said as much.

> I think it's important to respect everybody, but also to understand, to try and find out, to listen to them and see where they're coming from and what their issues are. Because until we understand where they're coming from we're not going to meet any middle ground. (NC Liberals 7, Woman)

> Yeah, I mean I think it's a few different things, you know, I think she was qualified, you know, being a senator, you know also she was in the unique position of being the First Lady and you know, being in the White House before even though it's not in necessarily—it's kind of a different role than like a staffer or something like that. (NC Conservatives 4, Man 1)

Yet these moments of understanding and empathy in our focus groups were less frequent than the comments of anger and accusation and derision (which was mirrored in our surveys). We also heard many comments reflecting a deep struggle to grant respect to their fellow citizens, people caught between their higher ideals and their political fears.

It is this struggle that is at the heart of the liberal respect paradox: liberal citizens believe firmly in their view of justice *and* that it is important to respect all citizens. While one might think that respect and justice need not stand in tension with each other, many liberal citizens have a hard time respecting opposing partisans. They think that opposing partisans are ignorant, misinformed, racist, or sexist. Acceptance of opposing views as reasonable is something that escapes many liberal (and conservative) citizens. We argue that the view of justice of many liberal citizens (and egalitarian theorists) leads to a belief that those who disagree are either ignorant or advocates of injustice. This belief makes respect hard to practice, leading to the paradox: liberal citizens believe in respecting others, but they disdain those with whom they have significant political disagreements. Moreover, as we show in chapter 6, both liberal and conservative citizens think everyone has a collective responsibility to implement their worldview—meaning that those who dissent are failing their responsibilities.

We explain our view of respect below, which we divide between recognition respect (Darwall 1977) and civic respect. *The liberal respect paradox focuses on recognition respect*, a respect that all humans are owed, and not civic respect, which is tied to an acceptance of a plurality of reasonable views, a refusal to think of one's political opponents as ignorant and misinformed, while not stereotyping one's political opponents.

In the rest of this introduction, we explain why respect should be studied empirically and we distinguish it from tolerance. We then situate our argument in the relevant normative political theory literature, conceptually define recognition and civic respect, and briefly explain their connection to pluralism. We end with a sketch of the rest of the book. We leave the description of the focus groups and surveys for chapter 2, where we begin our empirical analysis. Much (but not all) of the rest of this chapter is devoted to a conceptual defining of respect and situating respect within the normative political theory literature, which sets the stage for the empirical analysis of the next several chapters.

## Why Study Respect?

Why study respect? If respect is just another name for tolerance, or something close to it, there is little reason to study it separately. Tolerance, however, is conceptually distinct from respect, and both concepts have prominent places within political theory. In contrast, empirical political scientists have studied tolerance extensively but have rarely studied respect. We begin here by distinguishing tolerance from respect, and then we define respect more clearly.

Tolerance involves disliking, or even abhorring, an object or group but being willing "to put up with" it (Schirmer, Weidenstedt, and Reich 2012). When political scientists study *political* tolerance, it means more than just putting up with people one dislikes: "As typically defined by social scientists, political tolerance refers to a willingness to extend the rights of citizenship to all members of the polity—that is, to allow political freedoms to those who are politically different" (Gibson and Bingham 1982, 604). People are tolerant when they, at a bare minimum, allow even groups they heartily dislike to exercise their basic rights, including freedom of speech and assembly and due process rights (Sullivan, Piereson, and Marcus 1982). You may prefer not to live near them, but grudgingly agree that they deserve protected rights.

This definition of toleration mirrors that of many political theorists. Charles Taylor (1992, 22), for example, argues that it is important to "distinguish between tolerating and respecting differences. Toleration extends to the widest range of views, so long as they stop short of threats and other direct and discernible harms to individuals." Taylor argues that we tolerate amoral or immoral views, like racism or anti-Semitism. We put up with these views, but we do not view them as respectable. Similarly, John Horton (2011, 290) argues that "toleration is the willing putting up with the beliefs, actions or practices of others, by a person or group that disapproves of them, and who would otherwise be inclined to prohibit or suppress them, if they had the power to do so." An attitude of toleration is compatible with looking upon others with condescension, with an attitude of superiority.

Respect is a common enough and accepted idea in the liberal and egalitarian theory literature that hardly anyone argues against it.[2] It is hard for democratic citizens to feel equal if they are merely tolerated. Democratic equality is tied to respect. In a democracy all citizens should be seen as having equal moral worth by one another (Christiano 2008); this underpins the status of all citizens as equals. Elizabeth Anderson (2008, 264) argues that those vested in equality seek to establish "relations of equality—equal respect, power, and standing" (see also Gutmann and Thompson 1996; Mansbridge et al. 2012; Anderson 1999; Scheffler 2005). Jonathan Wolff (1998, 107) argues that respect is an essential part of democratic citizenship: "Let us define my 'respect-standing' as the degree of respect other people have for me. If I am treated with contempt this will lead me to believe that I have low respect-standing; if treated decently I will believe that my respect-standing is high. It is insulting to be treated as if one is of lower respect-standing than is due." Democracy is in part about the right of each citizen to participate in government and elections, and this right is based on democratic equality. More broadly, if democratic citizens do not recognize the fundamental equality and dignity of each other, then a key basis of democracy is in trouble, and one foundation of democracy becomes wobbly.

Democracy also works better when it is underpinned by respect rather than toleration because democratic citizens must work together in a variety of settings, often in a collaborative way. Elected officials obviously need to work together across partisan divisions to make good policy, but democratic citizens work together in many ways as well: on citizen committees to bring broadband access to rural communities, on creating and cleaning parks, on building houses with Habitat for Humanity, on cleaning up their neighborhoods, and in the workforce. If many citizens do not respect each other, all this work becomes much harder to do. Moreover, it is far easier to negotiate and compromise with people you respect rather than those you tolerate. Patrick Henry, a Republican member of the US House of Representatives, entered office as a conservative firebrand and rabble-rouser, and was frequently seen yelling on the House floor or on cable news shows. But over time, he decided to actually try to legislate, which meant he had to work with others: "What changed for me was once I slowed down enough to respect the process and to respect the people that I served with in the institution. . . . I was able to get more done when I slowed down and had respect for others"

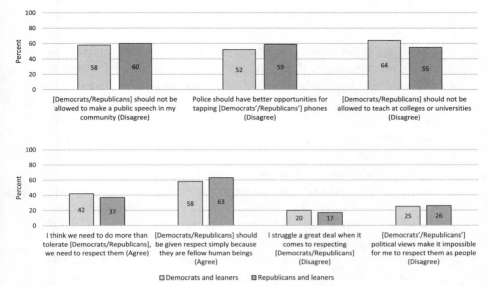

FIGURE 1.1. Tolerance and Respect by Party Identification. (a) Tolerance; (b) Respect.
*Source*: 2020 Social Justice and Solidarity Survey

(Edmondson 2023). Representative Henry's comment is similar to what Gutmann and Thompson (1996, 79) say about mutual respect: "It requires a favorable attitude toward, and constructive interaction with, the persons with whom one disagrees. It consists in an excellence of character that permits a democracy to flourish in the face of fundamental moral disagreement" (see also Parekh 2000, 1; Deveaux 1998; Ceva and Zuolo 2013; Ceva 2015). The idea that we should listen to each other illustrates another way in which respect is different from toleration.

We can also capture the difference between respect and toleration empirically. We asked in our 2020 Social Justice and Solidarity Survey questions about each. Figure 1.1 shows the percentage of Democrats and Republicans who gave tolerant or respect responses to the questions. Between 55 and 65 percent of respondents said opposing partisans should be allowed to make a public speech, teach in colleges and universities, and not have police tap their phones more easily. When we asked respondents if opposing partisans should be respected, not just tolerated, the percentages of respondents giving respect responses was generally much lower. While about 60 percent said opposing partisans should be respected simply because they are fellow human beings, less than half that many suggested it was possible to respect opposing partisans because of their views, and even fewer said they did not struggle when it came to respecting opposing partisans. We note that respondents did not respond in a way that suggests they found the question distinguishing between tolerance and respect nonsensical: about one-third said they neither agreed nor disagreed, which would be the go-to response if the distinction between tolerating and respecting made no sense to them. About 40 percent agreed that people should respect, not just tolerate, opposing partisans.

To practice respect is harder and more far-reaching than toleration. You can both tolerate and humiliate someone; but if you respect the person, you will not humiliate them. Tolerating someone may mean granting that person equal political rights in a narrow sense (equal right to assemble, to due process, to speech, and so on), but to respect someone means to affirm their equality in a positive way. Toleration is an acceptance, while respect is an affirmation. Toleration means I will refrain from trying to curtail your civil liberties, even though I may think they should be curtailed. Yet if I respect you, I accept you as a fellow human with moral agency and as my moral equal, whose claims on the state and other citizens should be treated with respect.

### Egalitarian Political Theory

When we discuss normative political theory in this book, we usually refer to what is commonly called egalitarian political theory (we note the exceptions as they arise). While equal rights or equality before the law may be part of equality, it is insufficient for many democratic theorists. The idea is that formal political and legal equality leaves considerable room for people to be treated unequally in ways that are unfair. We take what is commonly called liberal egalitarianism to be dominant within academic liberalism (Forrester 2019; Kymlicka 2002, 93), which places equality at the center of justice—indeed, justice and equality are often used interchangeably by liberal egalitarians. Though liberal egalitarianism is prominent within contemporary political theory, we place our argument within egalitarian theory, not just liberal egalitarian theory. We focus on what James Wilson (2019) (and others) calls *substantive egalitarianism*. Wilson explains the difference between what he calls merely basic egalitarianism and substantive egalitarianism: "Merely basic egalitarianism recognizes the equality of persons in some fundamental sense—for instance, their equal value or the equal status as holder of certain rights" (30). This egalitarianism is basic because it is compatible with different ways of satisfying basic norms of equality, "even if the result is substantial inequalities in people's life prospects, or in how people relate." Basic equality is intertwined with procedural equality—everyone's rights should be protected, the government should not discriminate against citizens, and legal rights are equal—but it allows for societies that are very unequal in economic, racial, or gender terms as long as people's procedural rights are not violated.

Substantive egalitarianism, by contrast, endorses a vision of equality that moves beyond equal rights or equality before the law. Wilson argues that it means people "conceive of themselves as equal in their social standing as well as in some fundamental moral sense." For many democratic theorists, equality is realized not only when the state recognizes citizens as equals, but when citizens recognize each other as equals. When people mutually recognize one another's equal status, they put themselves in an egalitarian relationship (Wilson 2019, 23). Respecting someone as equal involves expressing or manifesting respect through actions and maintaining a respectful disposition. We disrespect someone when we act in ways that express contempt or disregard (29).

We focus on egalitarian arguments that place respect *and* a sense of justice at their center—these are all substantive egalitarian arguments. Our main normative arguments about respect are twofold. First, nearly every respect theorist underestimates the difficulty of granting respect. It is easy to say that respect is important, but we will argue later in this book that challenges of granting respect should not be overlooked by theorists. Second, we argue that the more robust the idea of justice that is part of a theory of substantive egalitarianism is, the harder it will be to grant respect to those who disagree. In other words, respect theories often base their view of respect in a theory of substantive egalitarianism that makes it hard to respect those who disagree. If egalitarian theorists want to take respect seriously, they should say how their theories allow for respect, something we try to do in chapter 7 when we explain egalitarian pluralism.

Respect permeates egalitarian theory, but we focus on three schools of thought in this book. First, the idea that respect is a crucial part of liberal political theory is central to Rawlsian thinking (Rawls 1999, section 82; Stone 2022; McKinnon 2003; Arnold 2012; Zink 2011). Second, we examine the ideas of relational egalitarianism, where respect is twinned with democratic citizenship. The leading relational egalitarian, Elizabeth Anderson (1999, 289), writes: "In seeking the construction of a community of equals, democratic equality integrates principles of distribution with the expressive demands of equal respect" (see also Fourie 2012; Fourie, Schuppert, and Wallimann-Helmer 2015; Scheffler 2005; Wilson 2019; Wolff 2007).[3] Third, we examine theories of structural injustice, which emanate from Iris Marion Young. Young situates herself as a critic of Rawls and does not call herself a liberal, but she has influenced contemporary academic liberalism and liberal citizens. Young (1990, 27) argues that self-respect is not a matter of distributive justice like Rawls suggests, but it is "at least as much a function of culture, as it is of goods." Young focused on structural injustice in her later work, but the role of respect remained (Young 2006b, 118; Young 2006a, 95; Young 2009; Young 1989). Some of the recent structural injustice theorists focus mostly on Young's argument on responsibility, and they say little about respect; we argue later in this book that this absence is a challenge for these arguments.[4]

Our focus on egalitarian political theory and liberal citizens may seem to be a slight mismatch. Many structural injustice theorists do not identify with academic liberalism in the way that Rawlsians do, and the word *liberal* in everyday usage has a different meaning from academic liberalism. Yet our liberal focus group participants and survey respondents generally believed in substantive equality, including the importance of structural injustice, while our conservative participants and respondents tended toward procedural or basic equality. As we will explain below, many of our conservative participants were wary of the idea of equality, while many of our liberal respondents believed that equality cannot be merely granting everyone equal rights. Indeed, the idea of equity often arose in our liberal focus groups. Several people used similar imagery to this respondent:

> three people trying to look over a fence at a game and so you have a tall person and a medium-sized person and a short person. So equality is when everybody is given the same box but you still, that shorter person—and that means that person can't see over the fence. So that's equality, but what equity is when you get everybody the leg up that they need in order to achieve that same goal. So to me, that's the difference between equality and equity. (Chicago Liberals 4, Woman 5)

Equality is tied to justice for academic egalitarians and liberal citizens alike. Many liberal citizens accept the idea of structural injustice. Substantive equality ties together the normative literature that we examine and the liberal citizens we spoke with and who we surveyed, and when we speak of egalitarians, we speak of academics and citizens who are committed to substantive equality.

## Two Kinds of Respect

Despite the importance of respect, egalitarian theorists do not define respect precisely. We define egalitarian respect by offering a more precise definition here, or rather two different definitions for two kinds of respect: recognition respect and civic respect. Recognition respect is the respect given to people simply because they are fellow human beings and therefore equals in terms of the respect they deserve. Civic respect recognizes that there are many different beliefs and values and viewpoints and that we should respect people by being willing to listen to and engage with those with whom we disagree.

## RECOGNITION RESPECT

In his classic article, Stephen Darwall (1977, 38) defines recognition respect: "To say that persons as such are entitled to respect is to say that they are entitled to have other persons take seriously and weigh appropriately the fact that they are persons in deliberating about what to do." On Darwall's influential account, recognition respect means that we grant respect to people because they are people (39). All persons have equal fundamental moral worth and should be treated accordingly. This is based on the Kantian idea that "everyone, regardless of social station, talents, accomplishments, or moral record, should be regarded with respect as a human being" (Hill Jr. 1991, 170). Recognition respect means that we accept that everyone has intrinsic worth as moral agents and that we treat them as equals in this regard. To withhold recognition respect from someone is to say that the person's moral worth is less than that of other humans. Recognition respect is a universal matter: all people deserve this kind of respect, for the most part, regardless of what they have said or done. Our focus is mostly on how citizens look upon one another, so our framework is democratic citizenship. When people withhold recognition respect, they fail a basic element of democratic citizenship. (They also fail a basic element of humanity.)[5]

The importance of recognition respect to democracy is that it underlies the moral equality of all citizens—to deny others recognition respect is to deny them a rightful place in the democratic polity; it is to deny them the recognition due to all citizens (and humans). If recognition respect is denied, then the denier is suggesting that the other person fails the threshold of being a moral being who deserves the dignity that should be accorded to all humans. Indeed, even if someone refuses you recognition respect, this is no excuse to refuse the person recognition respect in turn. Granting recognition respect is not predicated on what the other person does (with rare exceptions). Citizens should grant recognition respect to one another in a democracy. To deny someone recognition respect is to deny the person's place as someone with the right to be part of the democratic community—someone with rights, with voice, and with the vote. What we call the liberal respect paradox is based on recognition respect—most liberal citizens believe in recognition respect, yet many struggle to grant it to opposing partisans.

## CIVIC RESPECT

The second aspect of respect that we study is what we call civic respect. Democratic theorists expect citizens to listen with care and intent to one another: to do so is to display mutual respect. We redefine mutual respect as civic respect, emphasize that it is respect among citizens (not the respect that the state should show its citizens), and distinguish it from recognition respect. To deny someone civic respect is to deny the person as a fruitful interlocutor; it is to suggest that the person denied civic respect has nothing worthwhile to contribute to political debate and discussion. A person can deny someone civic respect while at the same time granting them the basic equality of recognition respect, a second-best strategy that we suggest in chapter 7 should sometimes be pursued.

The overarching framework for civic respect is to take the views of one's fellow citizens seriously, and to allow for legitimate disagreement. There are three parts to our definition of civic respect. First, civic respect means listening in both interpersonal and impersonal ways to those with different views. Political theorists often discuss the importance of listening when it comes to mutual respect, but they seem to be thinking of face-to-face encounters, though the setting is rarely specified (Ryan and Spinner-Halev 2022). As with recognition respect, civic respect may arise in a personal encounter, but it also may arise when one is listening to the news or reading about the views of others. Civic respect does not obligate one to always listen; it means one must have seriously considered the views of others before dismissing them. If a topic is well-worn, people with different views do not have to listen to each other yet again, nor must they read about the views of others repeatedly. We argue in later chapters that there may be times when it makes more sense to practice impersonal civic respect, if practicing interpersonal civic respect will lead one to get angry with one's friends or relatives, to the point of not wanting to be near them.

Second, civic respect means listening or understanding without assuming the worst about the person who is talking. That is, civic respect means avoiding the temptation to engage in political stereotyping (Ahler and Sood 2018). Political stereotyping is common and perhaps hard to avoid, but it also allows the framing of opposing partisans in a worse light than is warranted. When citizens define opposing partisans by the most extreme elements in the opposing party, they engage in political stereotyping and undermine civic respect.

Third, civic respect means not assuming that citizens who vote differently do so because they are poorly informed, ignorant, or misled. Ascribing ignorance to opposing partisans repeatedly arose in our focus groups and was confirmed in our surveys. If you think that opposing partisans voted the way they did because of ignorance or misinformation, you implicitly assume that if these voters had the correct information or education, then they would in fact vote like you. This may be the most important aspect of civic respect, since to attribute different views to ignorance or misinformation is a denial that others can legitimately have different views from your own, which runs contrary to the pluralism that marks all modern liberal democracies.

At its core, civic respect means accepting pluralism. We will argue that many liberal citizens and egalitarian political theorists have a hard time accepting pluralism, which is also true for conservative citizens. We discuss pluralism in chapters 3 and 7, but here we can say that pluralism as we define it has two overlapping meanings. First, pluralism means that values will conflict. This means that some choices are difficult to make, and that different people will rank values differently. Second, pluralism means that even if a person has one predominant value, there will be times when that value tugs in different directions. An egalitarian concerned with the poor during the COVID-19 pandemic, for example, might have been concerned about the disease's disproportionate impact on the poor *and* about the impact of school closings on the same group. Liberty means the right not to wear a mask; yet liberty also means the right not to have others cause illness and sometimes death by indifferently spreading a highly infectious disease. Pluralism, too, means to have some humility—the world is complex and it is likely that all of us will make mistakes about how to solve our political and social challenges (Cherniss 2021). We will argue that the belief in substantive egalitarianism that many liberals hold crowds out pluralism, since this belief makes it hard to grant civic respect to those who disagree, but we will sketch an egalitarian pluralism in chapter 7 that allows for granting civic respect.

Civic respect means that we should respectfully listen to others as equal citizens in our democratic experiment. It does not mean that we must agree with them. Understanding that we can hold tight to our own views even when granting civic respect does not make civic respect easier to give. We show in subsequent chapters that granting civic respect is much harder than most theorists realize. Still, civic respect can be given in a more discriminating manner than recognition respect, though we think that it should be granted more widely than it is.

Unlike recognition respect, which is universal, there are bounds to civic respect: because we place our argument within the framework of democratic citizenship, we argue in chapter 7 that people who do not respect democratic procedures do not deserve civic respect. If someone refuses to respect democratic institutions and norms—say, if someone refuses to accept an election result and comes up with a conspiracy theory involving dead Venezuelan prime ministers to suggest why the election is rigged—civic respect is not called for. Similarly, if someone calls for martial law because the person dislikes an election result, civic respect is not called for, nor is it called for if someone thinks that Black people and Jewish people should not be able to vote.

Still, civic respect is not a binary concept; it is not always a matter of granting it or withholding it. Civic respect is both a belief and a practice. As a belief—the belief that there are reasonable ideas about political and social life beyond one's own—it is constant, but it is sporadic as a practice in two ways. First, there may simply not be times to practice civic respect daily—one might not have the occasion to talk politics with opposing partisans routinely, nor might one read opinion writers from the other side daily (though we think this is a good practice to do sometimes). Second, we do not have to practice civic respect every time we confront or hear an opposing idea. Civic respect does not demand that we listen carefully to views about Jewish space lasers that are supposedly causing fires in California, or that we listen attentively to the conspiracy theory that says that many politicians are involved in a child sex ring centered in a pizza parlor in Washington, DC. Civic respect expects us to listen to the beliefs of others, but once we listen to a conspiracy belief, and understand it as one, we need not listen to it again. If someone has one view after another that is deeply and factually mistaken, civic respect does not demand that we continue to listen attentively to that person. Once we understand that a person is a QAnon supporter, for example, we need not continually engage in conversation with the person. Belief in conspiracy theories is not limited to one ideology, of course, with liberals as likely to believe them as conservatives (Enders et al. 2022). One might say that holding conspiracy beliefs is a sign of civic disrespect, as certain kinds of political conspiracies are more likely to be held by partisans who are out of power (Uscinski, Klofstad, and Atkinson 2016). These kinds of beliefs are a way to avoid taking the ideas of one's political opponents seriously. A belief that Democrats are running pedophile rings in pizza parlors is a way to demonize one's political opponents, which dismisses their ideas, and this obviously runs against the idea of civic respect.

We do not have to listen carefully to a person who believes in QAnon conspiracies, but we should also not conflate QAnon supporters with all conservatives (QAnon support has not increased much over the last few years and remains relatively small) (Grossman, Anders, and Uscinski 2021). Civic respect also means we should not assume that because people have one or two views that are clearly outlandish, all their views are of the same ilk. Some of their ideas might be quite reasonable. Nor should we assume that people's views will never change. Permanently withdrawing civic respect is a problem because people can change their minds, and civic respect allows us to see when this happens.

Moreover, withholding civic respect may allow people to evade introspection: it allows them to avoid asking why others might not want to vote for their party or agree with them. When citizens assume that opposing partisans are all racist or anti-American, they avoid asking themselves the hard question of why so many of their fellow citizens don't agree with them. It is easy to write them off as deluded or deeply wrong, but the refusal to grant civic respect to opposing partisans is an avoidance strategy that allows one to evade being thoughtful in the way that civic respect demands. In many national elections, about half of the electorate votes for Republican candidates. Our argument is not only that refusing Republicans civic respect is dismissing half of Americans, but that doing so allows Democrats to avoid being introspective about their own party's flaws or lack of appeal. Latino voters in parts of Texas and Florida have moved quickly and decisively from the Democratic to the Republican Party in the last few years. A Democrat practicing civic respect would want to know why, instead of simply accusing Republican voters of being racist and sexist. Of course, the same is true for those Republicans who refuse to grant civic respect to Democrats. The Democrats gained a seat in the Senate in the 2022 elections; Republicans practicing civic respect would ask why their candidates did relatively poorly compared to expectations rather than dismissing Democrats as ignorant and misinformed. Dismissing civic respect means not taking seriously the people who left your party or decided not to vote. Dismissing civic respect allows one to bask in the glory of self-righteousness while refusing to consider that one might be wrong about some or many political issues or that there might be reasonable disagreement.

We have no doubt that civic respect is hard to practice. What we cannot show, however, is that civic respect (or recognition respect) has declined in the United States over the last several decades. We think this is the case, but our evidence is circumstantial and suggestive, not definitive. The combination of polarization and media silos, which are more extreme now than, say, thirty years ago, makes it harder for people to see the other side as anything but a deep threat to their way of life. There have been culture wars for years, but until recently liberals and conservatives spent much time arguing about the budget size—and budgets are something over which people can negotiate and compromise. As we explain in the second half of this book, different conceptions of justice, the nation, and liberty push liberals and conservatives

to moralize social and political issues, making compromise hard to accept—
and when these issues define opposing partisans, it makes granting civic respect difficult. This is circumstantial, not definitive, evidence for the decline
of civic respect. It is also a partial explanation for why civic respect is hard to
grant, but an explanation is not an excuse.

## A Short Note on Party Identification and Ideology

Throughout our book, we use ideology and party identification interchangeably. That is, we sometimes use *liberals* and *conservatives* and at other times
*Democrats* and *Republicans*. We fully recognize that ideology and partisanship are not the same thing, but we use ideological and partisan terms for
several reasons. First, the two major political parties in the United States have
sorted ideologically in recent decades. Whether this sorting is due to party
members becoming more homogeneous not only in terms of self-reported
ideology but also in terms of the social groups (race, geography, religion,
and so on) that identify with the parties (Mason and Wronski 2018; Iyengar,
Sood, and Lelkes 2012), or because partisans have aligned more cohesively
across numerous issue and ideological positions (Abramowitz and Saunders
2008; Levendusky 2009; Webster and Abramowitz 2017; Layman, Carsey, and
Horowitz 2006), it is clearly the case that at the elite and public levels, Democrats increasingly identify as liberal and hold more liberal issue positions,
whereas Republicans increasingly identify as conservative and hold more
conservative issue positions.

Second, a key interest in our research is people's willingness to give respect
to those with whom they disagree. In current American politics, some of the
most vitriolic disagreements have taken place between opposing partisans. As
the research on affective polarization shows (Iyengar et al. 2019), Americans
feel increased animosity toward opposing partisans in relation to their feelings toward their own party (Druckman and Levendusky 2019; Finkel et al.
2020; Mason 2018). Party polarization is related to several negative outcomes
directed at opposing partisans, including decreased trust (Carlin and Love
2018; Iyengar and Westwood 2015), unwillingness to interact socially (Chen
and Rohla 2018; Huber and Malhotra 2017; Iyengar and Westwood 2015; Shafranek 2021), dehumanization (Cassese 2021; Martherus et al. 2019), and a willingness to use violence (Kalmoe and Mason 2022). Ideology does not result
in the same level of animosity, in part because many Americans are unable
to use and identify with ideology as easily as they do party identification. We
therefore test our arguments about respect by focusing on opposing partisans
rather than ideological opponents. We use ideological labels, however, when

TABLE 1.1. Party identification and ideology

|  | Democrats and leaners | Pure independents | Republicans and leaners |
|---|---|---|---|
| **2018 Equality Attitudes Survey** | | | |
| Liberal | 71.2 | 19.0 | 10.9 |
| Moderate | 19.5 | 53.4 | 12.3 |
| Conservative | 9.3 | 27.6 | 76.8 |
| N | 697 | 116 | 604 |
| **2019 Pluralism and Respect Survey** | | | |
| Liberal | 71.5 | 13.8 | 7.7 |
| Moderate | 24.9 | 58.0 | 13.6 |
| Conservative | 3.6 | 28.2 | 78.7 |
| N | 663 | 174 | 638 |
| **2020 Social Justice and Solidarity Survey** | | | |
| Liberal | 72.4 | 8.6 | 9.7 |
| Moderate | 20.4 | 70.7 | 12.0 |
| Conservative | 7.2 | 20.7 | 78.3 |
| N | 677 | 116 | 566 |

Note: The Liberal, Moderate, and Conservative cell entries are percentages. The N cell entries are the number of cases.

discussing broad theoretical arguments (e.g., arguments made by liberal and conservative theorists), ideological worldviews (such as social justice and national solidarity worldviews), and our focus group participants, whom we recruited via calls for liberal or conservative participants.

Results from our surveys show that using party identification and ideology interchangeably is not a problem empirically. Party identification and ideology do not map perfectly, but Democrats overwhelmingly claim to be liberal and Republicans overwhelmingly claim to be conservative. Table 1.1 shows the ideological breakdown of partisans in the three surveys used throughout the book. We include with their partisan groups those who say they are Independents but lean toward one of the major parties, making this a tougher test of ideology. Even so, Democrats and leaning Democrats consistently self-identify as liberal, Republicans and leaning Republicans as conservative, and pure Independents as moderate or middle of the road. In general, fewer than 10 percent of partisans identify with the out-party ideology.

## Plan of Book

This book is divided into three parts, with chapters 1 through 3 in part one exploring respect. Part two includes chapters 4 through 6 and explores why respect is so hard to grant. Part three includes chapters 7 and 8 and explores the normative implications of our argument.

Chapter 2 focuses on recognition respect. We show that liberal citizens are both more apt to believe in recognition respect than conservative citizens and, by a modest margin, less likely to grant recognition respect. Even when liberals grant recognition respect to the opposition, they admit to experiencing a deep struggle when it comes to offering this respect, a struggle that few conservatives experienced.

Chapter 3 examines civic respect, where we define it more fully than we have in this chapter. The second half of the chapter focuses on our empirical results, where we show that Americans believe in civic respect in the abstract but have a hard time practicing it. We note several reasons why this is the case, but an important one is that many Americans define people by their vote. This might make some sense in a multiparty system, but in a system where two parties dominate, defining people by the way they vote is political stereotyping. Political stereotyping leads to people making many mistakes about opposing partisans' beliefs. The dynamics surrounding civic respect point to the struggle many Americans have with genuine pluralism.

The second part of the book focuses on explaining why many citizens cannot grant respect, even as they believe in the idea in the abstract. Chapter 4 examines liberals' social justice worldview, a combination of beliefs about social justice and structural injustice, issue stands, and the moralization of these beliefs, and it argues that it is this moralized worldview that explains Democrats' lack of respect for Republicans. Democrats believe strongly in social justice and that Republicans oppose them on these issues, making it hard to grant Republicans respect. We also show that liberals are devoted to a certain kind of equality, which conservatives are suspicious of. Since liberals link equality (or equity, as many of our focus group participants said) to justice, they think that those who disagree with them are advocates of injustice. Conservatives believe that fairness is about how individuals act. Even if they believe that structural injustice exists, they believe the way to dismantle it is for individuals to act differently and better.

In chapter 5, we turn to trying to understand why Republicans react against the social justice agenda pursued by liberals. We find that Republicans' belief in a moralized national solidarity worldview leads them to refuse to grant respect to Democrats. In their view, Democrats' insistence on thinking about Americans in terms of racial, ethnic, and gender identity groups breaks down the solidarity of the American people, which they see as morally wrong. Our findings show, however, that liberals and conservatives are not as divided on these issues as many people believe, but they are divided on what issues they moralize. The difference between an issue that citizens see as simply a preference and those that they moralize is that they do not see the latter as debatable. If someone is on the wrong side of a moralized issue, it becomes very hard to grant them respect.

In chapter 6 we link the moralized worldviews to collective responsibility. Here we argue that both liberals and conservatives believe that individuals have a responsibility to act in concert with others to address the issues they moralize—dismantling structural injustice for liberals, maintaining national solidarity for conservatives—and that respect hinges on these collective efforts. The idea that all citizens are obliged to act politically in certain ways bursts forth in some of the egalitarian political theory literature; and while it is less present among conservative political theorists, it can be found there as well. And many citizens have a collective responsibility view. Creating the good society demands that all citizens do their share. We argue, too, that while both liberals and conservatives have collective responsibility views, these views run across a larger number of issues for liberals than conservatives—for example, conservatives think that most consumer choices are simply a matter of individual choice, while liberals are more apt to think that individuals should make consumer choices in collectively responsible ways. When it takes everyone, or almost everyone, to achieve a good society, people judge those not doing their share harshly and find it hard to give them respect.

The third part of the book draws on the empirical findings to make a normative argument. It is unsurprising that we argue in chapter 7 that the notion of collective responsibility undermines a belief in pluralism. We argue that civic respect does not have to be granted to everyone, as recognition respect requires, but it should be granted to those who believe in what we call (following others) procedural democracy. While worldviews can illuminate issues and focus people on an important collective effort, they can also lead people to a quick and not particularly thoughtful denial of other views. In today's world, liberals welcome the age of diversity, while conservatives complain that liberals welcome all kinds of diversity except when it comes to conservative ideas. The problem, however, is that neither liberals nor conservatives are nearly as pluralistic as they think they are. Each side is quick to accuse the other of failure, but each side should also look for its own failures within. Our book ends with some thoughts on the importance and limits of respect and on possible remedies to increase respect among democratic citizens.

# Is It Possible to Respect Opposing Partisans?

So there's respecting the person versus respecting the choice, that choice. I can, I can, I can, I can make a division there. I can enjoy somebody's company who voted for Hillary, and not like the fact that they voted for Hillary. (NC Conservatives 1, Woman 1)

We live in a time when belief in equality is more widespread than at any time in the recorded past and calls for civility and inclusivity are rampant, which all make respect a key value and practice. At the same time, Americans are experiencing off-the-charts polarization, white nationalists feel emboldened, and "cancel culture" is a hot-button issue, all of which make practicing respect a challenge. We bring data in this chapter to the topic of recognition respect both in terms of people's abstract principles concerning recognition respect and by placing respect within a particularly difficult context in current times: partisan and ideological differences. We therefore aim to put recognition respect to a tough test by asking people if they respect those who disagree with them both in their party and in their vote for the opposing party's presidential candidate. What we find is that while Democrats tend to hold more strongly to the principle of recognition respect, they are no more able, and are often less able, than Republicans to give this respect to opposing partisans and voters. We call this the liberal respect paradox, signaling the paradox of holding to a principle dearly but not being able to carry through with it in practice even though one believes one should.

In the last chapter we discussed the research in political theory on respect, and these debates guide our research in important ways. In this chapter, we briefly address what psychologists say about respect. Much of the research in psychology focuses on the experience of being respected or disrespected (see, e.g., Renger and Simon 2011; Simon and Grabow 2014; Renger et al. 2017), including Tom Tyler's (1990) work on procedural justice (see also Tyler and Smith 1999). We are more interested in people's willingness to give respect to those with whom they disagree and how this affects what they think of their

IS IT POSSIBLE TO RESPECT OPPOSING PARTISANS?

adversaries. Fortunately, there is some recent work in psychology that addresses our notion of recognition respect.

The focus of our chapter is an empirical analysis of respect. Drawing on data from several focus groups and three surveys, we examine people's belief in the abstract principle of recognition respect and their application of this principle to opposing partisans. We conclude the chapter by addressing the argument that the liberal respect paradox is simply a Trump effect, that liberals would be equally or even more respecting than conservatives if only Republicans had not elected as president and followed Donald Trump, who liberals find particularly odious. While we cannot create a different outcome to the 2016 election and thereby test our argument under a Jeb Bush or Marco Rubio presidency, we think the evidence that this is not just a Trump effect is compelling. We also think that the distance between Trump and the Republican Party has diminished, at least at the time of this writing, making the idea of a Trump effect less meaningful now than right after the 2016 election.

### What Is Recognition Respect and Why Is It Psychologically Important?

Recognition respect is the acceptance of the idea that all people are fellow human beings who have intrinsic worth as moral agents. Democratic theorists argue that we must recognize this worth in people to be able to see them as equals. In contrast to democratic theorists, who have addressed extensively the role of respect, psychologists have not focused much attention on the concept and when they have, they have primarily been interested in people's responses to feeling respected or disrespected (see, e.g., Renger and Simon 2011; Renger et al. 2016; Renger et al. 2017; Simon and Grabow 2014; Tyler 1990; Tyler and Blader 2003). When people feel respected, they are more likely to engage in pro-group behaviors (Renger and Simon 2011) and social cooperation (Renger et al. 2017), suggesting that respect is an important interpersonal and intergroup concept. While the effects of feeling respected or disrespected are important, our main interest is in people's willingness to grant respect to others. Much less work has been done on this topic, but it has garnered some attention and parts of the conceptual framework deployed by psychologists are similar to those in philosophy.

Psychologists distinguish among three types of respect: status respect, achievement respect, and unconditional respect. Status and achievement respect are contingent on people having earned respect through their place in society or their actions, and are therefore referred to as contingent respect. They are inherently hierarchical: some people can have more status or achievement respect than others (Lalljee, Laham, and Tam 2007). Contingent respect is especially important within one's ingroup, where group status and leadership selection matter a great deal (Janoff-Bulman and Werther 2008) and where people care about what fellow ingroup members think of them (Ellemers, Doosje, and Spears 2004). Contingent respect is like what philosophers, following Stephen Darwall (1977), call "appraisal respect."[1]

Our interest, however, is in recognition respect, which is like psychologists' understanding of unconditional respect. Unconditional respect is given to everyone because all people have moral worth and deserve respect regardless of what they have said or done (Lalljee, Laham, and Tam 2007). Since everyone deserves this type of respect, there is no hierarchy. Everyone is equal. Unconditional respect is especially important in intergroup contexts and is primarily based in morality (Janoff-Bulman and Werther 2008). People within a group tend to automatically attribute positive, moral intentions to fellow ingroup members and just as automatically attribute negative, immoral intentions to outgroup members (Janoff-Bulman and Werther 2008, 10). If adversaries disagree with the ingroup, ingroup members are quick to jump to the conclusion that the outgroup members are biased, self-interested, and immoral, making unconditional respect difficult to give.

Unconditional respect is related to behaving respectfully toward others even when they have behaved disrespectfully (Lalljee, Laham, and Tam 2007), being less likely to avoid or act aggressively toward an adversary (Lalljee et al. 2009), not reacting negatively toward moral transgressors (Laham et al. 2010), not feeling or behaving negatively toward outgroups (Laham et al. 2009), and being more politically engaged and satisfied with democracy (Lalljee et al. 2013). Respect has these positive effects because it "involves treating adversarial others as equal participants even if you do not like their views. It calls for a sort of attributional generosity in interpreting the words and intentions of the other, holding one's harshest delegitimizing appraisals in abeyance, and allowing for inputs and influence by all parties to the conflict" (Janoff-Bulman and Werther 2008, 15). These are some of the reasons why unconditional—or recognition—respect is so important to democracy. We use the term *recognition respect*, rather than *unconditional respect*, because it highlights the important role respect plays in providing the basis for equality, but recognition respect is clearly unconditional.

Since very little empirical research has been done on the concept of recognition respect, or unconditional respect in psychology, our main purpose in this chapter is to explore people's belief in the abstract principle of respect and their willingness to grant recognition respect to their partisan adversaries. We specifically explore this research question: Do Democrats and Republicans differ in their willingness to grant recognition respect to their political opponents? The liberal respect paradox is the idea that liberals believe more strongly in equality and the necessity of recognition respect to achieve equality but that they are no more likely than conservatives to put it into practice. The liberal respect paradox is nicely captured in a comment by one of our focus group participants:

> Even as old as I am I have trouble sorting out the intellectual side from the emotional side. And I wonder, can you intellectually respect people and emotionally not respect them? Is that okay, or is that like "nope, you can't do that." Do the two have to go together to be an integrated person? But I can say, intellectually I understand that I respect those people, they're other human beings and they do what they do because they have as many fears and stuff as I do. But emotionally I really don't like them and honestly don't wish the best for them. I wish that stuff that Trump does hurts them so that they'll say, "wow, I made a mistake there," you know, that they lose their—And it's awful, I know, I hate myself for that, but what else would convince them? (Chicago Liberals 3, Man 1)

The bulk of the chapter explores this paradox drawing on a wide array of focus group and survey data we have gathered.

## Focus Group and Survey Data

Over the course of working on this book, we administered three online surveys and two experiments and conducted twenty-seven focus groups, eighteen with liberals and nine with conservatives. The surveys were fielded each year from 2018 to 2020 and used Dynata (formerly SSI) for the panels of participants. The focus groups were held in a variety of locations across the United States. We had a harder time getting conservatives to agree to speak with us, as they expressed more suspicion of academics than liberals did. On several occasions we had to try to prove that we would be fair to the conservative groups, who think that liberal academics are out to "get them" by showing them to be racist or sexist or homophobic. Our liberal groups were created much more readily.[2]

We recruited focus group participants via existing social groups, such as book clubs, church groups, dinner groups, and the like, so most participants within any given group knew one another and often met regularly. We found the existing groups by contacting people we knew or through inquires at bookstores and churches to ask about any existing social groups whom we could contact. We specifically asked for groups that self-identified as liberal or conservative and that included college-educated members. Research on tolerance shows that education is positively related to the willingness to give disliked groups their basic civil liberties (Sullivan, Piereson, and Marcus 1982). We assumed that the college educated would also value the idea of respect more highly and therefore potentially be more respectful of opposing partisans, putting our argument to a hard test.

The focus groups took place in two rounds (see appendix A for details). We focus on the first round of focus groups in this chapter. The first round of liberal focus groups took place in Chicago and North Carolina between February and May 2018. The first round of conservative groups took place in North Carolina, Nebraska, and Alabama between July 2018 and January 2019. We donated $50 to a charity of each group's choosing for its members' participation. Groups ranged in size from four to thirteen, with liberal groups having an average of 7.3 participants and conservative groups an average of 5.8 participants. Nearly all participants had a college degree. Most participants were white but there were Black and Latino/Latina participants in both the conservative and liberal groups. Fifty-eight percent of the liberal participants and 46 percent of the conservative participants were women. Altogether, we spoke with ninety-five liberals and thirty-five conservatives.[3] The focus group sessions lasted approximately 1.5 hours and were audio recorded. A graduate student transcribed the recordings, and we hired two graduate students to code the transcriptions.

We also conducted three national surveys (see appendix B for details). The first was a national survey of 1,600 respondents, the Equality Attitudes Survey, administered by ResearchNow SSI, an Internet survey company. The survey took place between December 3 and 9, 2018. The second survey, the Pluralism and Respect Survey, was also a national survey of 1,600 respondents administered by Dynata (formerly ResearchNow SSI) between October 23 and 29, 2019. The third survey, the Social Justice and Solidarity Survey, was administered by Dynata from July 30 to August 3, 2020, and had 1,600 respondents. ResearchNow SSI/Dynata recruits participants to be part of their online community and then, after screening, invites them onto the panel. Participants are randomly selected from the panel to participate in a particular study. We set the population of the samples as American citizens twenty years old or older, and oversampled college-educated respondents.[4] We included an attention test question and those who failed the test (13 percent for the first survey, 11 percent for the second survey, and 10 percent for the third survey) were dropped from the analyses. The Equality Attitudes Survey had a median completion time of 7.8 minutes, the Pluralism and Respect Survey had a median completion time of 11.2 minutes, and the Social Justice and Solidarity Survey had a median completion time of 11.4 minutes. We weighted the data in all three data sets to reflect US Census data from 2017 on education, sex, and race/ethnicity.

Since the focus of this chapter is on recognition respect, we begin by briefly examining the extent to which people believe in respect as an important aspect of equality and as an obligation they have toward fellow citizens and those with whom they disagree. These abstract beliefs in respect tell us something important about how people think about respect, but as Prothro and Grigg (1960) showed many years ago when looking at political tolerance, abstract views do not always lead to the application of the value when faced with a disliked group (Sullivan, Piereson, and Marcus 1982; Marcus et al. 1995). We therefore focus most of our analyses on people's respect for opposing partisans and voters, which places respect in the context of the current heightened partisan animosity.

### Who Holds the General Principle of Recognition Respect?

We begin by testing the first part of the liberal respect paradox. According to the paradox, liberals believe more strongly than conservatives in the principles of equality and equal, or recognition, respect. We know from previous research that Americans tend to believe strongly in general democratic principles, such as freedom of speech and assembly, majority rule and minority rights, and equality before the law (Prothro and Grigg 1960; McClosky 1964; Sullivan, Piereson, and Marcus 1982). Almost all respondents to the 1978 Political Tolerance Survey agreed that public officials should be chosen by majority vote (95 percent), that people should be entitled to legal rights and protections regardless of their political beliefs (93 percent), and that free speech should be given to all (85 percent; Sullivan et al. 1981). Equality is also a core element of Americans' political values, although liberals tend to hold the value of equality more strongly than conservatives, who are more likely to value freedom and individualism than liberals (McClosky and Zaller 1984; Feldman and Zaller 1992; Feldman 1988). If Americans, and liberals in particular, continue to give their strong support to the abstract principle of equality, we expect them to include respect in their understanding of equality.

We asked respondents in the 2018 Equality Attitudes Survey about what they think equality means: "People disagree about what equality means. Please indicate to what extent each of the following reflects your understanding of equality." Ten different meanings of equality were listed, and respondents were asked to indicate the extent to which the meaning reflected their own understanding of equality on a scale ranging from 1 (Does not at all reflect my understanding) to 7 (Completely reflects my understanding), transformed to

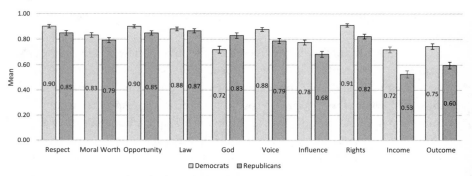

FIGURE 2.1. Meaning of Equality by Party Identification
*Source*: 2018 Equality Attitudes Survey
*Note*: Columns are means for Democrats and Republicans. The partisan groups include partisans and leaners. The error bars denote the 95% confidence intervals. All the mean differences are significant at the $p < 0.001$ level except for "Equality before the law" ($p = 0.098$).

range from 0 to 1. Figure 2.1 shows the mean scores for Democrats and Republicans.[5] The idea that equality means that everyone deserves equal respect was one of the most strongly supported understandings of equality among both sets of partisans, especially Democrats. Equal moral worth or value did not get as much support, but it still received a mean score over 0.8 among Democrats and was highly supported by Republicans as well. Partisans did not differ in their acceptance of one meaning of equality, equal under the law, and Republicans outscored Democrats only on equal under God. On all other items, Democrats were significantly more likely than Republicans to say the meanings were important to their understanding of equality. It is important to keep in mind, though, that people in both parties believe that respect is a key aspect of equality. We get the same results when we use liberals and conservatives instead of Democrats and Republicans (data not shown).

We asked our focus group participants an open-ended question: "What do you mean by equality?" Whereas survey respondents were provided with various meanings of the word, the focus group participants had to call to mind spontaneously what equality meant to them. Forty-five liberals (54 percent) and twenty-five conservatives (71 percent) commented on this question, and each mention of the meaning of equality was given a code.[6] We used fewer coding categories than the survey options, but the results are telling. Table 2.1 shows that the statements from the conservative focus group participants most often were about equal opportunity, followed by equal before the law and equal before God. Only 5 percent of conservative statements on the meaning of equality mentioned moral equality, which encapsulates the concept of respect and moral worth. Nearly 30 percent of conservative statements

TABLE 2.1. Meaning of equality among focus group participants (%)

|  | Liberals | Conservatives |
| --- | --- | --- |
| Equal before the law (law, rights) | 17 | 22 |
| Equal opportunity | 21 | 56 |
| Moral equality (value, worth, respect) | 26 | 5 |
| Equal before God | 5 | 11 |
| Fairness (affirmative action, equity, fairness) | 17 | 0 |
| Equal access or voice | 14 | 6 |

Source: 2018 Equality Attitudes Focus Groups

Note: Cell entries are percentages of statements conveying the particular meaning of equality given all statements on the meaning of equality.

said that equality did *not* mean equality of outcome, something mentioned only once by our liberal respondents. Liberals, on the other hand, discussed many different conceptions of equality, with moral equality being the most mentioned understanding (26 percent of all mentions), followed by equal opportunity, equal under the law, fairness, and equal access or voice.[7] When talking about equality in their own words, liberals are much more likely than conservatives to emphasize equal respect.

The results from the survey and the focus groups show clearly that liberal citizens have a rich and varied understanding of equality, along the lines of substantive equality. They also, much more than conservatives, talk spontaneously about respect and moral worth as central to their understanding of the concept. Conservative citizens, in contrast, are almost as likely as liberal citizens to highlight respect when prompted in a survey, but they are much less likely to do so spontaneously—their dominant view of equality is procedural. This evidence suggests that the first part of the liberal respect paradox is accurate: liberals are more likely than conservatives to believe that respect is fundamental to the ideal of equality.

While a strong belief in the centrality of respect and equality is important, we asked in two of our surveys more direct questions about beliefs in the abstract principle of recognition respect. In the 2018 Equality Attitudes Survey, we asked how important respondents think it is for citizens to respect each other. In the 2019 Pluralism and Respect Survey, we gave respondents a battery of statements that pushed them to consider respecting people no matter what they have done or said. In figure 2.2, we compare the mean scores of Democrats and Republicans on these measures. Almost all respondents, especially among Democrats, heartily endorsed the idea that giving respect to citizens is very important. Respondents also gave a high level of support to the statements that most directly capture political theorists' understanding

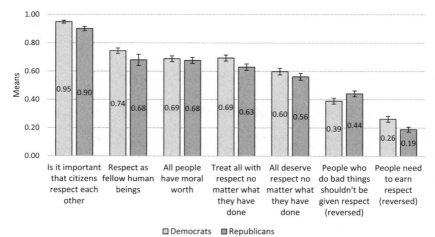

FIGURE 2.2. Support for the General Principle of Recognition Respect by Party
*Source*: 2018 Equality Attitudes Survey and 2019 Pluralism and Respect Survey
*Note*: Responses were reverse coded for the last two statements above so that all responses were coded to range from 0 = strongly do not support recognition respect to 1 = strongly support recognition respect. Response options in the 2018 survey ranged from "Very unimportant" to "Very important." Response options in the 2019 survey ranged from "Strongly disagree" to "Strongly agree." $T$-tests for the mean differences are two-sided. All the mean differences are significant at the $p < 0.05$ level except for "All people have moral worth" ($p = 0.451$).

of recognition respect, that all people should be given respect because they are fellow human beings, that all people have moral worth, and that people ought to be respected regardless of what they have said or done. When respondents are reminded, however, that some of the things people have said or done might be bad, support for recognition respect plummets. For the last two questions, someone high in recognition respect would need to disagree with the statements, with the idea being that everyone should be respected, and that no litmus test is needed. It is possible that respondents agreed with the "respect needs to be earned" statement because they were thinking of appraisal respect instead of recognition respect, but the rejection of respect being unconditional is clear. The number of Democrats and Republicans willing to reject the idea that respect must be earned is small (with mean scores of 0.26 and 0.19, respectively). The unconditionality of respect is further undermined by support for the idea that only good people deserve respect. Few Democrats and Republicans can bring themselves to respect people who have done or said bad things (means of 0.39 and 0.44, respectively).

The two surveys and the focus groups provide evidence that Americans believe in equality and accept the idea that everyone ought to be respected, but they walk back this strong support when faced with contingencies. This is true for liberal and conservative citizens, suggesting that few people accept a completely unconditional respect. Nonetheless, the liberal respect paradox argument that liberals are more likely than conservatives to believe in the general principle of respect is supported by the data. While the differences in survey responses are small, Democrats are significantly more likely than Republicans to believe that everyone ought to be given respect. The differences are more pronounced in the focus group discussions, where liberals were much more likely than conservatives to talk about the ideas surrounding substantive egalitarianism and respect. The bottom line is that the data support the first half of the liberal respect paradox. The exception is respect for bad people: Democrats are less likely than Republicans to think people need to earn respect, whereas Republicans are less likely to disrespect those who have said or done bad things. We address next the application of respect to those we dislike.

## Respecting Opposing Partisans and the
## Struggle to Grant Recognition Respect

While many theorists place the notion of recognition respect in the context of multiculturalism, diversity, income inequality, or democratic deliberation, our research focuses on the increasingly difficult context of partisan polarization in the United States. Over the past thirty years, Americans have become more negative toward those in the opposing party, registering colder temperatures on feeling thermometers (Iyengar, Sood, and Lelkes 2012), anger toward opposing party candidates (Mason 2013), preferential treatment toward in-party members (Lelkes and Westwood 2017), and discrimination toward out-party members (Iyengar and Westwood 2015). The increased incivility can lead to greater distrust (Mutz and Reeves 2005) and to delegitimizing the opposition (Mutz 2007; Brooks and Geer 2007). In terms of putting recognition respect to a tough test, asking partisans if they respect opposing partisans is particularly difficult.

Respecting other citizens across political divisions is something democratic theorists take for granted as important for democracy, and many citizens, especially liberal citizens, agree with theorists on this matter. They believe they ought to respect citizens with opposing views, but they have a hard time actually practicing respect. This is the second half of the "liberal respect paradox." We show that the belief in respect and the practice of respect often diverge. While this is true of most citizens, the finding that liberal citizens are at best no more likely than conservative citizens to respect opposing partisans, even though they value respect more highly, helps us understand the second half of the liberal respect paradox.

We test this second half by focusing on people's willingness to respect those who support the opposing party. If liberal citizens are more willing to respect their political opponents than conservative citizens, then the liberal respect paradox does not hold. If, on the other hand, liberals are no different from conservatives in their willingness to respect opposing partisans, or if they have less respect, then the liberal respect paradox holds. We test the paradox using both opposing partisans and people who vote for the opposing party's presidential candidate. The opposing party's top candidate for office is an easy target for much of the animosity people feel about the opposing party, and people judge others based on their vote choice (see chapter 4). We begin by looking at party identification using the 2020 Social Justice and Solidarity Survey and then focus on voters for opposing party candidates using the 2018 Equality Attitudes Survey before turning to the focus groups.

We gave respondents in 2020 four statements about respecting opposing partisans: (1) "I think we need to do more than tolerate [Democrats/Republicans], we need to respect them," (2) "[Democrats/Republicans] should be given respect simply because they are fellow human beings," (3) "I struggle a great deal when it comes to respecting [Democrats/Republicans]" (reverse coded), and (4)"[Democrats'/Republicans'] political views make it impossible for me to respect them as people" (reverse coded). The response options ranged from Strongly Agree to Strongly Disagree. We transformed the variables to range from 0 to 1, with 1 signifying greater respect. We also included one of the recognition respect statements in the 2021 Politics in the Field at UNC (PFUNC) survey that asked the extent to which people agreed or disagreed with the statement "The political views of those in the opposing political party make it impossible for me to respect them as people."[8] We transformed the variable to range from 0 to 1, with 1 signifying greater respect.

Figure 2.3 provides the results of the difference of means tests. Democrats and Republicans are very similar in their responses to the opposing partisan respect questions. The one significant difference between partisans is in the 2021 survey where Democrats are significantly less likely than Republicans to say they can respect opposing partisans given their views. Also telling, though, in terms of the liberal respect paradox is a comparison of responses in figure 2.2 with those in figure 2.3. The most comparable statement says that people should be respected as fellow human beings. Democrats have a mean of 0.74 on the question that simply refers to "all people" but drop to 0.65 when asked about Republicans. Republicans drop from 0.68 on the abstract question to 0.67 on the question about Democrats. The bottom line, though,

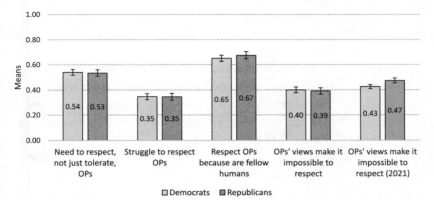

FIGURE 2.3. Recognition Respect and Opposing Partisans
*Source*: 2020 Social Justice and Solidarity Survey and 2021 PFUNC Survey
*Note*: The question labeled "(2021)" is from the 2021 PFUNC Survey; all the other questions are from the 2020 Social Justice and Solidarity Survey. The column data are means. One-sided *t*-tests show that the only significant mean difference is for the 2021 question ($p < 0.001$).

TABLE 2.2. Recognition respect for opposing partisans (%)

|  | Democrats | Republicans |
| --- | --- | --- |
| I find it easy to respect [Republicans/Democrats]. | 10 | 21 |
| I try to respect [Republicans/Democrats] but it is sometimes really hard to do so. | 49 | 48 |
| I used to respect [Republicans/Democrats] but I have given up trying to do so. | 29 | 25 |
| I have never respected [Republicans/Democrats]. | 12 | 6 |

*Source*: 2018 Equality and Respect Survey
*Note*: The cell entries are percentages of those who chose that response option.

is that Democrats, who believe more in equal respect than Republicans, are at minimum no more likely than Republicans to respect opposing partisans.

People were asked the extent to which they agreed or disagreed with the recognition respect statements in figure 2.3. Perhaps if they are given respect options, they will be able to indicate more accurately where they stand on respecting opposing partisans. We therefore asked respondents in our 2018 survey which came closest to their view on respecting opposing partisans and gave them four response options ranging from "easy to respect" to "never respected." Table 2.2 shows that almost half of Democrats and Republicans indicate that they try to respect opposing partisans but find it difficult, and another quarter say they have given up on respecting the other side. There is strong evidence, though, that Democrats are the ones who have a harder time respecting the opposition. Only 10 percent of Democrats say they find it easy to respect opposing partisans, compared to 21 percent of Republicans. Twice as many Democrats, compared to Republicans, say they have never respected opposing partisans.

We also asked respondents about their respect for opposing party voters. Some partisans do not vote for their party's candidate for president, but most do. In our 2018 Equality Attitudes Survey, we found that 83 percent of Democrats said they voted in 2016 for Hillary Clinton, while 89 percent of Republicans said they voted for Donald Trump. With the high level of animosity people feel toward the opposing party's presidential candidates, an argument we return to later, we expect people to struggle even more giving respect to opposing party voters. We draw on data from our 2018 survey where we asked Donald Trump and Hillary Clinton voters specifically about their respect for people who voted for the other candidate in the 2016 presidential election. Our recognition respect statements applied to opposing party voters were "I might disagree with [Donald Trump voters/Hillary Clinton voters] but I still respect them as people" and "I struggle a great deal when it comes to respecting people who voted for [Donald Trump/Hillary Clinton]," with response options ranging from Strongly Agree to Strongly Disagree. Democrats are less likely than Republicans to say they respect opposing voters (means of 0.62 for Democrats and 0.76 for Republicans, $p < 0.001$) and they are more likely to say they struggle to respect opposing voters (means of 0.69 for Democrats and 0.53 for Republicans, $p < 0.001$).

The survey results show that there is either no difference in respect between Democrats and Republicans or Democrats have less respect than Republicans for opposing partisans or opposing party voters, both of which are a problem for liberal citizens given their belief in the principle of equal respect. The focus group discussions illustrate in even starker terms than the survey responses the liberal respect paradox in action. We asked the liberal focus group participants, "Do you respect Trump supporters?" and the conservative focus group participants, "Do you respect Clinton supporters?" Fifty-nine liberals (62 percent) and twenty-two conservatives (63 percent) made comments that were coded. Table 2.3 shows that conservatives readily said they respect Clinton supporters. Liberals, in contrast, either struggled in trying to come to an answer or simply said they did not respect Trump voters. Both responses, struggle and no respect, support the liberal respect paradox, and they made up 77 percent of liberal comments and 0 percent of conservative comments.

The most frequent response among liberal participants, making up almost half (45 percent) of their comments, was the struggle between their belief in moral worth and respect and their views of Trump supporters. These people lived the liberal respect paradox, even if they did not name it as such:

TABLE 2.3. Focus group comments on respect for opposing party voters (%)

|  | Liberals | Conservatives |
|---|---|---|
| No struggle—respect | 8 | 83 |
| No struggle—do not respect | 28 | 0 |
| Struggle | 45 | 0 |
| No struggle—it depends | 20 | 17 |

Source: 2018 Equality Attitudes Focus Groups
Note: Cell entries are the percentage of all comments made about respecting the voters of the opposing party candidate coded into the particular category. Columns may not add up to 100% due to rounding.

For myself, I experience it as creating a lot of internal conflict and cognitive dissonance because I like to think of myself as someone who has respect for anyone and everyone. At the same time, I find it frightening and horrifying that we're talking about potentially being at the brink of a nuclear war, and our president is taunting this mentally ill leader of North Korea. (NC Liberals 2, Woman 4)

But does that suggest that anyone who voted for Trump are bad people? This is where I am so torn, because it can't possibly be. You know, I am a firm believer that everybody has good in them. (Chicago Liberals 1, Woman 1)

I mean it's a struggle, it's a struggle for me because, you know, we're Christian folks and we have this value that says you're supposed to be respectful and loving. (Chicago Liberals 4, Man 3)

The second most frequent response (28 percent of comments) showed that liberal participants did not struggle because they straightforwardly had no respect for Trump supporters, contrary to theorists' ideal.

There are a couple people that are still doing, like, #TrumpTrain, and that does actually instantly trigger disrespect, because I think it's the celebrating of something that is clearly flawed from any perspective. (NC Liberals 1, Man 4)

[I] have a hard time looking at someone who says to me "I voted for Trump" because what it says to me is "I voted against you." It's always going to say that to me: "You were marginalized, what you wanted was marginalized." (Chicago 1, Woman 4)

In contrast to the liberals who struggled with respect, these liberals accepted that they did not respect Trump voters and felt no hesitancy in saying so.

The absence of respect was not lost on our conservative participants, who noted strained and lost relationships with sorrow.

[A] good friend of mine, former friend I guess now, I had voted for Omaha's mayor back in 2013, and so when he found out that's how I voted and not only voted but volunteered for her quite significantly, he said "You know, you don't support me, you don't care about me" and cut it off, and cut off our friendship. I haven't spoken to him till this day, and won't make attempts to because he sees it as a—because of this one thing in my identity, you supported someone who voted against one thing, that impacted my identity, therefore you're as horrible as you know, somebody who's in the Ku Klux Klan. Which . . . was hurtful but you kind of accept it over time. (Nebraska Conservatives, Woman 2)

A good example is when my sister and I realized that we are at such an impasse and I chose to keep my sister, rather than keep my politics. And so I said to her, "X, I love you and I know what a good person you are. So I know that your choice, your liberal thoughts and choice, is because you are a good person and you are trying to do what's right." But she could not give me the same. (NC Conservatives 1, Woman 3)

It is important to note that a small number of liberal participants' comments (8 percent) showed they respected Trump supporters.

Definitely some of them. I mean, some of them I know, I totally respect. I think they were misguided, but that doesn't invalidate their worth as, as human beings. (Chicago Liberals 3, Woman 3)

Most liberal comments, however, fit the liberal respect paradox. Some liberals experience serious conflict between their beliefs and their practice; others are tossing asunder respect, a cardinal belief of nearly all liberal citizens; some are turning their backs on friends and family that they have known for many years because of a vote. The conservative comments from our focus groups, in contrast, were straightforwardly respectful of Clinton voters.

The focus group comments reveal that liberals think they ought to respect Republican voters, but they hold them in such disdain, a large majority just cannot give them that respect. To ascertain what characteristics people ascribe to opposing party voters, the 2018 Equality Attitudes Survey respondents were asked, "What comes to mind when you think of the people who voted for [Donald Trump/Hillary Clinton] in the 2016 presidential election?" They were given ten bipolar adjectives on a 7-point scale, which we recoded to range from 0 to 1 with the most positive characterizations at 1 (see table 2.4). Looking at the overall perceptions of opposing party voters, what is striking is how negatively Democrats characterize Republican voters. The midpoint of the measures is 0.5. Democrats were highly negative in their characterizations of Republican voters with means not reaching 0.3 (column 1) and with over 50 percent giving extremely negative characterizations (column 2) on eight items. The lowest scores were given for unwilling to compromise, intolerant, and closed-minded. Democrats also view Republican voters as racist and

TABLE 2.4. Perceptions of opposing voters

| | Democrats think Trump voters are . . . | | Republicans think Clinton voters are . . . | |
| --- | --- | --- | --- | --- |
| | Mean | Percent negative | Mean | Percent negative |
| Racist / Not racist | 0.27 | 58 | 0.51 | 22 |
| Sexist / Not sexist | 0.28 | 58 | 0.45 | 32 |
| Intolerant / Tolerant | 0.22 | 69 | 0.32 | 52 |
| Uneducated / Educated | 0.32 | 47 | 0.46 | 27 |
| Closed / Open to new ideas | 0.23 | 66 | 0.33 | 48 |
| Misled / Well informed by media | 0.28 | 57 | 0.25 | 62 |
| Unwilling / Willing to compromise | 0.20 | 70 | 0.29 | 59 |
| Unintelligent / Intelligent | 0.30 | 49 | 0.42 | 31 |
| Follows others / Acts independently | 0.27 | 61 | 0.29 | 55 |
| Condescending / Not condescending | 0.27 | 59 | 0.33 | 49 |

Source: 2018 Equality and Respect Survey
Note: The bipolar adjective items range from 0 (most negative) to 1 (most positive). "Percent negative" is the percentage of respondents who gave one of the two most negative answers on the scale (a 1 or 2 on the original 7-point scale). The mean differences are significant at the $p < 0.05$ level for all bipolar adjectives except "Misled / Well informed by the media" and "Follows others / Acts independently."

sexist. Liberals believe in the abstract principle of respect, but they balk when asked to respect people they think are bad, and Republican voters, they think, are bad. In contrast, Republicans were less negative in how they characterized Democratic voters, with means dipping below 0.3 on only three items (column 3) and exceeding 50 percent giving the most negative responses on only four items (column 4). None of these lower-scoring items signal that Republicans think Democratic voters are immoral or bad people. Two of these items, "misled by the media" and "follows others without thinking," were characterizations applied equally by both sides.

We directly asked the liberal focus group participants why they thought people voted for Trump. Responses were wide-ranging and included the usual motivations of party loyalty; policy concerns; Trump's promises on the campaign trail; and ignorance or being misled by the media; along with the frustrations felt by white, rural Americans. Participants in every liberal focus group, though, said people voted for Trump because of racism, sexism, homophobia, and intolerance, with fear as the underlying motivator.

> I think it's fear. Fear because of the changing populace. (NC Liberals 2, Woman 2)

> I think part of it also, and it's one of the fears, is this, for years we've been— open the newspaper and you see a chart that shows that within a short period of time whites are going to be the minority, in the minority, and I think that

is frightening to people who have been in the majority and been in control and been privileged and so I think part of this is, a lot of what Trump spoke to was that fear that, you know, immigrants, you know, are going to take over. (Chicago Liberals 3, Man 1)

The focus was often on President Barack Obama as a catalyst for a racist Trump vote.

I think that it was eight years of talk radio and inside jokes about Obama being black. I think it was all about, it was just a whole huge backlash from Obama being black. . . . I believe that all of those white people really were ready to just completely rebound and be openly racist again. (NC Liberals 6, Woman 3)

A subswath, and I don't know how big it is, there's no doubt to me it's racism. Just racism. Eight years of Obama, people hated it. (Chicago Liberals 1, Man 4)

I think there can, there were so many complex factors involved and yet I, all of it to me at some point feels like red herring. I, you know, I just have this image of when Obama was first elected of seeing, I can't remember where it was, but, you know there was a dummy of Obama that was lynched and burned essentially. So, that is so embedded at the core and the foundation of this phenomena. (Chicago 2, Woman 5)

A few (though surprisingly few) pointed to sexism:

You cannot explain how a man stands on a podium, tells you nothing of what he's going to do for the country, there was not a plan laid out in any way, shape, nuance or form, and a woman tells you what she's going to do, gives you the plan, gives you the gateway, has more experience than anyone who has ever attempted that seat, and she gets shut out that way. (Chicago Liberals 4, Woman 4)

Ascribing racism and sexism to Trump voters was not lost on the conservative focus group participants. When asked why his cousin refused to speak with him after the election, one conservative participant explained:

Oh, because I'm homophobic, xenophobic, racist, you know, anybody that voted for Trump, you're all these things that MSNBC told 'em they were. (Alabama Conservatives, Man 1)

What our data suggest is that liberals have a hard time distinguishing Trump from his supporters. Read carefully this response by a liberal to the question about respecting Trump supporters:

Very good question. I think that it goes to the heart of a kind of broader question which is, you meet somebody, you hate everything they say, you disagree with everything they say, you think it's horrible what they say. And in spite of that I, I am supposed to, you know, at my best level, to be able to see them as a human being who deserves my respect and deserves dignity just as much as anybody else does. . . . But I just think it's hard to pull that one off. It's a human to human problem, really. You know, every time I see Trump, to go back to Trump, I mean he just makes my blood boil just listening to the guy, right? Does he deserve respect? In theory he does, theoretically he deserves as much respect and dignity as somebody else. (NC Liberals 3, Man 3)

What is interesting about this response is not only the recognition of the tension between this man's beliefs about respect and his ability to implement this belief but that he changed the question, which was about Trump supporters, into a question about Trump himself. Many liberal participants ascribe what they perceive as Trump's traits onto his supporters. The liberal tendency to conflate Trump and his supporters is important, as is the liberal tendency not to entertain alternative (nonracist or nonsexist) reasons to vote for Trump.

While few of our liberal participants said they could readily separate a person's vote from the person's character, several of our conservatives volunteered they do just that:

You know, they're entitled, it doesn't, it doesn't frame them as, you know, how productive are they in society. It doesn't frame them as my neighbor, really. I mean, I try to put that aside to a certain extent because that's not the basis or the foundation of my relationship with them. (NC Conservatives 3, Woman 1)

I respect them, yeah, I respect their choice to do that and I, and I—there are probably many aspects of their lives that I do respect. (NC Conservatives 1, Woman 1)

Janoff-Bulman and Werther (2008) argue that recognition respect is based in morality judgments and that people tend to ascribe positive, moral characteristics to fellow ingroup members and negative, immoral characteristics to outgroup members. We find this tendency more among liberals than conservatives when talking about opposing party voters. Liberals take characteristics they associate with Donald Trump and generalize them to all the people who voted for Trump, making all Trump voters bad people. Conservatives, in contrast, hold more positive views of Clinton supporters. In chapter 4 we address the tendency of liberals to moralize the vote choice. What is clear at this point, though, is that the liberal respect paradox exists. Liberals believe strongly in the abstract principle of recognition respect but have a difficult time respecting Republicans and voters for the Republican presidential candidate.

## Is the Liberal Respect Paradox Simply a Trump Effect?

The survey and focus group results tell a compelling story. Liberals believe in the principle of recognition respect but find it difficult to respect opposing partisans and people who voted for Donald Trump. We address two possible arguments in the remainder of this chapter that could undermine the importance we attribute to the liberal respect paradox: (1) liberals respect conservatives and Republicans, it's just Trump voters they disrespect; and (2) we have unfairly put liberals to a tougher test than conservatives because Donald Trump is singularly horrible.

### LIBERALS RESPECT CONSERVATIVES AND REPUBLICANS, THEY JUST DISRESPECT TRUMP VOTERS

When people are asked about their respect for opposing partisans, Democrats and Republicans are similar in their unwillingness to grant respect (see figure 2.3). When asked about opposing party voters, however, Democrats' respect is significantly lower than Republicans' respect. Perhaps it is not party that is driving respect but the impact of Donald Trump. We can test this argument using an experiment we embedded in the 2018 Equality Attitudes Survey. Respondents read a short vignette about a hypothetical person we named Bob. We randomly assigned respondents to a liberal or a conservative vignette and to one of three conditions embedded in the vignette: policy, party, or vote choice. In the policy condition, respondents read about Bob's issue positions (either liberal or conservative). In the party condition, respondents read about Bob's issue positions and a sentence at the end that declared that Bob was a Democrat (if his policy stances were liberal) or a Republican (if his policy stances were conservative). In the vote choice condition, respondents read about Bob's issue positions and a sentence at the end that declared that Bob had voted in the 2016 presidential election for Hillary Clinton (if he held liberal policy stances) or Donald Trump (if he held conservative policy stances). The vote choice condition did not mention Bob's party. Table 2.5 shows the vignette conditions.

Following the vignette, we asked people how much respect they have for Bob (from 1 = no respect to 5 = total respect) and how they would characterize Bob on a series of polar adjectives. If the liberal respect paradox is driven simply by a Trump effect, we should find that liberals are more respecting of Bob than conservatives in the policy and party conditions. The one condition that should lead liberals to be significantly less able to respect Bob is the vote choice condition in which they are told that Bob voted for Trump. If, on the other hand, liberals disrespect conservatives not only because of Trump but

TABLE 2.5. Experiment vignette and conditions

| Policy condition | Party condition | Vote choice condition |
|---|---|---|
| [*Conservative*] Bob believes that large government means wasteful spending and too much regulation, which can hurt small businesses. He thinks unions often protect lazy and bad workers. He favors charter schools because he believes that competition will improve education and help all children, especially poor children. He thinks affirmative action is reverse discrimination. He believes that raising the minimum wage will lead to job losses, mainly among the poorest citizens. If labor costs too much money, he says, employers will turn to automation. Indeed, he favors restrictions on immigration because he thinks too many immigrants will depress wages for many American citizens, particularly the poorest, or leave them unemployed. | *Policy condition plus a sentence at the end of the vignette:* Bob is a Republican. | *Policy condition plus a sentence at the end of the vignette:* Bob voted for Donald Trump in the 2016 presidential election. |
| [*Liberal*] Bob believes in the positive role of government in people's lives and that government regulation often protects many citizens, especially the most vulnerable. He thinks unions are important to protect the wages of many middle- and lower-income people. He is against charter schools because he thinks they undermine support for public schools, which are important for nearly all children but particularly the poor. He thinks affirmative action is important for certain groups of people to be treated fairly. He believes that raising the minimum wage is important so the poorest citizens can earn enough to live decent lives. Without a minimum wage, there will be a "race to the bottom" among employers to pay employees less and less. With a good minimum wage set in place, he thinks many immigrants can be allowed into the United States because they add so much socially and economically to the country. | *Policy condition plus a sentence at the end of the vignette:* Bob is a Democrat. | *Policy condition plus a sentence at the end of the vignette:* Bob voted for Hillary Clinton in the 2016 presidential election. |

more generally (based on policies or party), we should not find a difference between liberals in the vote condition compared to the other two conditions.

We analyzed the data using analysis of variance with party identification and experimental condition as the two independent variables. The dependent variables (respect and characterizations) were transformed to range from 0 to 1 to allow for easier comparison across variables. We focus on the data for those who read about Bob whose ideology did not align with the respondent's party (i.e., Democrats who read about a conservative Bob and Republicans who read about a liberal Bob). Figure 2.4 shows the results for respect and table 2.6 shows the results for the characterizations of Bob.

As with our focus group and survey measures, we find in our experiment that Republicans are much more likely to say they respect Bob than

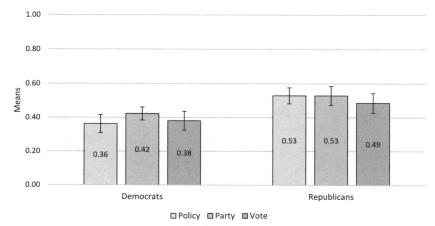

FIGURE 2.4. Respect for Opposing Ideology Bob
*Source*: 2018 Equality and Respect Survey
*Note*: The data, from an ANOVA, are the mean scores on respect for Bob, which was recoded to range from 0 (low respect) to 1 (high respect). Only the main effect of Democrats/Republicans is significant at $p < 0.001$.

Democrats, even though both sets of partisans read about a Bob who held an opposing ideology. Overall, the mean Bob respect score among Democrats is only 0.39 compared to Republicans' mean score of 0.52. The main effect for this difference is highly significant ($F_{(1,614)} = 35.75$, $p < 0.001$). Experimental condition was not significant. Figure 2.4 shows that Democrats who were told that Bob voted for Donald Trump in 2016 were reluctant to say they respected Bob (a mean score of 0.38), but they had almost the same level of respect for Bob when they were just told his policy stances (0.36; a t-test of this difference is not significant). The Democrats who scored highest in respect for Bob were those in the party condition (a mean score of 0.42), but even this high mark for Democrats did not come close to the respect levels of Republicans.

To understand more fully people's respect for Bob, we examined their responses to the same series of polar adjectives discussed above, this time specifically characterizing Bob. If people are open to respecting people with whom they disagree, they will give them the benefit of the doubt and not assume the worst of them. Liberals associate Trump with racism, sexism, and other negative qualities, as the liberal focus groups made clear, and tend to attribute these same qualities to his voters. Are people in our survey experiment more likely to attribute negative qualities to Bob, especially racism and sexism, when they know he voted for Trump? Table 2.6 provides the means of Democrats and Republicans on each of the characteristics within each experimental condition. As we found with respect, Democrats are significantly less likely than Republicans to ascribe positive characteristics to Bob on eight out

TABLE 2.6. Characterizations of Bob

| Characterizations | Democrats (mean) | | | Republicans (mean) | | | Main and 2-way effects (F statistic) |
|---|---|---|---|---|---|---|---|
| | Policy | Party | Vote | Policy | Party | Vote | |
| Racist / Not racist | 0.43 | 0.42 | 0.40 | 0.77 | 0.66 | 0.63 | Party ID = 126.16***<br>Condition = 4.12* |
| Sexist / Not sexist | 0.45 | 0.53 | 0.42 | 0.68 | 0.59 | 0.63 | Party ID = 43.36***<br>2-way = 4.77** |
| Intolerant / Tolerant | 0.28 | 0.32 | 0.28 | 0.62 | 0.60 | 0.55 | Party ID = 142.18*** |
| Uneducated / Educated | 0.43 | 0.54 | 0.38 | 0.61 | 0.57 | 0.53 | Party ID = 25.18***<br>Condition = 6.75***<br>2-way = 4.32* |
| Unintelligent / Intelligent | 0.39 | 0.48 | 0.35 | 0.58 | 0.53 | 0.52 | Party ID = 34.58***<br>Condition = 3.57*<br>2-way = 3.86* |
| Closed-minded / Open-minded | 0.32 | 0.32 | 0.27 | 0.47 | 0.52 | 0.42 | Party ID = 50.89***<br>Condition = 3.78* |
| Misled / Not misled by media | 0.38 | 0.42 | 0.33 | 0.34 | 0.42 | 0.28 | Condition = 7.29*** |
| Follows others / Acts independently | 0.43 | 0.46 | 0.39 | 0.43 | 0.46 | 0.33 | Condition = 5.02** |
| Condescending / Not condescending | 0.26 | 0.40 | 0.31 | 0.49 | 0.43 | 0.48 | Party ID = 38.5***<br>2-way = 7.28*** |
| Not willing / Willing to compromise | 0.27 | 0.30 | 0.25 | 0.49 | 0.48 | 0.39 | Party ID = 49.32*** |

Source: 2018 Equality Attitudes Survey

Note: The data in the Democrats and Republicans columns are mean scores from ANOVAs on the characterizations that have been recoded to range from 0 (most negative) to 1 (most positive). The data in the Main and 2-way effects column are $F$ statistics. The 2-way effects are the interaction of party ID and condition. ***$p < 0.001$; **$p < 0.01$; *$p < 0.05$.

of the ten characteristics. The respondents' party identification is a significant main effect for all the characteristics except misled by the media and follows others. Experimental condition is a significant main effect for six of the characteristics, and there is a significant two-way interaction for four of the characteristics. Democrats tend to be more positive about Bob in the party condition than in the policy and vote choice conditions, whereas Republicans tend to be more positive about Bob in the policy condition.

To test specifically the impact of mentioning Bob's vote choice in comparison to the policy condition, we ran two-sided t-tests to determine whether the differences in means between these two conditions were significant. Among Democrats there were no significant differences between the policy and Trump vote conditions. Among Republicans, five of the t-tests were significant: uneducated, racist, misled by the media, unwilling to compromise, and follows others without thinking. Republicans rated a Clinton-voting Bob much more negatively on these characteristics than simply a liberal Bob. Contrary to there being a strong anti-Trump effect among Democrats, there actually is a stronger anti-Clinton effect among Republicans.

We can only speculate on the reasons why Democrats in the party condition tended to be more positive about Republican Bob than Democrats in the other two conditions. When people read the policy stances held by Bob, they possibly assumed he was a Trump voter. This would explain why there is little difference between the policy and vote conditions. It doesn't explain, though, why people wouldn't associate a conservative Bob who was a Republican with a Trump vote. Almost all Republicans voted for Trump in 2016 (92 percent according to a 2018 Pew Research Center survey, 89 percent according to our 2018 Equality Attitudes Survey), so a safe guess would be that a Republican Bob was also a Trump-voting Bob. We therefore think this is less of a Trump effect and more of a general acceptance of the two-party system. Democrats understand that there are conservatives who are Republicans, and some of them begrudgingly accept this reality (see chapter 3). The main point, though, is that Democrats feel less respect for Bob and are more likely to ascribe negative characteristics to him than Republicans, regardless of whether they know Bob's policy stands, party, or vote. The liberal respect paradox exists, even when Donald Trump is not specifically mentioned.

## DONALD TRUMP IS SINGULARLY HORRIBLE

A second argument we need to address is one that liberals raised frequently in the focus groups for their disrespect for Trump voters: Trump is a singularly

terrible human being. In this view, Trump's words and actions make him particularly reprehensible and, therefore, good people wouldn't vote for him:

> It's just deplorable that you would vote for a man, I get voting Republican, I get
> voting for Marco Rubio, God forbid, but nonetheless, I do get that. I don't get
> voting for that man [Trump]. (Chicago Liberals 2, Man 3)

> I have a very large family and I think, out of my 30-some siblings and spouses
> and nieces and nephews, I may be the only one that didn't vote for Trump . . .
> And I, I'm very conflicted about it but I have certain areas of their life and
> their belief system and their values that I do respect. I know that many of them
> are good people, they do a lot of good work, they take care of the poor, they
> try their best, you know, to overcome some level of racism. I see that in them,
> I know them. And yet . . . you know, they . . . you know, I think that they're
> deplorable. (NC Liberals 5, Woman 3)

One could then say that asking liberals to respect Trump supporters is a test
that is too much to ask and even unfair, whereas asking conservatives to respect Clinton supporters is an easy test. This argument presumes, however,
that Hillary Clinton was a much less noxious candidate to conservatives than
Trump was to liberals, which is not supported by the Bob experiment or by a
wide array of data on the topic.

Our focus group results show that as much as liberals find Trump loathsome, conservatives find Hillary Clinton equally loathsome. Indeed, many of
our conservative focus group participants were mystified why anyone would
vote for Clinton:

> But Hillary herself as a person, I view her as just totally corrupt. The things
> she did. You know? The emails, destroying them. You know, those emails, us-
> ing BleachBit, and the FBI just—. (NC Conservatives 1, Woman 4)

> And I frankly viewed her as a crook. I just did. I didn't want to listen to the
> same stuff. Benghazi made me sick. I actually watched the movie, *13 Hours*,
> I couldn't believe this movie, that this went on. I, I just thought, I just, this
> woman cannot get into office, this is terrible. (NC Conservatives 2, Man 1)

American National Election Studies (ANES) data back up the idea that both
Clinton and Trump were viewed as particularly terrible people by opposing
partisans. ANES asks voters how presidential candidates make them feel.[9] In
2000, Republican candidate George W. Bush angered 45 percent of Democrats. In 2016, a whopping 96 percent of Democrats said Republican candidate
Trump made them feel angry. That high an anger level toward Trump is historically unusual for someone who has not already been president (President

Bush angered 86 percent of Democrats in 2004; Romney angered 64 percent of Democrats in 2012), yet when Republican voters were asked how Hillary Clinton made them feel, 95.5 percent said she made them feel angry. Similarly, the Pew Research Center asked Republican and Democratic voters before the election to rate Trump and Clinton on a feeling thermometer, from 0 (freezing cold) to 100 (very hot). The average rating for Trump among Democrats was 11, which is extraordinarily low. The average rating for Clinton among Republicans, though, was 12 (Gramlich 2016). In other words, both Trump and Clinton were beyond the pale for opposing voters.

The importance of the Clinton/Trump comparison is to show that nearly half of the population saw Clinton as unworthy to be president. If Trump and Clinton were equally hated, then we cannot say that Trump is singularly loathsome and therefore his voters are not to be respected. Trump may be hated by many, but so was Clinton. Pragmatic voters—those wanting to vote for a candidate with a reasonable chance of winning—voted for either Trump or Clinton in 2016, and for many people, voting for one or the other is impossible to imagine. Yet we find that while liberals struggle to respect Trump voters, conservatives are still willing to respect Clinton voters. The "Trump is singularly horrible" argument can't explain the liberal respect paradox.

It's a possibility, though, that Republicans had more respect for Clinton supporters because Trump won the presidency in 2016 and they simply felt more magnanimous. In other words, maybe we captured a loser effect among Democrats. Pew Research Center data suggests this argument is not viable. The Pew Research Center administered a survey on respect two weeks *before* the 2016 election, when many people thought Clinton would win and Trump would lose. Pew asked respondents to choose which statement came closer to their view: "I have a hard time respecting someone who supports [Hillary Clinton/Donald Trump] for president" or "I have no trouble respecting someone who supports [Hillary Clinton/Donald Trump] for President." Fifty-eight percent of Clinton supporters said they had a hard time respecting Trump supporters. Only 40 percent of Trump supporters said the same about Clinton supporters (Gramlich 2016). Even before the 2016 election, Republicans more willingly granted respect to the opposing side than did Democrats, even though both sides loathed the other party's candidate for president.

Other evidence that reinforces the point that we have not captured a Trump effect or a loser effect can be seen in the 2021 PFUNC Survey results in figure 2.3. While the difference is small, Democrats had lower respect than Republicans when asked if they could respect opposing partisans given their political views (means of 0.43 for Democrats and 0.47 for Republicans). What is especially important to point out is that Joe Biden was president during the time this survey was fielded. If election winners are more magnanimous than election losers, we would expect to find Democrats being more respectful than Republicans in 2021, and this is not what we find.

The findings from the Bob experiment, the Pew data, the PFUNC survey, and the equivalent disdain held by partisans toward the opposing party's candidate suggest that the liberal respect paradox cannot simply be pushed aside as a reaction to a Trump presidency. In chapter 4, we explore the reasons why liberals both believe more strongly in respect and equality and have such a difficult time granting respect to their political opponents. (There are also reasons for why some conservatives find it hard to respect their opponents, which we explore in chapter 5.) We do not see any compelling evidence for the idea that the liberal respect paradox is not real, that we have simply captured an ephemeral reaction to the Trump presidency.

It is also now hard to separate Donald Trump from the Republican Party. To be sure, many Republicans dislike Trump, and it is possible to envision a time when the Republican Party is no longer closely associated with Trump. Still, many of Trump's ideas (for example, immigration, foreign policy, and criminal justice) are part of the Republican Party, and Trump himself remains popular among many Republicans, even as that number has declined since 2016. Trying to create a wedge between the Republican Party and Donald Trump does not make much sense as we write this book.

## Conclusion

Political theorists herald the importance of recognition respect in liberal democratic societies. Social psychologists find that respect has a significant positive impact on such things as cooperation, relations with outgroups, and political engagement. Given the importance of recognition respect especially in liberal democracies, we have taken the first dive into understanding people's belief in the principle of recognition respect and their willingness to grant respect to their political adversaries. In these highly polarized times, respecting one's partisan opponents is not easy, and we found that liberals, who believe most strongly in the principle of recognition respect, struggled the most to respect their political opponents. Whether the focus is on Republicans or Trump voters, Democrats say they struggle to respect those across the partisan divide. Almost three-quarters of the comments made in the liberal focus group discussions demonstrated that liberals either struggle to respect or simply do not respect Trump voters. Conservatives are less likely than liberals to equate equality with respect and are equally likely or more likely to say they respect Democrats or Clinton voters. They reveal little struggle in that decision. We argue that this is not a Trump effect. That is, the liberal respect paradox does not exist because it is just about Donald Trump or because Donald Trump is so much more loathsome to liberals than Hillary Clinton is to conservatives.

The liberal respect paradox is real, and we explore in the second half of the book why liberals believe more in recognition respect and have such a difficult time respecting their political opponents. We also address why conservatives find it easier to respect liberals even as they believe less fully in respect. It comes down to questions about equality, justice, solidarity, and how people moralize the political choices others make. Before moving on to explanations for respect, we address in the next chapter a second type of respect: civic respect.

# 3

## The Failed Aspirations of Civic Respect

So she [a relative] couldn't bring herself to vote for Trump, but her husband I think did. And we like him. He's a wonderful guy. He's not stupid; he does not swallow bullshit from other people, he thinks about things. He just has his own agenda that's not ours. He's not prejudiced, they have friends of different races and gender, you know, he's as fully fleshed out as a wonderful person as I am, and you are. So, you know, he still found reasons to vote for Trump. And I think a big failing of Democrats is to not question what were those reasons and not to address them. (NC Liberals 3, Woman 1)

The hardest thing that I found with family members, close friends that don't agree with you at all, is getting a dialogue going. It's like, there's a sandbox right in front of 'em, plop. You know, it's frustrating, because you just want to get an honest discourse. (NC Conservatives 2, Man 2)

One little thing you mentioned, they don't, "well, if you stopped watching Fox News," that's all they have. And it's like, you don't understand. I don't always watch that. But I do read. Well "send me this," "send me that article," well, here's a book for you to read if you've ever read a book. Here's another book for you to read if you want to read about boom, boom, boom, boom. That's what I'm saying, here, here's some titles, here's a list, knock yourself out then we can talk about this. Then it's quiet. And that's how you get them to walk off or go away, because they just have nothing else to say. (NC Conservatives 2, Woman 3)

Recognition respect is fundamental to equality and the functioning of democracy. Civic respect, as we argue in this chapter, is fundamental to helping democracy function well. In any pluralist democracy, people are bound to hold a variety of different political beliefs and opinions. Some of these will be crackpot ideas that don't deserve to be taken seriously, but many will be reasonable or at least understandable. In a well-functioning democracy, people try to understand where opposing partisans are coming from, even if they don't agree with them, and find areas where there might be common ground. In a dysfunctional democracy, one or both sides refuse to listen to or engage with the other side's ideas and instead assume the worst of the opposition.

Civic respect means listening to and taking seriously the ideas of one's fellow citizens. This does not mean that people listen with the idea that their own mind or the mind of the other person will change, though the changing of minds is a possibility. It does mean that people should listen with the idea of understanding why fellow citizens think differently, if they do, and what their reasons are for their beliefs. Being willing to give civic respect demands a belief in pluralism. Accepting that there are multiple viewpoints and political parties, which is an acceptance of pluralism, is essential to civic respect (we give a fuller definition of pluralism in chapter 7).

We improve on theorists' idea of mutual respect—which we argued in chapter 1 is vague—through our conception of civic respect by giving the idea a more precise definition than is usually given and by noting how hard it is to practice civic respect. We use the term *civic respect*, instead of *mutual respect*, to emphasize that we focus on civic discourse, discourse that centers around social and political ideas. Where recognition respect is respecting a person simply as a fellow human being, people practice civic respect by listening (at least sometimes) to opposing ideas respectfully and accepting a real plurality of legitimate political views even if they hold firmly to their own beliefs and disagree heartily with others' views. One can grant recognition respect to a person, but not civic respect, though the reverse is rarely the case.

Civic respect potentially poses a difficult challenge. Talking about politics with those with whom one disagrees can lead to conflict and even ruined relationships, leading most people to try to stay away from the topic (Mutz 2006; Eliasoph 1998; Ulbig and Funk 1999; Testa, Hibbing, and Ritchie 2014). One focus group participant made this clear:

> Yeah, I'm surprised at the depth of visceral feeling that people have and the significant change in personal relationships. I mean, in my family of four I'm the only conservative. And so again, we don't talk politics at all. My wife didn't talk to me for probably 7, 8 days after the election. (NC Conservatives 3, Man 2)

We make an important distinction, though, between interpersonal and impersonal civic respect. Our argument that people need to be willing to entertain and understand the ideas of the opposing side does not mean they have to talk face-to-face to do so. People can learn a lot about opposing partisans' views by reading their articles or blogs or by listening to their podcasts or other media. We address this distinction between interpersonal and impersonal civic respect but focus more on personal relations because those settings are especially fraught.

Our argument in this chapter is that most citizens *say* they believe in civic respect, but they (both Democrats and Republicans) have a hard time *practicing* this respect. It is easy to believe that respect is important, but when faced with opposing partisans in a polarized environment, the legs on which civic respect stands become wobbly. Through our focus groups, two surveys, and an experiment, we identify two common ways in which many liberal and conservative citizens fall short of civic respect. First, being willing to grant civic respect depends on believing in the legitimacy of more than one's own political party or political views. Especially in a two-party system like the United States', the two major parties are umbrella parties that contain a wide range of issue stands and disagreement within the membership. Civic respect means not assuming the worst of opposing partisans and accepting that the other party's stands are for the most part legitimate. This acceptance of pluralism is difficult for people when affective polarization splits them so deeply. Second, civic respect is hard to practice when citizens define others by their political views and, especially, their vote. When citizens define others by their vote, they typically do so in a narrow way, stereotyping millions of voters who in reality vote as they do for a variety of reasons and motivations. We ask who is more likely to engage in civic respect and not stereotype opposing partisans, focusing on the heterogeneity of people's social networks and age. Before delving into the data, though, we begin by addressing more fully what civic respect is. We define civic respect, but we also address the notion that, unlike recognition respect, it is not a universal concept. We test civic respect empirically in this chapter and discuss its boundaries in chapter 7.

## Defining Civic Respect

Mutual respect means listening to and taking seriously the ideas of one's fellow citizens, even among disagreement. In what context, though, do we listen to and respect others? Social egalitarians often speak about respect in terms of face-to-face interactions. For example, two prominent social egalitarians suggest their focus is on individual interactions: Anderson (2008, 265) discusses individuals talking "eye to eye," while Scheffler (2015) illustrates the egalitarian deliberative constraint with a family discussing where they should vacation. Similarly, Philip Pettit (2013, 58), in his argument for neo-republicanism, argues that "people should have a publicly established and acknowledged status in relation to others; only this could enable them to walk tall and look others in the eye." In the deliberative context, Gutmann and Thompson (1996) discuss "constructive interaction with" people with whom one disagrees, which alludes to personal interactions.

Yet mutual respect theorists are interested in respect as part of justice, as part of the fabric of a just society. This is important for understanding the context of respect: it is not only about interpersonal interaction but also about impersonal interaction. Unsurprisingly, toward the end of his essay explaining the "egalitarian deliberative constraint," Scheffler (2015, 38) says that the question is how to scale up the constraint in a "society of equals" since the issue is how we think about "the institutions and practices that constitute the social framework." James Wilson (2019, 36) begins his argument about respect as part of democratic equality in small interpersonal settings, but he, too, scales up, as he discusses "beyond face-to-face relationships." He argues that we need to extend the "egalitarian ideal beyond familiar interpersonal relationships to more complex relationships and social structures." For Wilson, as for many of the theorists we discuss here, an egalitarian society is not just about face-to-face interactions but should infuse all of society.

If civic respect is to be part of a good society, then it should encompass both personal *and* impersonal interactions. One reason why this is important is that many people do not discuss on a personal level divisive social and political issues with people with whom they disagree. Sometimes this is because such people are not in their social circles; other times, it is because people routinely avoid political conversations when conflict might erupt (Mutz 2006). In our surveys, which we detail below, we ask people if they are willing to engage opposing partisans in a variety of ways. We want to know if people steer away from opposing partisans or seek them out. We test directly, using an experimental design, people's willingness to engage with those with whom they disagree in interpersonal and impersonal ways.

This leads to the first part of our civic respect definition: civic respect means listening to those with different political and social views in either or both impersonal and interpersonal ways. This definition highlights a difference between recognition respect and civic respect: listening to others about political and social matters is necessary for the latter but not the former. Listening should be earnest, with the intent to learn, not just to be able to rebut the views of others. It means trying to understand why others do not think as one does and why they vote differently, even if some of the views expressed are not worthy of being taken seriously (Cohen 2014, 3). Listening respectfully does not mean one must agree with the views of others, but it does mean that one takes people seriously, as people with ideas worthy of consideration. Even in the face of disagreement, one should presumably find *some* views among one's political opponents that are reasonable or that provide an understanding for why opposing partisans reject voting for one's own political party. It is also the case that one does not have to listen to the same arguments repeatedly. Since many people have settled views on issues, more listening is not necessarily important or useful once one understands the views of others. Listening with the goal of understanding is key to civic respect, not repeated listening to the same arguments. We want to emphasize again that some views are not worthy of consideration—the idea that Bill Gates implanted a chip into COVID vaccines is ridiculous. Yet civic respect means an acceptance of the idea that issues change over time, as do people, and in these cases, it is important not to dismiss others because you have disagreed with them on a different set of issues in the past.

The second part of our civic respect definition involves not engaging in political stereotyping. Political stereotyping occurs when people define others by their vote or their party. It is easy to think of "Biden voters" or "Trump voters" or "Democrats" or "Republicans" and then attribute many beliefs to these people based on the candidate or party. When we engage in political stereotyping of opposing partisans, we often assume the worst about them (Ahler and Sood 2022; Ahler and Sood 2018). These assumptions may be true for some opposing partisans, but people have many different motivations for their vote or party choice. Most American citizens see their choice as a binary one, Republican or Democrat, Biden or Trump. Votes are compromises for most people: voting for a candidate does not mean voters agree with all or even most of the positions taken by a particular candidate. The many Obama 2012/Trump 2016 voters show this; so, too, do the many people who voted for Biden but then for Republican candidates in the House and Senate races in 2020. This may seem obvious, but our research shows that many people ascribe clear, narrow, and base motives to opposing partisans, and when they do, they stop listening. If your political opponents are all socialist or fascist or unpatriotic or racist, for example, why listen to them? Political stereotyping cuts out opposing partisans from further consideration.

Third, because civic respect involves trying to understand the other side's positions, people should not assume that citizens who vote for the opposing candidate do so because they are poorly informed, ignorant, or misled. In some ways this is the most important part of civic respect because it suggests that pluralism is based on ignorance, not legitimate disagreement. To say that millions of people vote for the opposing party because they are ill-informed, don't understand the issues, or are misled by copartisans or the media is to assume that if people were better educated or informed, they would vote as you do; it is to assume a kind of hubris, that everyone should vote for one's side. Making these dismissive assumptions about one's political opponents reveals a serious lack of acceptance of pluralism, and this is certainly a rejection of civic respect. We do not deny that some voters are ignorant or misinformed—*of course* some are—and if one realizes that another's views are in fact misinformed, or the person refuses to accept obvious facts, civic respect does not demand that one continually engage with this person (though there may be reason to reengage in the future). But it is a violation of civic respect and common sense to assume that all opposing partisans are ignorant and misinformed. What is true is that voters have different priorities, that voters are motivated by different policies and values, and that voters sometimes vote against a political party as much as they vote for one.

It should be clear from this three-part definition that civic respect is both a belief and a practice. As a belief, civic respect is an openness to learning about others and their views and accepting the legitimacy of divergent views and political parties. We argue that people ought to believe in civic respect in their everyday lives. As a practice, civic respect means listening to and engaging with the opposing side to learn about their ideas and arguments, and it means not ignoring people entirely because they have a few views with which one disagrees or because one assumes they are ignorant or misled. Unlike the belief in civic respect, its practice is likely to be sporadic. Some people live or work with opposing partisans, and these people will likely face practicing civic respect daily. Other people rarely run into opposing partisans, so their opportunity to practice interpersonal civic respect will be limited. They can still, of course, practice impersonal civic respect routinely. Regardless of one's life circumstances, we do not envision the practice of civic respect as something people must engage in every day. People can choose to take a break from talking about politics or they can decide not to read a blog from a political opponent. Opposing views might be harder to listen to coming from a close relative than from someone more distant. Someone might not be able to listen to opposing partisans at one moment but be able to at some later date, particularly if the topic or situation changes. Someone might understand what opposing partisans think about a particular issue, and so they do not have to listen to the arguments again and again. While people ought to practice civic respect as the best options, it is all right for people to take a break.

An outcome of civic respect is the acceptance of the idea that it is reasonable for people not to vote or identify as one does, that there are good reasons why people vote for or identify with a different political party. Our definition of civic respect is based on the idea that a democratic society is pluralistic and that people hold different values. People will also weigh evidence differently from one another, yet we also think that people's normative frameworks shape the way they look at evidence. To think that one might be mistaken, or to think that one is correct but the beliefs of others are nonetheless worth hearing, is not easy. Jonathan Rauch (2021) refers to the willingness to accept that one might be wrong as the principle of fallibilism. This type of humility surrounding one's beliefs would, we think, contribute to increased civic respect. If we are confident that we are right, then why shouldn't we think that others are wrong, that any disagreement is based on their unreasonableness or their ignorance or their misinformation? This is what many citizens believe, though doing so undermines civic respect.

We know some readers will want to know why the opposing political party deserves civic respect. For example, Democrats might believe that many Republican elected officials have worrisome views about democracy and elections (where vote counting is nearly always accurate) and spew hateful views about Democrats. We have little doubt that this is true for some Republican leaders, yet the leaders of a political party are not the same as their voters. Voters may wish they had a different slate of candidates to vote for in the general election, since it is often the case that only a small percentage of voters choose the winners in a primary, but they must choose among the candidates on the ballot. People often hold their nose when they vote. Moreover, liberals must wrestle with the fact that over half of voters (50.6 percent) chose a Republican candidate in the 2022 House of Representatives elections, while 47.8 percent chose a Democrat. If the Republican leadership is so crazy, why do so many voters reject the Democratic message? If the Republican Party is so racist, why did the percentage of people of color voting for Republicans *increase* in 2022 compared to the previous midterm election (Foster-Frau and Rodriguez 2022)? Are liberals really willing to say that over half the electorate does not deserve any civic respect, that there is no worthy reason why so many voters rejected the Democrats? Doing so certainly allows liberals to avoid being self-reflective.

While the Republicans gained more votes than Democrats in the 2022 House elections, they gained fewer seats than is normal for the party out of power in a midterm election. Republicans, too, should wonder why they did not gain more votes, and why so many of their Senate candidates lost. Of course, many scholars and commentators have noted rural residents' move away from the Democratic Party and toward Trump in 2016 (Muravchik and Shields 2020). Similarly, many suburban women have shifted toward the Democrats in the last few years. People practicing civic respect want to understand why others are leaving their political party, and they look for reasons that are not based in ignorance or misinformation. Few major political parties are bereft of any reasonable ideas, and few political parties have a monopoly on all reasonable ideas.

## The Belief and Practice of Civic Respect

We showed in the previous chapter that people believe in the abstract principle of recognition respect but that Democrats are less likely than Republicans to grant recognition respect to opposing partisans in practice. We test whether civic respect is similarly supported in the abstract and whether this support dissipates when people are asked to grant civic respect to opposing partisans. Most Americans are taught, after all, that people are entitled to their own opinions on issues, that debate and discussion are good. We hypothesize that people will agree with the idea of civic respect in the abstract, but when they are asked about actually talking with and listening to opposing partisans, they will be less eager to support civic respect. That is, people will hold a belief in civic respect more than they put it into practice.

We begin with our 2019 Pluralism and Respect Survey. Our measure of abstract civic respect is agreement or disagreement with the statement "Respecting others means being willing to listen to what they have to say, even if one disagrees with them" (mean 0.802, sd 0.194). We posed several statements that measure the *practice* of civic respect. We used responses to these statements to create two scales, one reflecting a willingness to listen to opposing political beliefs and the other a willingness to engage with opposing partisans. The former, what we call the civic respect-listen scale, was created adding together responses to four statements: "I can't listen to someone when I disagree with their political views," "Respect is impossible to give to someone whose political views are different from my own," "Honestly, I don't really listen to what people say about politics if they belong to a different political party than I do," and "I sometimes feel it would be better if people in different political groups didn't try to mix together" (mean 0.632, sd 0.247, alpha 0.849). This scale, particularly the first two statements, leaves open the idea of whether civic respect takes place in personal or impersonal settings. The civic respect-engage scale is more directly about personal interaction and is an additive scale that consists of responses to two statements and one question: "I like meeting and getting to know people with political beliefs different from my own," "I often spend time with people who have political beliefs different from my own," and "How often do you talk about politics with people who belong to a different political party than you?" (mean 0.529, sd 0.205, alpha 0.608). Response options for the statements ranged from strongly agree to strongly disagree. For the "How often do you talk" question, response options were never, occasionally, sometimes, and often. The abstract civic respect statement and the two scales were coded to range from 0 = low civic respect to 1 = high civic respect.

Table 3.1 shows the mean responses among Democrats and Republicans on civic respect. As we expected, Americans say they agree with the abstract ideal, scoring right around 0.8 on a 0 to 1 scale, but they are much less likely to support civic respect when focused on opposing partisans. Respondents scored just above 0.6 (on a 0 to 1 scale) when asked the civic respect-listen questions. Respondents believe that listening is an important aspect of respect, but this principle doesn't necessarily apply to those who hold opposing political views. They are even less likely to acknowledge that they engage

TABLE 3.1. Abstract and practical civic respect

| | Abstract civic respect | | Civic respect—listen | | Civic respect—engage | |
|---|---|---|---|---|---|---|
| | Mean | Percent agree | Mean | Percent agree | Mean | Percent agree |
| Democrats | 0.802 | 87 | 0.615 | 58 | 0.538 | 42 |
| Republicans | 0.806 | 89 | 0.638 | 64 | 0.516 | 36 |
| t value | −0.406 | | −2.42* | | 1.919 | |

Source: 2019 Pluralism and Respect Survey

Note: Means based on 0 = low civic respect, 1 = high civic respect. The t values are from independent sample t-tests (two-sided). N = 1,300. "Percent agree" is the percentage of those who agree or strongly agree with the abstract civic respect question or who score 0.6 or higher on the civic respect—listen and civic respect—engage scales. *p < 0.05.

with opposing partisans, garnering a mean response just above 0.5 for both Democrats and Republicans. There is a statistically significant (or nearly so) difference between the responses of opposing partisans on the two practical civic respect scales, with Republicans scoring higher on Civic Respect-Listen and Democrats scoring higher on Civic Respect-Engage. The bottom line is that civic respect sounds good in the abstract to many Americans, but they have trouble practicing it across partisan boundaries.

## Interpersonal and Impersonal Civic Respect

Our measures of civic respect in practice do not explicitly distinguish interpersonal from impersonal civic respect, although civic respect-engage assumes personal interactions with political opponents. It is important, however, to make explicit the idea that civic respect as we envision it can include engaging with and listening to opposing partisans' ideas from a greater distance. People can practice civic respect not only by being willing to talk to opposing partisans but also by being willing to read or listen via mass media to the opponents' views. People shy away from conflict, and being in a face-to-face discussion with a partisan opponent can lead to conflict. It might be easier for people to practice civic respect impersonally, from a distance.

We conducted an online (Dynata) experiment in May 2021 to directly test the impact of disagreement on both interpersonal and impersonal civic respect. People were randomly assigned to one of five conditions. Those in the control condition read a series of five statements on the benefits of hiking; those in the experimental conditions read five pro or five anti statements on a political issue.[1] Following the statements, we asked the respondents, "To what extent do you, personally, agree with the point of view on [hiking or the political issue] reflected in the five statements listed above?" The response options ranged from strongly agree to strongly disagree.

We then randomly assigned respondents to an interpersonal or impersonal civic respect condition. Those in the impersonal condition were asked, "After reading the statements you just read, some people are interested in learning more about the point of view taken in those statements. We have chosen a couple of articles that more fully lay out that point of view. You'll have an opportunity to read the articles immediately after you have finished the survey. Are you interested in reading the articles after the survey?" In the interpersonal condition, respondents were asked, "After reading the statements you just read, some people are interested in learning more about the point of view taken in those statements. We have put together a panel of people willing to talk or text with our survey participants and therefore have someone available who strongly holds this point of view. You'll have an opportunity to talk or text with this person immediately after you have finished the survey. Are you interested in talking or texting with this person after the survey?" Response options for the impersonal and interpersonal questions were yes or no. We then asked all respondents a series of questions on civic and recognition respect. At the end of the survey, respondents were given a debriefing form explaining the experiment and that there were no articles to read or people with whom to talk. Respondents were asked if they wanted their data withdrawn once they understood the nature of the experiment. Of those who participated in the experiment and passed the attention check question, eight people asked that their data be withdrawn and the remaining 320 said they continued to give consent to use their data. We removed the data of the eight people who asked us to do so.

Many people are not eager to talk to a stranger, so it is likely that in general people will be more amenable to reading some articles than to talking to someone about a political issue. While we expect both kinds of civic respect to be lower when people disagree with the issue compared to when they agree, we thought impersonal respect would be higher than interpersonal respect even in the context of disagreement. Being willing to engage with the opposing side's ideas by reading about their point of view is an easier way to show civic respect than talking directly with an opponent. Figure 3.1 provides the results on the control group (hiking) as well as a breakdown of responses based on the respondents' agreement or disagreement with the political issue position taken in the statements they read. Since no one disagreed with the statements on the benefits of hiking, the hiking results include only those who agree with the statements.

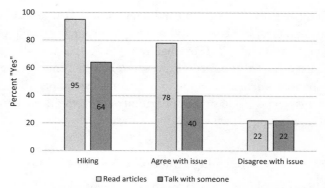

FIGURE 3.1. The Impact of Agreement and Disagreement on Impersonal and Interpersonal Civic Respect
*Source*: Civic Respect Experiment (2021)
*Note*: Percent "Yes" is the percentage of people who said yes, they would be interested in reading articles or talking to someone about the issue covered in the statements they read. "Agree" or "disagree" register whether the respondent agreed/strongly agreed or disagreed/strongly disagreed with the statements they read.

The results show clearly that people are more willing to read articles than to talk or text with someone about an issue. Even on the benign issue of hiking, many fewer people said they would be willing to talk to someone (64 percent) compared to those who said they would read articles on the topic (95 percent). A second general finding is that people are more willing to learn more about a nonpolitical topic than about a political one. Comparing those who agreed with the political issue to those who agreed about the benefits of hiking, we see that 17 percent fewer people said they would read articles on the political issue and 24 percent fewer people said they would talk with someone about the political issue compared to the hiking group. The major story, though, is the pronounced drop in the percentage of people willing to read or talk about an issue with which they disagreed. Almost half as many people said they would talk with someone about an issue when they disagreed with it compared to when they agreed with it (a drop from 40 percent to 22 percent), but this pales in comparison to the drop in people who were willing to read a couple of articles on the issue (a drop from 78 to 22 percent).[2] Impersonal civic respect is easier than interpersonal civic respect overall, but not when disagreement is brought into the mix. Our argument about civic respect is that people need to be willing to try to understand where opposing partisans are coming from, even if they disagree with their views. Contrary to our expectations, our experiment results show that only about one out of five people is willing to extend civic respect to their political opponents, even when it involves reading a couple of articles on the topic.

The findings from our experiment are important because they provide a direct behavioral test of people's willingness to engage in civic respect. The survey data results in table 3.1 show that from 50 to 65 percent of respondents claim to practice civic respect. In the experiment, however, only just over 20 percent of respondents actually commit to practicing civic respect. These results suggest that when people have the opportunity to practice civic respect, very few people are willing to step forward.

## Accepting a Multiparty System

People are much less likely to listen to and engage with opposing partisans than to believe in the ideal of civic respect. We argued earlier that civic respect is interconnected with a belief in pluralism, which we examine by looking at support for a multiparty system. Most democratic countries have at least two political parties that jockey for the allegiance and votes of the citizenry. The two major parties in the United States represent a vast array of interests, with the Democratic Party including under its umbrella the interests of liberals and the Republican Party including under its umbrella the interests of conservatives. People can say they are open to the ideas of others, but they must also accept that one or more political parties beyond one's own will compete for votes. Unsurprisingly, most Americans do believe in a multiparty system—or at least they *say* they do. We asked respondents in our 2019 Pluralism and Respect Survey to respond to a basic statement: "Having at least two political parties that compete in close elections is a good thing." Both Democrats (70 percent) and Republicans (76 percent) agreed or strongly agreed with this statement.

People have a much harder time, however, accepting that the opposing party ought to win on occasion. We posed to respondents three statements that specifically raised the specter of the opposition in a multiparty system: "Our country would be better off if everyone voted for my party," "I can't think of any good reasons why someone would vote for the [Republican/ Democratic] Party," and "Our country would be better off if the [Republican/ Democratic] Party won very few elections." Response options ranged from strongly agree to strongly disagree, and respondents were asked about the party with which they did not identify for the latter two questions. People who support a multiparty system and are open to the idea that there might be legitimate reasons for people to vote for the other party would disagree with these statements. People who reject this pluralist stance would agree with these statements.

Figure 3.2 shows that when respondents were asked if it would be better for the country if everyone voted for their political party, many more people

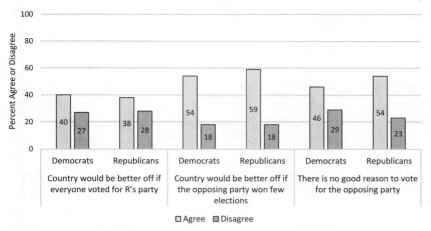

FIGURE 3.2. Support for a Multiparty System
*Source*: 2019 Pluralism and Respect Survey
*Note*: Cell entries are the percentage of respondents who agreed/strongly agreed or disagreed/strongly disagreed with the statements. The excluded category is "Neither agree nor disagree."

agreed than disagreed. Only about a quarter of respondents thought it might not be such a good idea for everyone to vote for their own party. People may have balked at the idea that "everyone" should vote for their party as they were even more approving of the idea that the opposing party should win few elections. Over half of Democrats and Republicans want the opposing party to win few elections, with only 18 percent disagreeing. About half of respondents also say that there is no good reason to vote for the opposing party. If about half of Americans cannot think of a good reason why someone would vote for the opposing political party (with another quarter saying they "neither agree nor disagree"), and if a similar percentage thinks the country would be better off if *everyone* voted for their party and the other party lost just about all of the time, then they are not practicing civic respect. This inability to accept a basic pluralist premise that more than one party exists to represent people's interests provides additional evidence that most people in the United States do not practice civic respect.

## The Problem of Defining People by Their Party and Vote

One way that civic disrespect is manifested is when people define others by their party choice and their vote in a way that negatively simplifies opposing partisans and their motivations. Stereotyping people based on their party and vote is a problem given that people choose a party and cast the vote they do for a number of reasons, not least of which is that the United States has only two major political parties that are umbrellas for a wide variety of issue stands and interests. A person who is conservative politically will likely identify as a Republican and want to elect a representative who is different from the representative of choice of a liberal person. With the limited options offered in a two-party system, people might vote for their party's candidate even if they don't particularly like the candidate because they do not care for the issue stands of the opposing party's candidate. In addition, political scientists know that many people vote *against* a candidate as much as they vote *for* a candidate. In 2016, many people found Hillary Clinton to be an unappealing candidate, whereas others found Donald Trump to be unappealing. Defining people by their vote choice, then, as if their motivations and their interests can be assumed, is a sign of civic disrespect. Of course, defining people by their vote may make sense if a political party explicitly defines itself around one or two issues, but that is not the case for the Democratic or the Republican Party.

People willingly acknowledge that they define people by their political attitudes and their vote choices. In our Equality Attitudes Survey (2018), we asked respondents if they agreed with the following statement: "People's political views say something deeply about who they are as a person." Three-quarters of Democrats (75 percent) and 63 percent of Republicans agreed or strongly agreed.[3] In our Pluralism and Respect Survey (2019), we asked people to agree or disagree with the statement "Who people vote for in an election says a lot about the voter." We again found that most people agreed with the statement; 74 percent of Democrats and 62 percent of Republicans agreed or strongly agreed. People overwhelmingly agree that they judge other people based on their vote even though they also agree that "we shouldn't judge people based on who they voted for" (61 percent of Democrats and 74 percent of Republicans agreed).

These responses would not be troubling if what people thought the vote said about opposing voters was nuanced in both positive and negative ways, or based on listening to and understanding why people voted as they did. Instead, we found in both our surveys and in the focus groups that people attribute opposing partisans' vote choice to sweeping negative motivations and characteristics, not party affiliation or issue stands or concerns about the country.

We asked our focus group participants a basic question: Why did people in the opposing party cast the vote they did for president in 2016? Among our liberals, a few participants mentioned abortion; a few mentioned job loss and fear of change; a few mentioned lower taxes, but usually with a sneer and the implication that the desire for lower taxes was motivated by greed. Beyond that, mentions of policies driving conservative votes were rare. Terrorism, economic growth, abortion, and immigration are all issues that motivate conservative voters differently than liberal voters, yet these issues were hardly mentioned by our liberal participants. All in all, only 17 percent of the reasons liberals gave for a Trump vote mentioned policies or partisanship.

Our conservative focus group participants mentioned policies as a motivator for Clinton voters even less than the liberal participants. No conservative mentioned health care, the environment, or the treatment of people of color as a reason why liberals voted for Clinton. Among all conservative comments given in answer to the question, only 14 percent focused on policies or partisanship; while these two categories were coded together, none of our conservative participants mentioned policy reasons. Eighteen percent of all conservative comments did say that Democrats perceived Clinton to be better qualified than Trump, while no Democrats suggested that anyone might think that Trump was better qualified than Clinton.

To be clear, we asked our participants why they thought opposing partisans voted the way they did, not to express agreement with their positions or their vote choice. A conservative can recognize that government-supported health care is important to many liberals without agreeing with the idea. A liberal can recognize, without agreeing with the argument, that conservatives might want smaller government because they believe the government does not always do the right thing with its power.

What we found in our survey was that many people view opposing voters in highly negative terms. We asked both Clinton and Trump voters in our Pluralism and Respect Survey (2019) to what extent they agreed that people who voted for the opposing candidate are immoral and intolerant. Because we heard many times in our liberal focus groups that Trump was racist and sexist and in our conservative focus groups that Clinton was condescending and, especially, dishonest, we also asked Clinton voters whether Trump voters are racist and sexist and Trump voters whether Clinton voters are dishonest and condescending.[4] Figure 3.3 shows the percentage of Clinton and Trump voters who thought opposing voters fit each characteristic. Clinton voters were more negative in their evaluations than Trump voters. One-third (34 percent) of Clinton voters said Trump voters are immoral, and about half said Trump voters are intolerant, racist, and sexist. Trump voters were less likely to call Clinton voters immoral and dishonest (about a quarter of them did), but over 40 percent said Clinton voters are intolerant and condescending. If respondents figured that some proportion of opposing voters had these negative characteristics but that most did not, they could have answered "Neither agree nor disagree" or even given opposing voters the benefit of the doubt by disagreeing with the characterizations. Many voters, especially among Clinton supporters, assumed the worst about opposing voters.

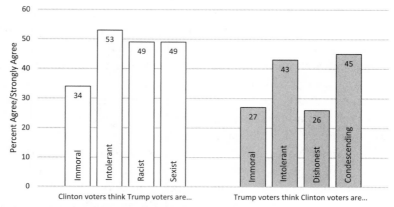

FIGURE 3.3. Characterizations of Clinton and Trump Voters
*Source*: Pluralism and Respect Survey (2019)

We dig more deeply into the idea, expressed by many of our focus group participants, that a driving motivation behind the votes of opposing partisans was a perceived characteristic of the candidate for whom they voted. We saw this among our focus group conservatives when some participants argued that the only or a main reason people voted for Clinton was because she was a woman.

> Well, people voted for Hillary because she was name recognition. Her name was out there, book's been on the news for twelve years or whatever since Bill was in. And she was to be the first woman president. I know women that voted for her, just so she could be the first woman president. Not qualified, but they automatically qualified her because, well, she was Secretary of State: stamp. You know, and nothing in the background, associated with Bill or anything else. She had a credential, and she had name recognition, she was a woman. (NC Conservatives 2, Man 2)

> And I think a little bit of it might even be "She's a woman, I'm a woman, I want a woman." (NC Conservatives 3, Woman 1)

> And I know several people who voted for her because she was a woman and then that was the, they were a one-topic voter and that's the only thing that mattered to them. (Nebraska Conservatives 1, Man 3)

> I thought it was demeaning to women. I mean, I'm a retired physician so I thought, you know, if you're going to vote because somebody has ovaries rather than testicles, you're pretty stupid. (NC Conservatives 2, Man 1)

Here we see that some conservatives assume that a large percentage of Clinton voters were motivated solely by gender considerations. Twenty-three percent of all reasons mentioned by conservatives for why people voted for Clinton pointed to her gender.

This tendency to attribute a particular characteristic associated with the candidate to the voters was especially apparent, though, among the liberals in our focus groups, who focused primarily on race. Many liberals think that Trump is racist and therefore that his voters are as well.

> I still hold that anybody who voted for him at their core is racist, because they couldn't have listened to those words and not been racists. (NC Liberals 6, Woman 3)

> [T]here's no doubt to me, it's racism. Just racism. Eight years of Obama, people hated it, and there was all kinds of, yeah—And the fact that whenever that would raise its head during the election, Trump did not denounce it, to me shows that he knew perfectly well that that was a subswath that was important to his election. Not only did he not denounce it, he courted it. (Chicago Liberals 4, Man 4)

The data in figure 3.3 corroborate the focus group comments: about half of Clinton voters do in fact think that Trump voters are racist.

What is striking in both sets of focus group comments is that some liberals and some conservatives think many or nearly all voters on the other side are motivated by one issue. The idea that many liberals would vote for Hillary Clinton mostly or solely because she is a woman is obviously wrong. That Clinton is a woman might be an extra reason to vote for her, but it is hard to believe that many liberals would have voted for Trump if the nominee of the Democratic Party had been a man. While the specter of race was on the minds of many liberals when thinking about Trump voters, it is too simple to say that racism was the main motivator for most Trump voters. We will not deny that some Trump voters are racist, but stereotyping all Trump voters— millions of people—will obviously lead one to mischaracterize many, many fellow citizens. A few of our conservative participants noted the negative stereotyping aimed at them because of their vote:

> I've been placed in situations where my political ideology has been assumed, based off the color of my skin and so when people come up to me like "Wait, wait a second. You're this and you voted for that, how, you know, how dare you?" And I've been confronted by that several times. (NC Conservatives 4, Man 3)

> Yeah, and obviously being a female and people in this room being a minority, not identifiers, it's almost like "Well, why do you hate yourself?" And I'm like "That's not at all what I'm doing" and when you try to explain your position, you're immediately shouted down, you're being called a racist, a sexist, which that's new to me. Yeah, I betray my own gender, "you're a homophobe," and

I'm like "You don't even know my stances when in fact I'm the minority of the conservatives." (NC Conservatives 4, Woman 1)

Before I left Atlanta I had a couple of friends that were liberal in their politics, and that was fine. You know, we didn't get into it, we tried to talk a little bit. But then when Obama ran and they found out that I did not vote for him, all of a sudden, I'm a racist. And so I experienced that, quote, what was supposed to be a friendship dissolved very quickly. So I did not even try to discuss issues. And you just said something that was very true about the labelling, and you know, you don't have to say hardly anything and all of a sudden you're pounced upon as a "you're a this" or "you're a that," and so it makes it very difficult to even have discussions, because some people don't want to discuss, they want to dictate what you're supposed to think, and that's a huge part of the problem. (NC Conservatives 2, Woman 3)

People vote for their candidate for many different reasons. This seems so obvious that it seems odd to even say it. We are not denying that race is a factor in the vote of some conservatives, but there are clearly other issues motivating them: social solidarity and liberty (issues that we focus on in chapter 5), fear of socialism and "big government," abortion, tax rates, guns, and so on. Moreover, there are many "Obama-Trump" voters, while the percentage of Black and Latino voters for Trump apparently *increased* from 2016 to 2020 (though the vast majority of Black and Latino voters cast their ballots for Biden). As we noted in chapter 1, conservatives are more positive about Black conservatives than white liberals (Brandt et al. 2014; Chambers, Schlenker, and Collisson 2013), suggesting that ideology can trump race. None of this means that race is rarely a factor in people's voting decisions, but a counterfactual is a useful heuristic: if race were not a factor, would nearly all Trump voters have supported Clinton in 2016? We think the answer is obviously no. The reasons why over 70 million people voted for Donald Trump in 2020 (and over 60 million in 2016) are multifocal—different reasons motivate different voters, and it surely defies pluralism and civic respect to assume that 60 million or more people are motivated to vote for a candidate for the same reason.

### IGNORANT AND MISLED

Another common argument among both liberal and conservative focus group participants was that the other side is ignorant and misled by the media. Some conservatives pointed to Clinton's past and determined that a vote for her could only be caused by ignorance or media misinformation:

Well and I think—I mean there's—as we all know there's a certain segment of the population that votes because it is told, they're told how to vote. They're given a piece of paper or they're taken to the polls, they are influenced in that way, in one regard or another. (NC Conservatives 1, Woman 2)

I just think of them [Clinton voters] as—you know, I—this would be private in my own little head, I think, "you know, they're just misinformed." (NC Conservatives 1, Woman 1)

Many liberals echoed the idea that it was ignorance or being misinformed by the media that propelled people to vote for Trump:

I also think the misinformation, or disinformation, whatever you want to call it in our country propelled him as well. The lack of decent media coverage, you know, the media not doing their job. I think they didn't, they didn't press Trump enough on issues. I think people didn't have a clear idea of what he even stood for, I mean [he] flip flops all the time. You don't even, even now, then and now, who knows what the man believes really, if anything? He doesn't even know. So I think the media was at fault, I think the social, the mainstream media and social media. (Chicago Liberals 2, Woman 1)

And I just want to pick up on your word of "uninformed." Because I've been trying really hard not to say "uneducated" because who am I to say, I don't know. Like, is there research that shows that people in rural communities are less educated? I don't know. But, my question is, where did the information come from? Was there any even sought? And if it's given to them, why would they believe it, you know? So I just ask myself I have to imagine that so many of the people who voted for Trump were uninformed. (Chicago Liberals 4, Woman 1)

What is striking in these comments is the implicit suggestion—by both liberals and conservatives—that if voters of the opposing party were educated or better informed or tuned in to the right media outlets, they would change their vote. If ignorance explains their vote, then presumably a well-educated and informed public would all cast their votes for one party. Ignorance may well play a role in how some citizens vote, but the idea that ignorance is the key factor in how most or all opposing partisans vote is quite astounding.

The idea that "if people were just educated and informed enough, they would vote for my party" reveals an inability to accept the political pluralism that is a feature of all modern democracies. Civic respect means understanding that one's fellow citizens will disagree on key issues, and that these differences are not rooted in ignorance but in different worldviews, political perspectives, and so on. Some of our participants understand this. After two women complained that liberals were getting all their information from the liberal media, a third responded:

> But again, it's the, right it's the—they say exactly the same thing about Fox—I'm not making a value judgment with this analogy, but it's like Flatlander. Right? I mean, you know, here's one group is working in this two-dimensional world and another group is talking about something up here in the third dimension and there's like, I mean, you might as well be talking ancient Greek to me. You know, whatever you're talking about, it doesn't mean anything. Like, it's not even in my realm. (NC Conservatives 1, Woman 1)

We showed in chapter 2 that partisans are quick to characterize opposing voters negatively on several bipolar adjectives (see table 2.4). Democrats are significantly more likely than Republicans to characterize opposing party voters as uneducated (means of 0.32 among Democrats and 0.46 among Republicans) and unintelligent (means of 0.30 among Democrats and 0.42 among Republicans). Partisans are equally likely to characterize the opposition as being misled by the media and following others. Indeed, Republicans' harshest evaluation of Clinton voters was on being misled by the media (a mean of 0.25, compared to Democrats' mean of 0.28). Their second lowest score, and one that was only slightly higher than that of Democrats, was "acts independently" or "follows others" (0.29 for Republicans and 0.27 for Democrats). In other words, most voters think that the opposing voters vote because they are part of a large group of ignorant, like-minded people who are misled by the media.

We asked a question in our Pluralism and Respect Survey (2019) that got at whether respondents attributed a vote for the opposing party to ignorance (vs. immorality, an idea we address in chapter 4). We asked respondents, "Do you think a vote for [Donald Trump/Hillary Clinton] was more a vote based on ignorance, a vote that was immoral, or a vote that was neither?" Respondents were only asked about a vote for the opposing party's presidential candidate. If people attributed opposing partisans' vote to policy stands or partisanship, the easy answer to the question is "Neither." Less than half of Republicans (44 percent) answered "Neither," and only about a quarter of Democrats (23 percent) gave that response. The most common response among both sets of partisans was "Ignorance": 42 percent of Republicans and 63 percent of Democrats said a vote for the opposing party's candidate was based on ignorance. When people are so sure of their views that they assume that the main reason why others vote differently is that they are ignorant or misled, they are not displaying a belief in civic respect; they are certainly not welcoming of pluralism.

## Social Networks and the Practice of Civic Respect

We have compared Democrats and Republicans on civic respect and the difficulties they face granting this kind of respect to opposing partisans, but are there any groups that shine when it comes to civic respect? Are there some groups of people that are more accepting of legitimate disagreement, that do not think that opposing partisans are misled by the media and by their misinformed friends, that exhibit civic respect? Prior research suggests that when people are exposed to diverse viewpoints in heterogeneous social networks, they become more tolerant of opposing viewpoints (Mutz 2002; Levendusky and Stecula 2021; Kalla and Broockman 2020), likely decreasing affective polarization (Iyengar et al. 2019). It is likely, then, that people with social networks that are more heterogeneous in terms of partisanship, and who must therefore interact more frequently with opposing partisans, will be less likely to stereotype them and more likely to listen to and try to understand them and their views. Democrats and Republicans obviously think poorly of each other, but social network heterogeneity might increase people's willingness to be respecting of opposing partisans.

We begin by comparing the reported partisan vote makeup of people's social networks. We asked respondents in the Equality Attitudes Survey (2018), "We want you now to think about the people you are close to and with whom you work (your family, friends, and co-workers). What is your best guess about how many of them voted for [Hillary Clinton/Donald Trump] in the 2016 election?" Response options were very few or none, about one-quarter, about half, about three-quarters, and all or just about all. People who voted for Clinton were asked about Donald Trump while people who voted for Trump were asked about Hillary Clinton. Figure 3.4 shows the distribution of responses among Clinton and Trump voters. A majority of respondents have few people in their social networks who voted for the opposing party's candidate: 69 percent of Clinton voters and 56 percent of Trump voters said that a quarter or less of their family, friends, and coworkers voted for the other candidate. In contrast, only 9 percent of Clinton voters and 13 percent of Trump voters have social networks composed of three-quarters or more of opposing party voters.

We reasoned that age was an important factor to consider when looking at the partisan makeup of social networks given that social networks appear to shrink across the life cycle (Wrzus et al. 2013) and party identification crystallizes in one's thirties (Sears and Funk 1999; Jennings and Markus 1984; Niemi and Jennings 1991; Markus 1979). Older people, we reasoned, might have more homogeneous networks since their networks are smaller and they

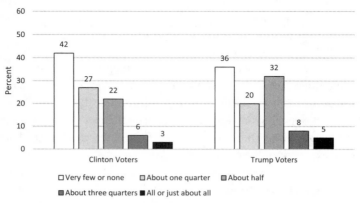

FIGURE 3.4. Partisan Heterogeneity of Social Networks by Clinton/Trump Vote
*Source*: 2018 Equality Attitudes Survey

are better situated to choose people with whom to interact based on their crys-tallized partisanship. Younger people, in contrast, are more fluid in both their partisanship and friendships and might therefore have more heterogeneous networks. We define a heterogeneous network as one in which at least half of one's family, friends, and coworkers voted for the opposing party's candi-date. A homogeneous network has a majority of people sharing the same vote choice, consisting of less than half of opposing party voters. Using this mea-surement, we examine the heterogeneity of people's social networks broken down by vote and age cohort and then connect it to civic respect.

First, do younger people have more heterogeneous social networks in terms of vote choice? Younger people are indeed more likely to have hetero-geneous networks (43 percent) than older people (36 percent), but what is driving this difference is younger Trump voters. Fifty-five percent of Trump voters aged twenty to thirty-nine have social networks in which half or more of their family and friends voted for Clinton in 2016, far more than any other group. Only 33 percent of Clinton voters in the same age cohort had hetero-geneous networks, far fewer than the younger Trump voters. Among those forty and older, 30 percent of Clinton voters and 40 percent of Trump voters had heterogeneous networks.

Our argument is that people who have more heterogeneous networks will be more likely to exhibit civic respect toward opposing partisans by being willing to listen to and not politically stereotype them. We draw on both the 2018 Equality Attitudes Survey and the 2019 Pluralism and Respect Survey to test our argument. We asked the social network questions only in 2018, so the results in table 3.2 are broken down by social network heterogeneity for those

TABLE 3.2. Civic respect, vote choice, and age

| | Clinton voters | | | | Trump voters | | | |
| | 20 to 39 | | 40 plus | | 20 to 39 | | 40 plus | |
| | Not mixed | Mixed | Not mixed | Mixed | Not mixed | Mixed | Not mixed | Mixed |
|---|---|---|---|---|---|---|---|---|
| **2018 Survey** | | | | | | | | |
| *Political stereotyping* | | | | | | | | |
| Uneducated / Educated | 0.24 | 0.42 | 0.28 | 0.37 | 0.51 | 0.58 | 0.40 | 0.51 |
| Unintelligent / Intelligent | 0.24 | 0.38 | 0.27 | 0.37 | 0.50 | 0.57 | 0.33 | 0.47 |
| Misled / Well-informed by media | 0.18 | 0.39 | 0.24 | 0.34 | 0.38 | 0.42 | 0.21 | 0.24 |
| Follows others / Acts independently | 0.27 | 0.37 | 0.21 | 0.35 | 0.39 | 0.44 | 0.22 | 0.31 |
| **2019 Survey** | | | | | | | | |
| Abstract civic respect | 0.79 | | 0.80 | | 0.87 | | 0.80 | |
| Civic respect—listen | 0.59 | | 0.65 | | 0.51 | | 0.66 | |
| Civic respect—engage | 0.56 | | 0.51 | | 0.63 | | 0.50 | |

*Source:* 2018 Equality Attitudes Survey and 2019 Pluralism and Respect Survey

*Note:* Cell entries are means from ANOVAs. All the two-way interactions between Vote choice and Age are significant at the $p < 0.05$ level. "Not mixed" means the social networks were homogeneous (less than half voted for the opposing candidate). "Mixed" means the social networks were heterogeneous (at least half voted for the opposing candidate).

data. Nonetheless, the pattern of younger Trump voters exhibiting greater civic respect holds up across almost all measures.

Table 3.2 shows the analysis of variance results when Clinton and Trump voters are broken down by age and, for the 2018 survey, the heterogeneity of social networks. Looking first at political stereotyping, the one group that consistently gives the most positive characterizations of opposing voters are young Trump voters in heterogeneous social networks. Younger Trump voters are less likely to stereotype Clinton voters regardless of social network makeup, but those who have a lot of friends, family, and coworkers who voted for Clinton are especially reluctant to stereotype. Interestingly, the heterogeneity of social networks has a positive impact on people's perceptions of opposing voters regardless of age or party. Being around a significant number of people who disagree with one's politics appears to decrease the negative stereotyping component of civic respect. Of course, we cannot rule out the possibility that the causal arrow goes in the other direction. It could be that people who are higher in civic respect are more likely to have more heterogeneous networks.

While we cannot test the impact of social network heterogeneity on people's willingness to listen to and engage with opposing partisans, we can test whether younger Trump voters are more likely to believe in and practice these aspects of civic respect. The bottom part of table 3.2 shows that Trump voters under the age of forty are more likely than any other group to believe in the abstract value of civic respect and to say they engage with opposing party voters. The one exception is our civic respect-listen scale, where young Trump voters are less likely than others to be willing to listen to the other side. All three of the age by vote choice interactions are significant. We do not have an explanation for why civic respect-listen would differ from the other measures.

We can further test whether younger Republicans differ from others in their willingness to put civic respect into practice using a series of questions from the 2018 Equality Attitudes Survey about how the 2016 presidential election affected their relationship with close friends and family members. We started by asking people if the election of Donald Trump had a negative impact on any of their relationships with friends and family members.[5] We then asked respondents who answered yes a series of questions on actions they personally had taken against family and friends after the 2016 election: "We'd like to start by asking about *your* actions after the 2016 presidential election. Did the election of Donald Trump lead you to . . . argue with a family member or close friend . . . stop talking to a family member or close friend . . . block a family member or close friend on social media . . . end a relationship with a family member or close friend?" Response options for all the relationship im-

TABLE 3.3. Party, age, social network heterogeneity, and civic respect actions

| | Argued with (%) | Stopped talking to (%) | Blocked on social media (%) | Ended relationship (%) | Mean number of actions |
|---|---|---|---|---|---|
| Clinton voters | 76 | 46 | 54 | 39 | 2.14 |
| 20 to 39 | | | | | |
| Homogeneous | 88 | 47 | 61 | 46 | 2.42 |
| Heterogeneous | 83 | 59 | 76 | 58 | 2.76 |
| 40 and older | | | | | |
| Homogeneous | 68 | 35 | 37 | 28 | 1.68 |
| Heterogeneous | 65 | 49 | 50 | 27 | 1.91 |
| Trump voters | 72 | 35 | 48 | 36 | 1.90 |
| 20 to 39 | | | | | |
| Homogeneous | 91 | 55 | 83 | 64 | 2.92 |
| Heterogeneous | 69 | 31 | 42 | 34 | 1.77 |
| 40 and older | | | | | |
| Homogeneous | 69 | 21 | 13 | 14 | 1.16 |
| Heterogeneous | 56 | 27 | 41 | 22 | 1.46 |

Source: 2018 Equality Attitudes Survey

Note: Cells under each action are the percentages of "yes" responses. The mean number of actions ranges from 0 (no actions taken) to 4 (all four actions taken).

pact questions were yes or no. In addition to the individual items, we created an additive scale using these four questions. The scale ranges from 0 (the respondent took no actions against close friends and family members) to 4 (the respondent argued with, stopped speaking to, blocked social media from, and ended relationships with close friends and family members). Table 3.3 shows the percentage of respondents in each category who answered yes when asked if they had taken the action against friends and family and the mean of the total number of actions taken.

People in heterogeneous networks are more likely than people in homogeneous networks to have the opportunity to take actions against family members and friends who voted for the opposing party's candidate simply because there are more of these people in their social networks, yet these are also the people who are more likely to engage with opposing partisans. The results in table 3.3 reveal interesting patterns related to civic respect actions. Overall, Clinton voters were more likely to take negative actions against friends and family who voted for the opposing party's candidate than were Trump voters, as were younger people compared to the older cohort. Looking at the mean number of actions, the more heterogeneous people's social networks were, the more actions they took compared to those in homogeneous networks, with one exception: younger Trump voters. These younger Trump voters were consistently less likely to argue with, stop talking to, block on social media, or end relationships with Clinton voters than their homogeneous counterparts. It is important to keep in mind that younger Trump voters are more likely to have heterogeneous networks, and those who experience this political diversity are less likely to negatively stereotype, less likely to take actions against, and more likely to engage with opposing party voters. In other words, they were more likely than any other group to practice civic respect.

## Conclusion

The results in chapter 2 demonstrate that people believe in recognition respect but struggle to respect opposing partisans, and that this is especially true for Democrats. In this chapter, the results make it clear that it is even more difficult to give people civic respect. Whether listening to or engaging with opposing partisans face-to-face or impersonally via various media, people are reluctant to try to understand the other side. In part this reaction stems from an unwillingness to accept the pluralism of American society and in part it stems from a tendency to think of opposing partisans in stereotypical terms. To think that only one's own party should ever win elections or that the only reason people would vote for the opposing party's candidate is because of ignorance or being misled by the media is quite astounding. In a pluralistic society, people hold diverse political views and would not agree on for whom they should vote even in the best of times.

Practicing civic respect means being genuinely pluralistic in a way that is hard for many citizens. Indeed, many Americans fail the civic respect test. We will argue in chapter 7 that practicing civic respect is a sign of a well-functioning democracy, but that civic respect should not be granted in all circumstances. The limits of civic respect are placed at the boundaries of democracy: if some citizens do not respect democratic institutions or norms, putting these institutions in doubt without evidence, they do not warrant full civic respect. The data used in this chapter, however, were gathered well before the January 6, 2021, insurrection at the US Capitol. Being willing to listen to and engage with people with whom one disagrees will likely not change minds, but doing so can lead to a better understanding of why people think and vote the way they do. Making assumptions about why opposing partisans vote the way they do, and most often assuming that they are simply ignorant or misled, does little to contribute to the health of the democratic process.

# PART II

# Loathing: Why Is Respect So Hard to Grant?

# The Social Justice Worldview and Moralization

In a healthy democracy, people treat each other as equals, and this means giving all the respect they are due as fellow human beings, regardless of differences. It also means respecting those with whom one disagrees. Yet giving recognition respect to someone who holds political views at odds with one's own is hard to do. Democrats are put to a harsher test than Republicans simply because they are more likely to believe that respect is fundamental to equality. From the perspective of egalitarians and liberal citizens, equality demands that people respect one another, and not being able to give respect goes against this belief.

In this chapter, we begin the process of digging deep into why respect is hard to grant to opposing partisans. Among Democrats, it is precisely because of the centrality of egalitarianism in their view of what constitutes a just world, what we call the social justice worldview, that they struggle to give Republicans respect. Democrats think that achieving a just world requires individuals to think and act in socially just ways and to oppose injustices that are in place and as they arise. For justice to be achieved, many believe that structural injustice must be recognized and then dismantled. This belief in social justice is not only a personal value; it is a core political value broadly applied to politics and society (Schwartz, Caprara, and Vecchione 2010). Democrats hold these beliefs as moral convictions. People perceive moralized issues or vote choices as a matter of right or wrong, good or bad, just or unjust and as universal (Skitka, Bauman, and Sargis 2005; Skitka and Morgan 2014; Ryan 2014). Even if people behave in a just way in their individual actions but disagree with the importance of dismantling structural injustice, this view suggests, they contribute to injustice. By not being willing to eliminate a cause of injustice, they accept what is bad or even evil and therefore condone harming others. We argue that the Democrats' social justice worldview leads them to be unable to respect Republicans, even though they believe respect is central to equality. If Republicans cannot get on board in terms of social justice, the thinking goes, then they do not deserve respect.

This chapter and chapter 5 are a pair. We focus in this chapter on how Democrats' social justice worldview explains why they have a hard time respecting Republicans; in the next chapter we argue that Republicans' national solidarity worldview explains their lack of respect for Democrats. A key finding in these two chapters is that partisans underestimate opposing partisans' support for their issues. That is, Democrats underestimate Republicans' support for social justice and Republicans underestimate Democrats' support for national solidarity. An important difference, however, is the extent to which opposing partisans moralize these issues. While many Republicans think social injustice exists, they do not moralize these issues as much as Democrats do. Similarly, Democrats do not moralize national solidarity issues as much as Republicans do. It is these moralized worldviews that help explain the respect challenges so many American citizens experience.[1]

We complete our empirical argument about respect in chapter 6, where we argue that each side thinks that there is a collective responsibility to act in concert toward the goals that each moralizes in its worldview. Partisans believe opposing partisans are not doing what is needed to achieve the goals set out for society in either the social justice or the national solidarity worldview. This failure to act is another reason to withhold respect from opposing partisans. In chapter 7, however, we suggest that the moralization of certain issues and the idea of collective responsibility too readily mask the contradictions and challenges that beset these ideas.

## Worldviews

What makes for a good society? What values would be upheld and, ideally, what beliefs and behaviors would people prioritize to create that good society? Answers to these questions get at what we call worldviews, a concept that has been used in many disciplines and defined in many ways (see, e.g., Schultz and Swezey 2013; Sire 2015). Worldviews not only reflect assumptions, beliefs, and perceptions of reality but also contain beliefs about what ought to be (Johnson, Hill, and Cohen 2011). Mark Koltko-Rivera (2004, 4) defines the concept as such:

> A worldview is a way of describing the universe and life within it, both in terms of what is and what ought to be. A given worldview is a set of beliefs that

includes limiting statements and assumptions regarding what exists and what does not (either in actuality, or in principle), what objects or experiences are good or bad, and what objectives, behaviors, and relationships are desirable or undesirable. A worldview defines what can be known or done in the world, and how it can be known or done. In addition to defining what goals can be sought in life, a worldview defines what goals should be pursued.

Importantly, worldviews engage a person's moral convictions, "the value commitments we express in thought and action" (Stenmark 2021, 2). The goals that should be pursued are moral imperatives.

People have a sense of how society ought to be, and they hold core political values, such as equality and egalitarianism (Feldman 1988; McCann 1997) or liberty and individual freedom (Jacoby 2006; Ashton et al. 2005), that guide them to make choices in any given situation. These core political values are distinct from personal values (Schwartz, Caprara, and Vecchione 2010) in that they are applied to society or government as a whole, not just one's own individual beliefs and behavior. Worldviews are a combination of core political values, the beliefs associated with them, and moral convictions about them concerning how society works best. Worldviews therefore encapsulate how individuals should think and behave but also what should be prioritized for the society and the government.

Understanding people's worldviews is key to understanding respect for opposing partisans. The issues that have been a focus among Democrats in recent decades are those that fall under the broad umbrella of social justice issues. Social justice issues are concerned with inequalities, such as racial, gender, and economic inequality, but also the societal and global structures that exacerbate and further inequalities. For example, climate change is not inherently a social justice issue, but it becomes one when the negative impacts of climate change create or exacerbate injustices, such as by disproportionately affecting poor people and people of color around the world.

It is the moralization of beliefs that make them particularly potent. Moralizing about politics is a common occurrence. For example, some policies are widely considered to be more morally relevant than others, such as abortion policies or policies dealing with LGBTQ+ rights, and people tend to be more adamant about and more engaged on these issues (see, e.g., Mooney 1999; Haider-Markel 2005; Smith 2002). Our focus here, though, is on people's moral convictions. Moral convictions, according to Skitka and Morgan (2014, 96), are beliefs people have that an "attitude is grounded in core beliefs about fundamental right and wrong." They are not simply another way of talking about attitude extremity, strength, or relevance. Rather, beliefs that are held with moral conviction share distinct properties (Skitka, Bauman, and Sargis 2005; Skitka and Morgan 2014): they are experienced as objective and factual, such that "in the same way 2 plus 2 equals 4 and not 5, we experience moral convictions as inherently right or wrong, with no room for negotiation" (Feinberg et al. 2019, 1); they are universal in that they apply everywhere and to everyone regardless of context; they are based in emotion, and often intensely felt emotion; and they are autonomous and not swayed by social norms, peer pressure, or authorities. Moral convictions are particularly potent because they can lead to certain outcomes, such as greater political engagement and activism, more acceptance of the use of violence to solve political conflicts, and a greater likelihood of rejecting the rule of law (Skitka and Morgan 2014). When people hold beliefs about certain issues that are moral convictions, they are not simply indicating a preference; they are taking a stand such that someone with an opposing view is not only wrong but often bad or evil.

Particularly important for our purposes is that people vary in the extent to which they believe certain issues are morally relevant or irrelevant; that is, they vary in their moral convictions about any given issue. Some people might hold moral convictions on an issue, but not everyone will, even on issues often considered to be moral issues such as abortion or same-sex marriage (Skitka and Morgan 2014; Ryan 2014; Brandt, Wetherell, and Crawford 2016). Ryan (2014, 385) finds that while many, but not all, people moralize such issues as stem cell research and gay marriage, a significant number of people (20 percent or higher) moralize issues not normally associated with morality, such as social security and collective bargaining. Rather than assume that certain issues or considerations are morally based, people vary in where they place issues or considerations on a continuum from morally relevant to morally irrelevant (Brandt, Wisneski, and Skitka 2015). Beliefs about justice are based on subjective understandings of what is right and wrong, making these beliefs inherently about morality (Tyler et al. 1997), but we show that Democrats are much more likely to moralize social justice beliefs than Republicans. Moralized social justice beliefs and values, that is, the social justice worldview, significantly explain Democrats' lack of respect for Republicans.

## Beliefs about Social Justice and a Just Society

Conservatives and liberals view justice and what contributes to a just society in very different ways. In general, conservatives believe justice is based on individual actions, whereas liberals emphasize individual actions but also include structures and institutions as necessary foci when dealing with injustices. We distinguish between these views beginning with political theorists and then examining how everyday people talk about justice.

## THEORISTS' VIEWS OF SOCIAL JUSTICE

An important conservative political theory view about justice is straightforward. In his influential argument against the idea of social justice, written several decades ago, Friedrich Hayek argued that justice is only a matter of how people treat one another. Justice, Hayek (1976, 31) argued, is not a matter of institutions, but of human conduct: "Only human conduct can be called just or unjust." For there to be an injustice, there must be someone responsible to cause the injustice. Indeed, Hayek argues that if it is not the "intended result or foreseen result of somebody's actions," then a state of affairs cannot be called unjust. Hayek wanted limited government generally (though he supported social welfare programs). He thought that if people gave too much power to government authorities and institutions, they would inevitably make the wrong decisions.[2] Hayek (1945) famously argued that knowledge is diffuse, and central authorities cannot harness enough knowledge to make good decisions. If government officials try to solve one problem, they will probably fail; even if they succeed in some fashion, they will surely cause other unforeseen problems. Agreeing with Hayek, some contemporary conservatives accept that the state "should be given the power to provide a social minimum funded by a system of taxation" (Tomasi 2012, 92). Ensuring a social minimum is not, of course, the same as ensuring justice. There is a role for government in society, but it is a minimal one.

In contrast to the individual action and limited government view held by conservative theorists, egalitarian theorists have a much more encompassing understanding of justice. Achieving a just society does not simply entail individuals treating each other as equals or fairly. While individual action is important, such a focus ignores the important roles played by the oppression of certain groups in society, the structures and institutions that foster these injustices, and the state in eradicating injustices. Equality for many liberals means dismantling social barriers; it means a focus on oppressed groups, on structures and institutions, and on the need for government to address these problems.

Iris Young (2011), who we briefly discussed in chapter 1, began what can be called the "structural turn" in political theory: "Traditional theorizing about injustice has been premised on a picture of individual moral agents bearing responsibility for particular actions because they exercise freedom and rationality in choosing to act one way rather than another" (Zheng 2018, 871).[3]

John Rawls, for example, argues that we should work to make institutions more just; this would mean a focus on ensuring equal opportunity and the redistribution of wealth. While Rawls focuses on what he calls society's basic structure, structural injustice theorists argue that Rawls's focus on opportunity and wealth distribution is too narrow: "Rawls's overemphasis on redistribution misses the actual imbalance in the process, given the differences present in society. Rawlsian contractarianism is naïve to structural issues" (Maboloc 2019, 1190).[4]

The main idea animating the structuralist approach to structural injustice—or social injustice—is that justice is not only about how individuals treat one another. Because injustice is embedded in societal institutions, people who inhabit these institutions may act without intentional malice or prejudice, but the outcomes of the institutions may nonetheless be oppressive to members of some social groups. The practice of redlining undermined the ability of Black Americans to buy houses and reduced the value of the houses that Black Americans were able to buy (Hayward 2003). This in turn reduced the wealth that Black Americans were (and are) able to accumulate, since many families pass on wealth to their descendants through their homes. If we are to say right now that anyone can work hard in the United States and save the money needed to buy a house, we miss how members of certain groups were able to inherit more money than others because of the way discrimination worked in the housing market. What marks an injustice as structural—or institutional—is that the injustice is not now committed by a particular person (or persons) but is embedded within institutions. The people within the institutions may act without prejudice, but the institutional structure nonetheless unfairly discriminates against or oppresses certain groups of people.

If one thinks that structural injustice is a large obstacle to fairness, then justice is not only about changing attitudes and getting people to treat one another fairly—justice is also about structural change. Sometimes, like in the case of ramps for the disabled, the benefit for the group can be used by others as well (e.g., someone pushing a baby stroller). But often the structural disadvantage can only be remedied by changes that focus on one particular group. This is where the clash between the liberal and conservative way of viewing justice is stark: the division between seeing group-based injustice that needs group-based solutions versus seeing justice as only an individual matter. Group-based and institutional solutions are bigger than any given individual action and therefore, according to social injustice theorists, demand government action. Laws and policies must be in place that will ensure that these solutions are put into practice.

## SURVEY RESPONSES AND BELIEFS
## ABOUT SOCIAL JUSTICE

As is the case among theorists, our focus groups suggested a strong division between how liberals and conservatives see justice and social justice, but there was some surprising overlap as well. When we asked our liberal participants about the meaning of justice, justice quickly evoked social justice, and participants offered good understandings of social justice:

> Providing additional funding support for certain groups that have been denied justice over the years is a form of justice as well. So like additional allocation of resources, in, you know, African-American communities for example would be a form of justice. Not just equal application of resources. (Bay Area Liberals 1, Woman 2).

> I think for me it's, I mean equality is sometimes like treating everyone the same, versus equity, and that's like what I think social justice is about, to me is about equity. So like there's that classic picture with the three people watching the baseball game, but there's a fence. So, for example, if you like have a spinal cord injury, you might need a wheelchair and resources in the environment like a curb that allows you to get onto the sidewalk or public transit, so you might get more resources to make things equal for you. Versus equality, where everyone gets the same thing and it's like "Well, you all got the same thing, so you're equal now." But if you don't have this ability to take advantage of this same thing equally, then that's not just or socially not just, I guess. (Bay Area Liberals 2, Man 4)

> Well I mean I think it recognizes that the status quo right now isn't necessarily equal or fair for everybody so social justice is that awareness of that and trying to figure out how to correct or sort of even the playing field for the ones that are fighting uphill right now. So it being having the awareness that it actually exists. (Bay Area Liberals 1, Man 4)

Individuals play an important role in justice, and in social justice as well, but the responses of our liberal focus group participants highlighted the notion that social justice is more concerned with ensuring that groups are treated fairly, especially those groups that have historically been treated unfairly. Dealing with injustices at the group level inevitably raised the argument that injustices are embedded in structures and institutions. We asked some of our liberal groups their reaction to someone who believes that racial inequality is unfortunate but that everyone can get ahead by working hard. Many of the answers argued for the presence of structural injustice:

So my response is to think about how systemic it is, all the institutions that promote and enshrine racism, all the ways education does not address it. I mean, even looking at my own kids who are now in college and just past, their education was woefully, pitifully small. In district [X] and in Catholic schools, when it came to issues of racism, systemic injustice, I mean . . . they barely knew what the Civil War was or Jim Crow or those things. (Nebraska Liberals 2, Woman 1)

I'm going to borrow a phrase from our fearless leader [Donald Trump at the time of the focus group], "The system is rigged." And the more I go on, the more I have read and have talked to people and have observed, I do think housing, education, voting, I think there have been very conscious and long-term efforts to oppress and to prevent especially African-Americans from getting ahead. (Nebraska Liberals 2, Woman 2)

Bullshit. It's institutionalized, I mean, it's—and if it's institutionalized, I mean, how do you break, break into that institution? (Bay Area Liberals 1, Woman 1)

Participants were often passionate about wanting people to understand the insidious role played by structural injustice. Several of these comments focused on ignorance as the cause of people not seeing this type of injustice:

My first thought is, "okay, it's a white man," which isn't necessarily fair, but again, white man who is privileged and hasn't had barriers in his life, and he is not well-informed or exposed to people that are different from himself. And I immediately want to ask him a lot of questions, I kind of feel my stomach tightening up and I don't feel very comfortable with it. And I don't necessarily like him. (Nebraska Liberals 1, Woman 1)

I think it should be mandatory that everyone gets racial equity training as in elementary and high school. I went to a workshop called "The REI Racial Equity Institute" and one thing they showed a video that was, like, so eye opening about how the generation, how, how the generations build upon each other in terms of the inequities that we have and how, it doesn't just—it's not just slavery, it's everything that has been, the wheels that were turning with slavery, what's happened ever since then, is just set up against people to succeed. (NC Liberals 9, Woman 6)

Many liberals believe that conservatives are racist and sexist (see chapters 2 and 3). They also believe that conservatives are ignorant about the structural barriers faced by marginalized groups. But this view is mistaken. Many conservatives understand the meaning of structural injustice, but some (not all) disagree with the concept and believe that their approach to race will help people of color more than trying to dismantle structural injustice. The conservative view of equality, based in procedures and the idea of nondiscrimination, is different from the liberal view of equality and came through in several ways in our conservative focus groups. When asked about the person who views racial inequality as unfortunate but easily remedied by hard work, the responses of some of our conservative participants focused on individual awareness and actions:

> Just being aware. Not saying, and I wouldn't say—I mean, racism is wrong. But just accepting the fact that it's the way it is and it's just happened to turn out that way and it's just being cognizant of that fact. It's not saying that we have to do all of these things to fix it, but it's just saying, "We're aware, we know moving forward, you know, that hindsight's 20/20, whatever." But we can do something to affect positive change and it's not going to be cancel culture, it's not this, it's not that, it's just being aware. (Sacramento Conservatives, Man 4)

> I think that you know, there's always going to be some discrimination just because I think people are human and people are going to have built-in biases and prejudices. That doesn't make it right. I think that's just a human reality and I think that's the case in any society. . . . But I do believe in this country it is set up in such a way that nowadays, if you're willing to work hard—now it doesn't guarantee that you're going to be extremely wealthy, but I do think you can get along pretty good if you're willing to put in the effort and the work. You know, I understand that some people are starting perhaps disadvantaged . . . but I do believe that if you make sound decisions [you can succeed]. (NC Conservatives 5, Man 2)

Many conservatives believe that discrimination is real, but they also think that individual behavior is the key to change, whether it's a matter of being aware of racism or working hard to be successful. Not all our conservative participants, however, agreed that hard work is all it takes:

> I think there are, in my opinion, there are undeniable factors that lead to the reason that minority classes statistically have a harder time achieving what we call the American Dream. I do think that's real, I mean we're not that far removed from a very different time in our country . . . [and if someone says] "Hey, if you want more money, just make more. You know, if you want a better job just get one." I think that's . . . immoral and lacks the sort of depth that our country's capable of when looking at these problems. (Sacramento Conservatives, Man 2)

> I don't think they've travelled enough. I don't think they've seen enough people. Because I've met people who just because of life circumstances can't get a job in order to get ahead and they get caught in an endless loop that unfortunately it's just a reality at this point in time that that happens. But I don't believe that everybody can just work hard and get ahead in this life. (Tennessee Conservatives, Man 1)

Even when conservatives are sympathetic to social justice goals, few think that government can solve the problem of injustice. Individual actions lead to injustices, in this view, and individual actions are the solution as well. In answer to a question about how to solve the problem of racial discrimination, one conservative focus group participant said:

> Well, and to that point, like sometimes I think what you're getting at is a familiar experience of, why does it feel like sometimes working with social justice groups mean that we're creating social injustice for another group? (Sacramento Conservatives, Man 2)

The conservatives we spoke with understood the meaning of social injustice. There is little reason to think that the obstacle in dismantling structural injustice is ignorance, as some egalitarians think (Hayward 2017). Many American citizens simply do not believe that structural injustice exists. Conservatives are more likely to view injustices as the result of individuals making choices about how to behave toward other individuals.

Responses to our Social Justice and Solidarity Survey (2020) confirm our focus group findings, that most Republicans think that justice is about individual behavior, whereas most Democrats believe social justice encompasses not only individuals but institutions, structures, and processes as well. We asked our survey respondents a straightforward question: "When you think of justice, do you think more about . . . treating individuals fairly OR treating oppressed groups in society fairly?" Almost all the Republicans, 95 percent, chose "treating individuals fairly," compared to just under 70 percent of Democrats. Republicans balk at the idea of focusing on groups, a topic we cover more fully in chapter 5, but their emphasis on the individual when it comes to justice is clear. Democrats, in contrast, think justice involves individuals, groups, and structures—that is, all of society. If our question had had a third response option, "all of the above," it is likely Democrats would have picked that option most frequently.

Additional evidence for Republicans' focus on the individual comes from our 2019 Pluralism and Respect Survey. The idea that conservatives see justice as a matter of individual conduct is supported by a corollary idea: the contrast of divine versus human justice. We asked: "Some people believe in divine justice, the idea that it is God's will to ensure that every person receives his or her due. Other people believe that any justice that occurs has to be handled by people. On a continuum from divine justice (1) to human-based justice (5), where would you place what you believe?" Conservatives tend to be more religious than liberals, so it is perhaps not surprising that they believe in divine justice much more than liberals. The mean score for Democrats was 3.73 and for Republicans 2.85 ($t = 11.7$, $p < .001$). A majority of Democrats (56 percent) sided with human justice (a score of 4 or 5). Republicans were more likely to be either torn between the two options (a score of 3; 36 percent) or to side with divine justice (37 percent).

Divine justice is an individualistic notion: individuals will be judged in the afterlife based on their individual actions. If you are a just person then you will be judged well in the afterlife. While Republicans likely believe that people act unjustly at times, their belief in divine justice may give them a reason to worry less about justice in this world. If people will be judged in the afterlife, and if trying to ensure justice in this world may backfire by creating new injustices, the afterlife can be counted on to punish the unjust. For those who believe in human justice rather than divine justice, as many Democrats do, there is more urgency to see justice in the world. Injustices in this world will not be corrected in an afterlife but will remain here unless people take action.

We gave respondents to our 2020 Social Justice and Solidarity Survey a series of statements to gauge specifically their beliefs about social justice. These statements covered general beliefs about a just society and social justice along with beliefs about specific issues. The general statements focused on whether achieving a just society required the following: government efforts targeted to improve the lives of oppressed groups; the dismantling of systemic racism, sexism, and other forms of systemic injustice; and a focus not just on individual behavior but also on structures and institutions. Before asking about systemic injustice, we reminded respondents what this means: "We're going to ask some questions about social justice. We use the term *systemic injustice*, which refers to systems and structures that unfairly disadvantage oppressed groups." We then gave them the statements. (See appendix C for "Social Justice Beliefs" statements and response options.)

Do Democrats believe more strongly than Republicans that injustices are systemic? Table 4.1 shows that the answer is yes. The responses were coded so that 1 indicates the most extreme pro–social justice response and 0 the most extreme antisocial justice response. The Democratic means on the items were all above 0.8. A just society, according to Democrats, is a society in which government ensures that groups are not oppressed and where systemic and institutional injustices have been dismantled. In fact, a majority of Democrats gave the most extreme response, extremely important or strongly agree, to these items. Republicans do not reject these beliefs about justice—none of the Republican means falls below 0.5—but they are much less likely to hold these views as strongly as Democrats.

We also asked participants if they personally supported several political issues, three of which were social justice issues: combating climate change,

TABLE 4.1. Belief in social justice by party identification

| | Democrats | | Republicans | | Difference of means |
|---|---|---|---|---|---|
| | Mean | Percent | Mean | Percent | t value |
| Government must improve lives of oppressed | 0.83 | 56% | 0.54 | 19% | 18.7*** |
| Society must dismantle systemic injustice | 0.88 | 65 | 0.63 | 26 | 16.6*** |
| A just society is about structures, institutions | 0.84 | 56 | 0.63 | 23 | 13.9*** |
| N | 675 | | 567 | | |

Source: 2020 Social Justice and Solidarity Survey
Note: Cell entries under "percent" are the percentage of people who answered "Extremely important" or "Strongly agree." T-tests are one-sided. ***p < 0.001.

ensuring equal access to voting, and prioritizing social justice (see appendix C for the Social Justice Issue Stands questions). We include climate change since many theorists argue that "the climate crisis should be understood as a structural injustice" (Sardo 2020, 2; Kortetmäki 2018; Gabrielson et al. 2016; Zheng 2018; Banks 2013; Baatz 2014). No one person or set of persons planned to have carbon emissions induce climate change. Combating climate change may need individual as well as structural change: carbon taxes, incentives for electric cars, mileage standards for traditional vehicles, and so on. And climate change often hurts the poor and people of color the most, particularly but not only viewed from a global perspective (Sardo 2020; Kortetmäki 2018).

Given our interest in respect, we also asked respondents how much they think people in the opposing party support each of these issues. That is, we asked Democrats how much they think Republicans support these issues, and we asked Republicans how much they think Democrats support these issues. People often exaggerate the stands taken by outgroups, making the polarization between groups more extreme than it actually is (Bursztyn and Yang 2022; Graham, Nosek, and Haidt 2012; Levendusky and Malhotra 2016), although the extent of the misperception depends on how it is measured (Dias, Pearl, and Lelkes n.d.).[5] If people's perceptions of opposing partisans are wildly off the mark on social justice issues, it might help explain people's lack of respect for those on the other side of the partisan divide.

Figure 4.1 shows, by party, both the mean personal support for each issue (solid bars) and the support attributed to opposing partisans (bars with patterns). As expected, Democrats are much more likely than Republicans to support these social justice issues. The average difference between Democrats and Republicans is 0.29, almost a third of the scale, with Democrats always giving more prosocial justice responses. The patterned bars show where people think opposing partisans stand on the issues. The hatched bars are the mean levels of support Republicans attribute to Democrats, whereas the dotted bars are the mean levels of support Democrats attribute to Republicans. Both Republicans and Democrats underestimate opposing partisan support for social justice issues, with Democrats more seriously underestimating than Republicans. When Republicans underestimate Democrats' support for social justice issues, they assume that Democrats are closer to their own position than is actually the case. The average difference between Republican support and their estimate of Democratic support is 0.21 (compared to the actual 0.29 difference). When Democrats underestimate social justice support among Republicans, they assume that Republicans are much more opposed to these issues than is true. The average difference between Democratic support and their estimate of Republican support is a whopping 0.62, almost two-thirds of the response range.

These results are important for understanding perceptions of opposing partisans. In Republicans' eyes, Democrats of course support social justice issues more than Republicans, but not at a level that suggests an extreme divergence in views. Democrats, in contrast, perceive Republicans *much farther* from them on these issues they strongly support. While Republicans are somewhat moderate on social justice issues (around 0.5), Democrats perceive them to be opposed to social justice (around 0.25). These differences in perceptions could be benign if people believe these are just differences in simple

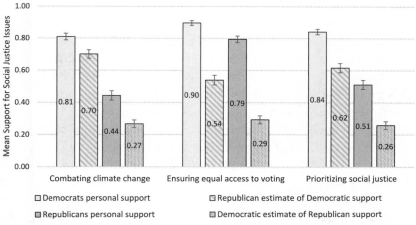

FIGURE 4.1. Partisan Support for Social Justice Issues and Attributed Support by Opposing Partisans
*Source*: 2020 Social Justice and Solidarity Survey
*Note*: The data are mean responses to the social justice questions, where 0 = anti–social justice beliefs and 1 = pro–social justice beliefs. The error bars are 95% confidence intervals.

issue preferences. If these issues constitute core moral beliefs for people, though, the differences take on much greater significance.

## Moralizing Social Justice Beliefs

The social justice worldview isn't only about policy preferences or the belief that injustices are systemic. Policy differences by themselves are unlikely to explain the lack of respect among American citizens in the face of partisan disagreement. People could disagree about foreign trade or tax rates or school vouchers and still respect each other. It is possible to do this even when the issues involve social justice concerns. What makes the social justice worldview so politically potent for Democrats is that they view Republicans as taking the wrong stands on these issues and hold their social justice positions as moral convictions. If these moralized issues cut across party lines, people who hold the moralized issue stance might disrespect those who disagree with them, but they wouldn't disrespect Republicans as a group. In a previous time, there were Democrats who wanted trade barriers, abortion restrictions, and stronger labor unions. There were Republicans who were pro-choice, for strengthening businesses, and for a government-sponsored health care marketplace. When there are issues that cut across party lines, moralized worldviews are unlikely to align in a partisan way.

We argue that Democrats are more likely to hold a moralized social justice worldview than Republicans because these issues are so integral to their beliefs about a just society. A good United States is one that has eradicated structural injustices and created a society where there is true equity among people, regardless of skin color or sexual orientation or income or ability status. We are not arguing that Democrats are more likely to moralize issues than Republicans. There is in fact little evidence that liberals and conservatives differ in their tendency to moralize policies or concerns.[6] Whether people are given a list of issues (Ryan 2014; Skitka, Bauman, and Sargis 2005) or a particular issue (Tagar et al. 2014), or select the issue themselves (Morgan, Skitka, and Wisneski 2010), liberals and conservatives are surprisingly similar in both the overall level of their moral convictions and the processes underlying their moral convictions (Brandt, Wisneski, and Skitka 2015; Skitka, Hanson, and Wisneski 2017).[7] What we are arguing is that Democrats are much more likely than Republicans to moralize social justice issues, and therefore to hold a social justice worldview that decreases their respect for Republicans.

We examine both people's moralization of social justice issues and their moralization of the vote choice, starting with issues. We utilize two surveys for these analyses: the 2019 Pluralism and Respect Survey and the 2020 Social

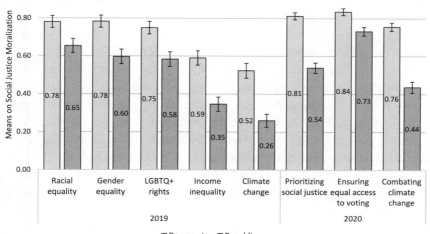

FIGURE 4.2. Mean Differences between Partisans on Social Justice Moral Convictions
Source: 2019 Pluralism and Respect Survey, 2020 Social Justice and Solidarity Survey
Note: The response options for the 2019 social justice issues are 0 = a policy preference or 1 = a core moral belief. The response options for the 2020 social justice moralization items are 0 = not a core moral belief at all to 1 = very much a core moral belief (on a 5-point scale). All the mean differences between Democrats and Republicans are significant at the $p < 0.001$ level.

Justice and Solidarity Survey. We asked our 2019 Pluralism and Respect Survey respondents to indicate if they thought an issue was a policy preference or a core moral belief. The social justice issues were racial equality, gender equality, LGBTQ+ rights, income inequality, and climate change. In our 2020 Social Justice and Solidarity Survey, we asked our survey respondents to indicate the extent to which their stand on an issue was a core moral belief, which let us measure how strongly they thought it was a moral belief. The social justice issues we asked about were the same as those used earlier for personal beliefs: combating climate change, ensuring equal access to voting, and prioritizing social justice. (See appendix C for the Moralization of Social Justice Issues question wordings within each survey.)

Figure 4.2 provides the means for Democrats and Republicans on the moralization of these social justice items. The differences in moral convictions on these issues are stark. Democrats are consistently and significantly much more likely than Republicans to view social justice issues as core moral beliefs, with means at or above 0.75 on six of the eight items. Republicans moralize some aspects of social justice as well, with relatively high moral conviction scores on racial equality and ensuring equal access to voting, but they are significantly less likely than Democrats to moralize these issues, especially when it comes to income inequality, climate change, and prioritizing social justice.

While researchers studying moral convictions focus heavily on issues, we argue that moral convictions can also be felt, and felt strongly, when thinking about one's own and others' vote choice. Voting for a particular candidate not only signals support for a set of policies (even if people cast their vote for other reasons); it also directly contributes to electing to office someone who will be in a position of power to work to enact those policies. The increase in affective polarization and vilification of opposing partisans as evil (Martherus et al. 2019; Iyengar et al. 2019) suggests that the moralization of vote choice is even more pronounced now than in years past. As we noted in chapter 3, people make assumptions about opposing partisans that ignore the broad array of reasons someone might vote for a candidate. The lack of civic respect helps foster an atmosphere where people can assume the worst of those who vote for the opposing candidate: that they are knowingly and willingly voting for someone who is vowing to do bad. It is no surprise that people moralize the vote choices people make when votes signal support for immoral outcomes.

We asked respondents in the 2019 Pluralism and Respect Survey the following questions: "To what extent is your attitude toward people who voted for [Donald Trump/Hillary Clinton] a reflection of *your* core moral beliefs and convictions?" and "To what extent is your attitude toward people who voted for [Donald Trump/Hillary Clinton] deeply connected to *your* fundamental beliefs about right and wrong?" (Skitka, Bauman, and Sargis 2005; Skitka 2010). Everyone was asked about Donald Trump and Hillary Clinton, so we have measures for both coparty voters and out-party voters. Response options ranged from not at all (1) to very much (5) and were recoded to range from 0 to 1. We created two scales, one that combined the two questions about the voters for the opposing party candidate (M = 0.392, sd = 0.367, alpha = 0.906) and the other that combined the two questions about the voters for one's own party candidate (M = 0.610, sd = 0.340, alpha = 0.942).

Figure 4.3 shows that coparty votes are held as moral convictions more than out-party votes. Partisans do not differ significantly in the extent to which they view the vote of their fellow partisans as a moral conviction, with both Democrats and Republicans seeing the in-party vote as a moral conviction. Partisans disagree, though, about people who voted for the other party's candidate when it comes to moral convictions. Democrats are significantly more likely to view a vote for Trump as a moral conviction than Republicans do a Clinton vote. Holding a strong moral conviction about other people's vote choice means that people are judging coparty voters as good and out-party

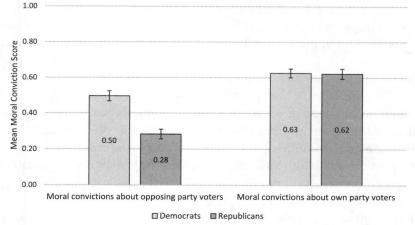

FIGURE 4.3. Party Identification and Moral Convictions about Vote Choice
*Source*: 2019 Pluralism and Respect Survey
*Note*: The figure is based on mean scores on the own party and opposing party moral convictions scales where 0 = not at all a moral conviction and 1 = very much a moral conviction. Difference of means two-sided *t*-tests show that the difference between Democrats and Republicans on own party voters is not significant (*t* = 0.46) whereas the difference is highly significant for opposing party voters (*t* = 11.2).

voters as bad, and Democrats are significantly more likely than Republicans to make this moral assessment of opposing voters.

The results on policy areas and vote choice point to a similar conclusion: Democrats are significantly more likely than Republicans to moralize social justice issues and the vote choices people make. These findings have important implications given the nature of moral convictions. Moral convictions are not simply more intense opinions. Rather, people's belief that some things are morally good or bad is, in their minds, objectively true, universal, intensely felt, and not open to change (Skitka, Bauman, and Sargis 2005; Skitka and Morgan 2014). Democrats are more likely than Republicans to support social justice issues and to hold them as moral convictions. Anyone who holds opposing positions on these issues and votes for candidates who similarly do not support them is supporting what is wrong, bad, and unjust.

## Who Holds the Social Justice Worldview?

Republicans believe in equality and a just society, but they do not believe in these values in the same way as Democrats. While they are more likely to believe in social justice than Democrats give them credit, they are significantly less likely than Democrats to support the constellation of beliefs that make up the social justice worldview. They are less likely than Democrats to believe that injustices are structural or institutional, and they are less likely than Democrats to hold their social justice beliefs as moral convictions. Democrats base their respect—or lack of respect—for Republicans in part on their perception that Republicans are strongly opposed to social justice as a goal for society, that they do not share the same worldview.

We created a social justice worldview scale that includes people's personal stands on social justice issues, their belief that injustices are often systemic and structural, and their moralization of these issues (see appendix C for the social justice worldview scale items). The social justice worldview scale ranges from 0 to 1, with high scores signifying support for and moralization of social justice beliefs (mean = 0.714, sd = 0.235, alpha = 0.912). Democrats score significantly higher on the scale than Republicans (a mean of 0.83 for Democrats and 0.58 for Republicans, $t = 21.9$, $p < 0.001$). Democrats are strong advocates of the social justice worldview, but as we have noted throughout, many Republicans do not oppose the social justice worldview, scoring above the midpoint of the scale.

In addition to political party, we look at a range of demographic and political attitude variables to see who holds the social justice worldview and who opposes it. Table 4.2 shows the results. First, Democrats always score higher on the social justice worldview scale than Republicans and have less variation in their scores, regardless of demographic breakdown. Social justice is a core issue to Democrats, and most people who identify as Democrats share these core beliefs. The only large difference among Democrats is between those who said they planned to vote in 2020 and those who said they wouldn't be voting, with voters being much more pro-social justice than nonvoters. Second, Republicans who share some of the demographics that are normally associated with Democrats are more positive in their social justice worldview than are other Republicans. Republicans who are younger, people of color, urban dwellers, and self-identified liberals (although the number of these is very small) score much higher on the social justice worldview scale than do Republicans who are older, white, rural, and conservative. Interestingly, higher education does not increase support for social justice among Republicans, although it does for Democrats.

## Respect and Social Justice

In the remainder of this chapter, we directly examine the relationship between social justice worldviews and respect. We argue that the more Democrats hold a social justice worldview, the less they will be able to offer respect

TABLE 4.2. Social justice worldview support

| | Total | Democrats | Republicans |
|---|---|---|---|
| Overall mean | 0.72 | 0.83 | 0.58 |
| Age | | | |
| Young (20–39) | 0.75 | 0.80 | 0.66 |
| Older (40 and older) | 0.70 | 0.86 | 0.55 |
| Sex | | | |
| Male | 0.70 | 0.84 | 0.57 |
| Female | 0.74 | 0.83 | 0.60 |
| Race | | | |
| White | 0.70 | 0.85 | 0.57 |
| People of color | 0.76 | 0.79 | 0.65 |
| Education | | | |
| Less than college | 0.72 | 0.82 | 0.61 |
| College degree | 0.69 | 0.83 | 0.54 |
| Post-baccalaureate degree | 0.74 | 0.87 | 0.56 |
| Place of residence | | | |
| Urban | 0.79 | 0.83 | 0.66 |
| Suburban | 0.71 | 0.83 | 0.58 |
| Rural | 0.66 | 0.83 | 0.55 |
| Ideology | | | |
| Liberal | 0.85 | 0.86 | 0.76 |
| Middle of the road | 0.74 | 0.76 | 0.72 |
| Conservative | 0.56 | 0.80 | 0.54 |
| Voting behavior | | | |
| Plan to vote in 2020 | 0.72 | 0.83 | 0.58 |
| Do not plan to vote in 2020 | 0.61 | 0.66 | 0.60 |

Source: 2020 Social Justice and Solidarity Survey
Note: Cell entries are mean scores on the social justice worldview scale (0 = anti–social justice worldview, 1 = pro–social justice worldview).

to Republicans and those who oppose them on social justice issues. In the eyes of Democrats, Republicans are opposed to social justice issues, and it is hard to respect those who take an immoral stance. Republicans are less motivated by social justice considerations, but when they are sympathetic to the social justice worldview, they are more likely to respect Democrats who have become such strong champions of these issues.

Using the 2020 Social Justice and Solidarity Survey, we measure recognition respect by asking people the extent to which they agreed or disagreed with statements directed at opposing partisans: "I think we need to do more than tolerate [Republicans/Democrats], we need to respect them," "I struggle a great deal when it comes to respecting [Republicans/Democrats]" (reversed), "[Republicans'/ Democrats'] political views make it impossible for me to respect them as people" (reversed), and "[Republicans/Democrats] should be given respect simply because they are fellow human beings." We created a Recognition Respect Scale (mean = 0.508, sd = 0.224, alpha = 0.761) that ranges from 0 to 1, with higher scores indicating greater recognition respect.

Our respect questions specifically tied to social justice opposition started with "we asked you some questions earlier about various issues. Now we're going to ask you questions about people who strongly disagree with you on these issues. How easy or difficult is it for you to respect someone who strongly disagrees with you on . . ." The social justice issues about which we asked were combating climate change, ensuring equal access to voting, and prioritizing social justice. Response options ranged on a 5-point scale from very difficult to respect to very easy to respect. We created a Social Justice Respect Scale from these three items that ranged from 0 (very difficult to respect) to 1 (very easy to respect) (mean = 0.444, sd = 0.277, alpha = 0.865).

We regressed Recognition Respect and Social Justice Respect on social justice worldview, party identification, and the interaction between these two variables, along with several control variables.[8] Our main interest is in the impact of the interaction on respect, since we argue that the more strongly Democrats hold the social justice worldview, the less willing they are to grant respect to those who disagree with them on these issues. Since Democrats think Republicans are anti–social justice (see figure 4.1) and they moralize these issues (see figure 4.2), the distinction they draw between those who are anti–social justice and those who are Republican is very slim, and both are bad. In contrast, Republicans are fairly moderate on social justice issues, and they are less likely to hold them as moral convictions, potentially leading to a less pronounced effect on social justice respect.

Figure 4.4 shows the regression results for the key variables in the models that do not include the social justice worldview by party identification interaction and those that do. Figure 4.5 shows the interaction effects.[9] In general, without considering the interaction, Republicans are more likely than Democrats to respect those with whom they disagree, and, at least for recognition respect, those who hold a strong social justice worldview are more likely to give respect. The interaction, which is highly significant, clarifies the picture. The more strongly Democrats hold a social justice worldview—believing in and moralizing social justice concerns—the less they respect Republicans and those who disagree with them on social justice issues. The results for Democrats are very similar for both kinds of respect: for recognition respect, Democrats drop from 0.66 among those low in social justice worldview to 0.42 for those high in social justice worldview; for social justice respect, Democrats

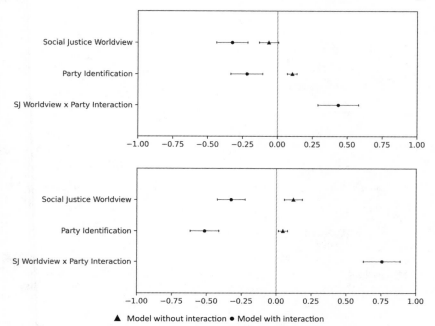

FIGURE 4.4. Social Justice Worldview, Party Identification, and Respect.
*Source:* Social Justice and Solidarity Survey (2020)
*Note*: Data are unstandardized regression coefficients with 95% confidence interval error bars from OLS regressions. The regression models included control variables for age, sex (male), race (white), rural, and education level (data not shown; see appendix D, table D.1, for the full models). Party identification is coded 0 = Democrats and leaners, 0.5 = pure Independents, 1 = Republicans and leaners. Recognition respect: Model without interaction—Constant = 0.404 (se 0.032), $F = 3.63^{***}$, Adj. $R^2 = 0.015$, $N = 1227$; Model with interaction—Constant = 0.741 (se 0.043), $F = 19.25^{***}$, Adj. $R^2 = 0.106$, $N = 1227$. Social justice respect: Model without interaction—Constant = 0.674 (se 0.035), $F = 31.63^{***}$, Adj. $R^2 = 0.136$, $N = 1358$; Model with interaction—Constant = 0.873 (se 0.048), $F = 32.62^{***}$, Adj. $R^2 = 0.157$, $N = 1358$. $^{***}p < 0.001$.

drop from 0.79 for those low in social justice worldview to 0.55 for those high in social justice worldview. The similarity of these results highlights our contention that Democrats think similarly about Republicans and those opposed to social justice. They are pretty much one and the same.

These results add to the evidence in this chapter that one way Democrats violate civic respect is through political stereotyping. Many Democrats assume that all Republicans oppose social justice, which of course is not true. While we think that political disagreement is usually not a good reason for disrespect, political disagreement based on a misunderstanding is even worse. Of course, Democrats might say that civic respect can correctly be withheld because many Republicans do not moralize social justice, even if they agree

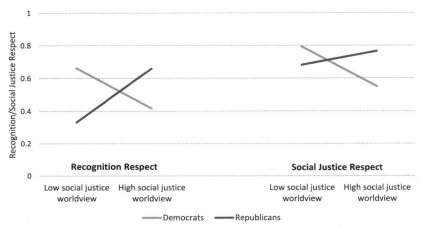

FIGURE 4.5. Respect and the Interaction of Party Identification and Social Justice Worldview
*Source*: 2020 Social Justice and Solidarity Survey
*Note*: The values for "high social justice worldview" were calculated using the highest score possible (a score of 1) on the scale. The values for "low social justice worldview" were calculated using a score of 0.244, which is 2 standard deviations below the mean of the scale, to reflect low scores more realistically since no one scored 0 on the scale.

that social injustice exists. But if respect is predicated on agreement about what issues are the most important and how they must be viewed, then many if not most Democrats do not accept pluralism (nor do many Republicans, as we show in the next chapter). If respecting differences is a core value in a democracy, then many American citizens have considerable work to do.

As expected, the strength of Republicans' social justice worldview has the opposite impact on recognition respect than it does for Democrats (see figure 4.5). Those who hold a strong social justice worldview have more recognition respect for Democrats than those who do not. Republicans' worldview strength has less of an impact on their social justice respect, which is perhaps a result of their view of Democrats as closer to them on these issues and on their reluctance to moralize these issues as much as Democrats.

We have argued that Democrats struggle giving respect to Republicans, and often fail in that struggle, because they moralize social justice as a societal goal and believe Republicans are unjust for opposing or not fully promoting a socially just society. Indeed, Democrats with a strong social justice worldview have a hard time giving respect to those who oppose them, including Republicans and those who specifically oppose them on social justice issues. While Democrats are wrong to suggest that almost all Republicans oppose social justice, clearly many do; those Republicans who do oppose social justice are much less likely to grant Democrats respect than other Republicans.

## Conclusion

We set out in this chapter to figure out why liberals, who believe more strongly than conservatives in equal respect, have such a difficult time respecting their opponents. We argued that the explanation lay in liberals' desire for a just world centered on social justice. A just world is one in which the oppression of marginalized groups is eradicated in individual behavior and in the country's institutions, structures, and processes, leading to equality for all. People who disagree with these goals, or who do not fully promote them, do not deserve respect. Among Democrats, there is a strong relationship between belief in the social justice worldview and a lack of respect for those who disagree with or who are perceived to disagree with social justice goals.

It is important to point out that Republicans support and moralize social justice issues less strongly than Democrats, but they tend not to oppose them. Conservatives, both theorists and the public, believe that it is individuals, not structures or institutions, that behave in unjust ways, which means that attaining a just society involves getting individuals to behave justly. While many of our liberal focus group participants attribute conservatives' more moderate support of social justice goals to racism or sexism or homophobia, conservatives argue that they disagree with liberals on what exactly a just society entails.

Partisans who buck their party's stance on social justice tend to be more respectful toward opposing partisans. That is, Republicans who hold strongly the social justice worldview and Democrats who do not support the social justice worldview are much more likely to respect opposing partisans. The problem, in terms of respect, is that relatively few partisans hold views on social justice that are contrary to their party's stand. Only 1 percent of Democrats score in the bottom quadrant of the social justice worldview scale (compared to 10 percent of Republicans in this quadrant). Over a quarter (27 percent) of Republicans score in the top quadrant (compared to 76 percent of Democrats). Our results show clearly that most partisans side with their party on social justice issues, and when they do, they have a hard time respecting those in the opposing party.

# 5

# The National Solidarity Worldview and Moralization

The liberal respect paradox is real. Liberals believe that respect is fundamental to equality, but they have a hard time respecting people who disagree with them, especially on their social justice views. The challenge felt by conservatives is different. They view the liberal agenda that emphasizes equality and the problems caused by the systemic oppression of marginalized groups as a problem for the United States. Conservatives believe that the United States is better off when its citizens embrace being American, which includes valuing freedom, being loyal to the United States, and understanding the special status of being a US citizen. When people divide Americans into multiple groups that are pitted against each other, when they criticize America and its history, and when they refuse to hold American values that are morally good, they are not just wrongheaded or mistaken, they are undermining national solidarity. National solidarity is at odds with liberals' social justice agenda, and conservatives find it difficult to respect those who disagree with them on the need to prioritize national solidarity and who contribute to the fraying of American culture.

The national solidarity worldview shares similar properties with the social justice worldview (see chapter 4). It is based on a moralized set of core political beliefs that help people understand how society ought to be for the common good of all. The national solidarity worldview encompasses a variety of beliefs all centered on fostering a strong nation, including beliefs about national identity, cohesion, loyalty, citizenship, and liberty. As is the case with the social justice worldview, national solidarity beliefs are moralized, meaning that disagreeing with them is not just a difference in beliefs or preference but is morally wrong. We argue that Republicans are more likely than Democrats to hold a national solidarity worldview, although we show that

Democrats do not oppose national solidarity. The more strongly Republicans hold the national solidarity worldview, the less they respect Democrats. In their view, Democrats are weakening America with their social justice views, and this cannot be respected.

In this chapter, we lay out the core components of the national solidarity worldview, including the beliefs that make up this worldview and the extent to which people hold their beliefs as moral convictions. While there could be other worldviews that motivate conservatives, we focus on national solidarity because it clearly motivates conservatives' reaction to liberals' social justice worldview: social justice focuses on the oppression that different groups faced and face in the United States, while national solidarity holds that the framework of dividing America undermines solidarity and weakens the United States. We show throughout this chapter how the national solidarity and social justice worldviews clash. For example, we examine immigration, since it is often perceived as a solidarity issue by conservatives and a social justice issue by liberals. We also examine two issues that conservatives moralize because they perceive them as liberty matters, gun control and religious freedom. The latter part of the chapter focuses on the impact of the national solidarity worldview on respect. If people believe that society is better off if the nation is kept strong, which Republicans believe intensely, then it is difficult to respect those who appear to want to weaken the country; that is, it is difficult to respect Democrats.

## The National Solidarity Worldview

### NATIONAL IDENTITY AND COHESIVENESS

National groups are "imagined communities" (Anderson 1991). People will never meet more than a small number of their fellow nationals and can therefore only imagine who else belongs to the national group. A sense of community among these strangers is based on their common bonds, established by a shared history, experiences, and sacrifices that hold the national group together as a people. This argument harkens back to J. S. Mill (1882, 1120; 1991 [1861], ch. 16), who argued for the importance of a principle of sympathy among a state's members, which can be supplied by nationality:

> The third essential condition of stability in political society, is a strong and active principle of cohesion among the members of the same community or state. We need scarcely say that we do not mean nationality, in the vulgar sense of the term; a senseless antipathy to foreigners; indifference to the general

welfare of the human race, or an unjust preference of the supposed interests
of our own country. . . . We mean a principle of sympathy, not of hostility; of
union, not of separation. We mean a feeling of common interest among those
who live under the same government, and are contained within the same natural or historical boundaries.

The United States is often held up as unique in the sense that its national
identity is not based on race, religion, ethnicity, history, territory, or culture
(Gellner 1983) and instead rests on a shared set of beliefs in liberalism, democracy, and the "American Creed" (Smith 1988; Schlesinger 1991; Huntington 2004).[1]

This argument suggests that a country is stronger when its people are
united, and it is weakened when people don't see themselves as members of
the same national group. What is needed is for the group's members to "constantly experience what happens to the collective to which they are loyal as
happening to themselves" (Hazony 2018, 71). This means, in the words of the
conservative British thinker Roger Scruton (2004, 10), that we often think of
the first-person plural: "Only where people have a strong sense of who 'we'
are, why 'we' are acting in this way or that, why 'we' have behaved rightly in
one respect, wrongly in another, will they be so involved in the collective
decisions as to adopt them as their own. This first-person plural is the pre-
condition of democratic politics, and must be safeguarded at all costs, since
the price of losing it, I believe, is social disintegration" (see also Lowry 2019,
47). We all understand when Americans say things like, "We beat the Soviets
to the moon" or "We won our match at the World Cup" or "I love the colors
of our flag." All these statements are in the first-person plural, and of course
people all over the world speak this way.

This tendency to think of the national group as "we" comes from people's strong commitment to their national identity. When a social identity
is salient, people's sense of self comes from their membership in the group
and their attitudes and behaviors reflect that group membership (Tajfel 1982;
Abrams et al. 1990; Hogg 2001). People who strongly identify with the group
often put the group's interests above their own, follow the group's norms,
think and act in ways that further the group's goals, and hold the group in
high esteem (Huddy 2003; Ellemers, Spears, and Doosje 1999; Hogg and
Abrams 1988; Jetten, Postmes, and McAuliffe 2002). Group identification increases cohesion (Turner et al. 1987) and loyalty (Van Vugt and Hart 2004;
Brown 2000), and when the group is threatened, people react strongly and
collectively to defend themselves against the threat (Ellemers, Spears, and
Doosje 1999). Conservative nationalists argue for the importance of national

solidarity in part because members of the same nation should want to defend one another from threats, whether the threats are external or internal. This reaction to threats motivates many Trump supporters in their desire to secure their ingroup (Hibbing 2020).

Yet people's commitment to their national group varies. Most Americans identify strongly as Americans, but not all do (Schildkraut 2014; Theiss-Morse 2009). People are born into their racial, gender, and national groups, and these group memberships are not always embraced. We asked respondents in our Social Justice and Solidarity Survey (2020), "How important is being an American to your identity?" The mean response, where 0 is not important at all and 1 is extremely important, is 0.68 for Democrats and 0.88 for Republicans. For both partisan groups, the mean is well above the midpoint and indicates a strong attachment to the national group. For Republicans, though, identifying as an American is significantly more important to them than it is for Democrats. Only about a third (37 percent) of Democrats gave the most positive response of "extremely important" compared to two-thirds (68 percent) of Republicans.

If strong identifiers value group cohesiveness, then promoting other identities, such as race or gender, can be a threat to the national group. According to Janoff-Bulman and Carnes (2013, 227), the emphasis on cohesiveness means that "a single defining category for all (e.g., American) is optimal. Thus, 'color-blindness' is a group value intended to blur or eliminate differences across societal subgroups." Prioritizing other group identities above that of the national group can weaken the national group. This argument arose in several of our conservative focus groups, even though we did not directly ask about it.

And what's happened is people who identify through identity politics have now disdained and find totally unacceptable, using "racist," you know, "homophobic," every worst adjective you can, labeled people who don't agree with them that way because they don't identify as Americans who believe in democracy and free speech and different points of view. They believe in their own identity and when they believe in their own identity, people who don't identify with that identity, disagree with that identity, unfortunately are marginalized. (Alabama Conservatives, Man 4)

I'd say if there were absolute, one thing, if I could make it happen that would improve equality, is have people say "I am an American." Period. I'm not an African-American, I'm not a conservative-American, [voiced assent] I'm not a liberal-American, I'm not a Pacific Islander-American. . . . There aren't 43 genders in New York City. We're all Americans and the more we start thinking

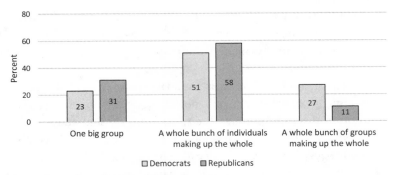

FIGURE 5.1. Perceptions of the American People as a Group
*Source*: 2020 Social Justice and Solidarity Survey
*Note*: Respondents were asked to pick one of the three possible response options.

of ourselves as Americans and not as special interest groups and subsets [the better off we will be]. (NC Conservatives 3, Man 2)

For many conservatives, everyone should be seen as a citizen of the state, and other identities should not change that relationship. People may have ethnic, religious, or racial identities, but none of them should have any legal status or interfere with people's identity as an American. When people don't do this, when they think of Americans in terms of multiple groups, the nation is weakened because the people are divided, not united. A divided nation cannot stand.

To get at the cohesiveness aspect of national solidarity, we asked the respondents of our 2020 Social Justice and Solidarity Survey a question on how they view the American people: "Which comes closer to your view? When I think of Americans . . . I think of one big group OR I think of a whole bunch of individuals who make up the whole OR I think of a whole bunch of groups that make up the whole." We expected Republicans to be more likely than Democrats to choose one of the first two response options. Either of these options allows for the centrality of a cohesive American identity. The third option, in contrast, allows for other group identities to compete with the national group. The results are shown in figure 5.1. While most people think of the American people as individuals making up the whole, Republicans (58 percent) are more likely to do so than Democrats (51 percent). Republicans are also more likely than Democrats (31 to 23 percent, respectively) to think of Americans as one big group. As we expected, however, Democrats (27 percent) are more likely than Republicans (11 percent) to say they see Americans as a bunch of groups.

We also asked specific questions on the cohesiveness of the American people. One question asked about the extent to which respondents agreed or disagreed with the statement, "It's better to think of us as Americans rather than by our race or gender." Republicans were much more likely to agree or strongly agree with this statement than Democrats, 94 percent to 72 percent, respectively. Almost three-quarters of Republicans, 73 percent, said strongly agree, compared to only 48 percent of Democrats. We also wanted to push respondents on the possible consequences of thinking of Americans as a united group, which we did with the statement "When people focus on Americans being united, they ignore the oppression of certain groups in American society." Republicans often argue for a color-blind America, where there would be greater equality if people saw each other as fellow Americans and not as white people or Black people or Hispanics or Asian Americans. Democrats recoil from this view, believing that a color-blind America gives the white majority leeway to oppress people of color. Responses to our question on a consequence of emphasizing American solidarity reveals the deep fissure between Democrats and Republicans. Democrats are much more likely to agree or strongly agree with the idea that focusing on united Americans leads to the oppression of marginalized groups (70 percent) than Republicans (29 percent). This reaction from Republicans is not because they deny the existence of racism, as we saw in chapter 4. Many Republicans believe that racism exists, but they see it as an individual-level problem that must be dealt with individually. What will help create better outcomes for all, regardless of color, is thinking of Americans as one.

## LOYALTY

In addition to cohesion, loyalty is a key component of the national solidarity worldview. According to Zdaniuk and Levine (2001, 502), "behavior is loyal to the extent that it enhances (or at least is meant to enhance) group welfare." In Jonathan Haidt's (2001) moral foundations theory, loyalty/betrayal is one of the binding foundations and encompasses such virtues as patriotism and self-sacrifice (see also Graham, Haidt, and Nosek 2009; Graham et al. 2013). Loyalty brings group members together when there is a threat, which is why people who strongly identify with a group value loyalty so much (Clifford 2017). Strong identifiers stick with the group, even during hard or bad times.

The nation can be seen as a joint project, one where we as a nation might make mistakes but where we as citizens remain loyal. Negative attacks and criticisms coming from outsiders can be expected and are fairly easy to rationalize or ignore. Criticisms coming from fellow nationals are harder to dismiss (Hornsey, Oppes, and Svensson 2002). When people who love their country point out problems or raise criticisms, strong identifiers assume their motive is to enhance the national group's well-being and to make the nation better. When people who some see as not loving their country are critical of it, other members will see them as disloyal and see their criticisms as threatening (Adelman and Dasgupta 2019; Hornsey et al. 2007; Hornsey 2006; Ellemers, Spears, and Doosje 1999).[2]

Loyalty to the nation is often contrasted to the globalized elite. In his book on nationalism, Lowry discusses the "treason of elites" who are no longer attached to their country and who criticize their own country as if it is not theirs (Lowry 2019, ch. 10). We asked a few of our conservative focus groups about criticism of the United States. They said that criticism was acceptable, as long as it came from a place of loyalty.

> We're not perfect, however, we're pretty good; there's always room for improvement. But I'll just finish on my original point which I think was in order for us to be thankful for what we have, we have to celebrate what we've done and what we've come from. (NC Conservatives 5, Man 3)

> The thing that bothers me I guess is that if you ever hear somebody who is critiquing, they're talking about the negatives of America like "I don't like this place at all, I hate it," that they . . . there's not that underlying, like, "yeah, I'm going to talk about what I think needs to be fixed with the country but I love the country and that's why I want to fix it." It's almost like you're talking about the critiques as if the entire country is your enemy. And that's when it would really bother me. As long as that's an assumption, that yes, we love the country and we care about the country and that's the reason why we're making these critiques, then it's fine. But that's, the moment you cross that line where it's like the critique isn't coming from a place of, you know, love and investment and interest in the future of the country, that's where it's just not helpful at all. (TN Conservatives, Man 2)

Loyalty is paramount. Scruton (2004, 35) argues that Britain is in crisis because "the loyalty that people need in their daily lives, and which they affirm in their unconsidered and spontaneous social actions, is constantly ridiculed or even demonized by the dominant media and the education system."

A major problem with the social justice agenda, in the eyes of Republicans, is that it is not only divisive, pitting groups against each other rather than bringing the American people together, but it also fosters disloyalty. Social justice advocates are deeply critical of America's racist, sexist, and homophobic past. Confronting America's prejudices and injustices is a key goal of the social justice agenda, with hard-hitting criticism that the United States is inherently racist and sexist starting off the process of change. One of our liberal focus group participants explained:

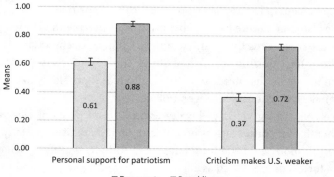

FIGURE 5.2. Solidarity Beliefs and Party Identification
*Source*: 2020 Social Justice and Solidarity Survey
*Note*: Higher scores reflect higher solidarity beliefs. The mean differences between Democrats and Republicans are significant at the $p < 0.001$ level using one-sided $t$-tests.

> Because I truly believe there's an underlying reality and it is complicated, we name different reasons and we come back to different, but there's an original sin, original reality of how America was formed in the first place that rarely gets acknowledged . . . [T]he underlying reality of stealing land and stealing people, that's in the DNA of who America is. So a Donald Trump does not surprise me at all. He just represents kind of some underlying realities of who we are as a nation. (Chicago 2, Man 5)

Republicans tend to believe that social justice advocates are not loyal Americans but are instead unrelentingly critical. In this view, the social justice advocates' passionate and often loud criticisms are potentially harmful to the nation because they are not coming, to quote the conservative Sacramento focus group participant, from a place of "love and investment and interest in the future of the country."

We asked a series of questions about patriotism and reactions to criticism of the United States in our 2020 Social Justice and Solidarity Survey. We asked respondents how much they personally supported "loving the United States (patriotism)," from "not at all" to "very much" on a 5-point scale. We also asked the extent of their agreement with the statement, "When people criticize America without recognizing its greatness, they make us weaker." Response options ranged from strongly agree to strongly disagree.

Figure 5.2 shows the mean responses among Republicans and Democrats to these two items. Republicans are significantly more likely to say they personally support loving their country (a mean of 0.88 on a 0 to 1 scale), although many Democrats say this as well (a mean of 0.61). Almost three-quarters of Republicans (72 percent) said they "very much" support patriotism, compared to only 29 percent of Democrats who gave the most positive response. Republicans are also much more likely to believe that criticizing the United States is bad because it weakens the country (a mean of 0.72). Democrats disagree (a mean of 0.37). Criticizing the United States, from Democrats' point of view, can highlight areas that need to be fixed, and fixing problems like social injustices makes the country stronger, not weaker.

These contrasting views of loyalty and criticism play out clearly in the views liberals and conservatives hold about American history. Many liberals question the motives of the founders, bring to light the racist behaviors of major historical figures (such as Thomas Jefferson's ownership and treatment of slaves), and frequently point to racist and sexist events or periods as exemplars of American hypocrisy. The treatment of Native Americans; the internment of Japanese Americans during World War II; the widespread support of slavery, then Jim Crow laws, and now the mass incarceration of Black Americans; and the enforcement of sodomy laws and treatment of homosexuals and transgender Americans all point, in many liberals' minds, to a history that is certainly tarnished and one about which Americans should hold collective guilt. There has been some progress, in this view, but that progress has been slow and uneven, while advances are often made only after criticisms and conflict have forced change. Criticism, then, is essential for creating the change that will make the United States a better, more just place.

Conservatives tend to view American history very differently. The founders of the country were great men who in their brilliance wrote a constitution that put in place one of the most successful social experiments in the history of the world. If there have been any mistakes, they were due to short-term forces and were quickly corrected. US history, then, is one of greatness flowing through time, and Americans need to embrace and celebrate that greatness. It's not that the United States is perfect, and progress has been made overcoming any imperfections, but it makes no sense for people to focus on the negatives. The positives far outweigh the negatives and ought to be celebrated.

We asked the Social Justice and Solidarity Survey respondents the extent to which they agreed or disagreed with the statement, "While our country has some flaws, overall the United States is a great country." Respondents overwhelmingly agreed with this statement, with 69 percent of Democrats and 92 percent of Republicans agreeing or strongly agreeing. We also asked them specifically about their view of America's history on racism: "Which comes closer to your view? The United States has made considerable progress on racial equality since the 1960s, and people should be patient as progress continues . . . OR . . . The United States has not made nearly enough progress on racial equality since the 1960s, and our society should prioritize racial justice." Partisans differ in their responses: 89 percent of Republicans chose the first statement, whereas 68 percent of Democrats chose the second. These competing views of history raise serious concerns among Republicans about Democrats' social justice agenda. Many Republicans believe this view of history is disloyal and harmful to the national group.

LIBERTY

Strong identifiers are more likely than weak identifiers to hold the norms and beliefs central to a group's identity. For Americans, these norms and beliefs include, especially, a belief in liberty or freedom as a core value (Schildkraut 2007; Schildkraut 2014). In our 2020 Social Justice and Solidarity Survey, a majority of Democrats (60 percent) and Republicans (79 percent) somewhat or strongly agreed with the statement, "One of the most important values we have as Americans is the freedom to do what we want."

Conservative theorists link national identity to democracy and collective freedom, and collective freedom in turn is what protects individual freedom. Hazony (2018, 125) explains this connection: "Only the national state, governed by individuals drawn from the tribes of the nation itself, can be a free state—because only rulers who are bound to this nation by ties of mutual loyalty, and who experience the things that happen to the nation as things that are happening to themselves, will devote themselves to the freedom and self-determination of this nation on a permanent basis" (see also Lowry 2019, 39–47; Scruton 2004, 22–32). Citizens bounded together will protect their freedoms. The British in World War II fought for *their* country, not for cosmopolitanism or a universal government. Moreover, it is not an accident that democracies are national states. States torn apart by tribal identities do not have collective freedom—they are riven by division and distrust that make democracy impossible. Empires, too, are not democratic—the government is too far removed from the people to make collective freedom a possibility. For people to be free, they must feel connected to one another. They must share an interest in defending themselves against threats, and they must be unified enough to want to engage in self-rule. Only under these conditions is individual liberty possible. A strong nation with loyal citizens is intertwined with liberty and democracy, but national solidarity and loyalty are the foundation on which liberty stands.

For many conservatives, justice is secondary to liberty, in part because justice is diffuse and hard to achieve but most importantly because the single-minded pursuit of justice may undermine liberty and be self-defeating. In

TABLE 5.1. The tradeoff between liberty and equality (%)

|  | Democrats | Republicans |
| --- | --- | --- |
| Value equality much more than freedom | 21 | 9 |
| Value equality somewhat more than freedom | 48 | 18 |
| Value freedom somewhat more than equality | 26 | 47 |
| Value freedom much more than equality | 6 | 27 |
| Total percent valuing freedom more than equality | 32 | 74 |
| Total percent valuing equality more than freedom | 69 | 27 |

Source: 2020 Social Justice and Solidarity Survey

contrast to liberals, then, conservatives think that the purpose of social institutions is to foster liberty, not justice. The fear haunting conservatives is that liberals will rob them of their liberty and undermine national solidarity in the name of equality and in the pursuit of social justice.

This division between conservatives and liberals can be seen in the disagreement between Republicans and Democrats concerning which value—equality or liberty—has priority. While public policy can pursue more than one goal, it often emphasizes some values over others. To get at this prioritization, we asked our survey respondents: "Americans tend to value both equality and freedom but often value one somewhat more than the other. What do you think? Where would you place yourself in terms of valuing equality and freedom?" Table 5.1 shows the differences between Democrats and Republicans on this question. When pushed to choose between values widely supported by most Americans, Republicans definitely side with freedom, whereas Democrats definitely side with equality. Three-quarters of Republicans said they value freedom over equality and over two-thirds of Democrats say they value equality over freedom.

These are of course blunt survey questions. Many people argue that liberty means very little to the impoverished or the oppressed; liberty in a sea of deep inequality means little to many people. Others argue that equality without liberty is, at best, hollow. Still, our survey questions get at the orientation of liberal and conservative citizens and their priorities. The social justice agenda puts equality front and center, making it one of the most important values Americans ought to pursue. Social justice advocates do not see themselves as anti-liberty, but they do think that social policy should focus on equality: to them, the main problem facing the United States is not about insufficient liberty but rather the downgrading of equality.

As we showed in chapter 2, conservatives believe in procedural equality, but they worry that liberals' more expansive view of equality will mean worrisome government intervention and the abridging of people's freedom.

When survey respondents were asked the extent to which they agreed with the statement, "If society tries too hard to become a just society, it will undermine liberty," 68 percent of Republicans agreed or strongly agreed, compared to only 22 percent of Democrats. From Republicans' point of view, of course people should not promote racial or gender inequality, but the way to create a just society is to give everyone a basic set of opportunities and then let them use those opportunities to achieve what they can. This means that there will always be inequality, and it is not government's role to deny the inevitable. If government gets involved, it only leads to more inequality and unfairness in the system.

## Group Boundaries

Having a strong national identity increases support for group cohesion, loyalty, and core group beliefs, one of which, among Americans, is liberty. It also increases the likelihood that people will set clear boundaries on who is in and who is not in the group (Theiss-Morse 2009). If the group boundaries are highly permeable and people can easily enter or leave the group, keeping the group together and ensuring that key norms and values are shared by group members become very difficult (Brown 2000).

Most conservatives believe that citizenship is a privileged status. Citizenship is not just a matter of belonging legally to a particular country; it also puts in place a set of obligations. States have more robust obligations to their citizens than to noncitizens, but citizens have stronger obligations to their own state than to others. This special status of citizenship leads conservatives to feel more empathy for their fellow citizens than for others. Conservatives and liberals alike think that everyone should be treated fairly, but for conservatives (though not libertarians) everyone's claims on justice are to their own state.[3] Procedural equality, in this view, is for fellow citizens, and the government has no obligation to apply it to noncitizens.

In contrast, egalitarian theorists are divided over the meaning of citizenship, as are liberal citizens. Some liberal theorists argue for the importance of citizenship and community (Miller 1995; Blake 2019; Walzer 1980; Walzer 1983), but others do not (Carens 2013). Many liberal citizens, given their social justice worldview and belief in equality, think Americans have an obligation to take in those from other countries, especially people who are refugees, yet others are more ambivalent.

We asked the participants in our first round of focus groups, "Some people argue that immigration is a problem because it leads to lower wages for low-skilled workers. So what would you think about limiting immigration to reduce income inequality?" Our conservative participants agreed that immigrants coming into the country illegally must be stopped, although some wanted to stop or slow all immigration, legal and illegal, whereas others wanted only to stop illegal immigration.

> I would approve immigration only under the same terms as my ancestors came to this country, which was legally, through Ellis Island, with a medical clearance, and being able to support themselves or somebody here said they would help them get through. Period. There's no controversy about the word illegal. If it ain't legal, it ain't legal. (NC Conservatives 2, Man 3)

> I'm not sure we have an immigration issue as much as we have an illegal immigration issue. I think our legal immigration system is for the most part fine. I feel like it does what it's supposed to do, where you're letting in people who are going to benefit the economy, you know, who are going to benefit the country, and you're kind of processing it just so we know who everybody is. (Nebraska Conservatives, Man 3)

Some focused on the question whether immigration hurt low-skilled Americans or not:

> Uncontrolled immigration is hurting our most vulnerable populations. Like, the rich people benefit from it, the big corporations benefit from it. The people who are injured by it are the marginal communities who are most at risk, who are having the hardest time. They're the ones, like, to say that we have no heart because we want to, because we want to limit immigration. No, we have a tremendous amount of empathy and it's for our own populations that are being hurt by it. (NC Conservatives 1, Woman 1)

> I would say keep immigration the same but kind of speed up the process. I don't, I don't really see anything coming out of people immigrating and taking jobs or lowering wages, because they're doing the jobs that like, I hate to say it, but the rest of us aren't doing. And they're working their butts off, they're not the ones mooching off the government. (NC Conservatives 4, Woman 1)

Many conservatives, though, addressed the topic of immigration in a way that was heavily steeped in American identity:

> And also, to me, huge is I want to live in America. I do. I want to live in America. I do not want to live in Saudi Arabia, I don't want to live in Mexico, I want to live in America and I am happy to welcome people from other cultures and other races, yes, I am happy and will be kind to them, but I don't want America to turn into a foreign country that I don't know anymore. (NC Conservatives 1, Woman 3)

Well I think another critical part is that anyone who is an immigrant to this country has to want to become an American and accept American values, and not impose Sharia law on us or you know, you can respect diversity, but the old melting pot idea was wonderful; it was you brought all of this rich culture, but there was an American identity that's now being bashed, white privilege among it, among the bashing, but absolutely I think immigrants need to prove that they want to become part of our culture. (NC Conservatives 2, Woman 2)

Our conservative participants said that people coming to the United States must do so through legal channels. They also expected immigrants to embrace fully American values. They must work hard and not be a drain on government resources. While conservatives disagreed about immigration controls, they felt a much greater obligation to Americans than to non-Americans. The debate among conservatives is not about the meaning of citizenship.

Our liberal focus group participants had a very different reaction to the question about limiting immigration to help the low-skilled American workforce. The swift response from liberals across all the focus groups was that the question itself was completely wrongheaded. One woman said, "That's such crap," and another said, "Oh, Lord, what a question!" A man responded, "No, because it won't. . . . That you even ask the question is mindboggling to me." Another man said, "It's racial code talk" followed by another participant's "Absolutely." We were surprised that the liberal participants did not engage with the income inequality aspect of the question. Their focus was solely on how terrible it would be to limit immigration.

We asked a follow-up question on whether the United States should try to ensure that people do not come to the United States without legal authorization.[4] Many liberal participants questioned the need for border enforcement:

But there's no way to make it sane. People have been migrating and moving around since the beginning of time, and you, we have even better ways of moving around now than we have ever had. And so what's the big fucking deal? (NC Liberals 6, Woman 3)

Yeah, I don't even know how big a problem it is. I think it's been drummed up as a huge problem. (NC Liberals 4, Woman 1)

Yet some liberals were more ambivalent.

But I agree with you there, there are some who are fleeing for their lives, literally, and we ought to offer, out of compassion we ought to offer a home to them. But there are some who just, you know, want a better life. Which is commendable in itself, but they don't have a right to be here, and you know, work here and all that kind of thing. (NC Liberals 8, Man 3)

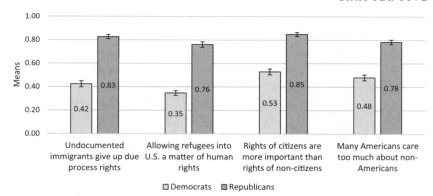

FIGURE 5.3. Status of American Citizens versus Noncitizens by Party Identification
*Source*: 2019 Pluralism and Respect Survey
*Note*: Higher scores reflect a more restrictive view of immigration and a stronger national solidarity view of American citizenship. The mean differences between Democrats and Republicans are significant at the $p < 0.001$ level using one-sided $t$-tests.

The debate among liberals couldn't be more different from the debate among conservatives. Whereas conservatives view citizenship as an important demarcation, some liberals question whether citizenship is even meaningful while others think people do have special obligations to their fellow citizens. Our 2019 Pluralism and Respect Survey results highlight this difference between and among partisans (see figure 5.3).

When it comes to placing the rights of American citizens above those of noncitizens, Republicans agree. Republicans overwhelmingly believe, with means over 0.8, that citizens' rights are more important than those of noncitizens and that undocumented immigrants have given up their due process rights when they come into the country illegally. Not surprisingly, Republicans reject the view that admitting refugees into the United States is a human right. For Democrats, people have an obligation to help each other, but the boundaries of the obligation are disputed. Democrats are split on whether citizen rights are more important than the rights of noncitizens. While many more Democrats think that letting in refugees is a matter of human rights than think otherwise (only 15 percent disagreed with the statement), the mean responses for the other statements hover around 0.4 and 0.5 (neither agree nor disagree).

Respecting rights is a bedrock of justice; many liberals think that if the United States does not respect the rights of noncitizens, then it is not merely falling short of justice but it may be following racist and xenophobic policies.

If you do not extend rights to noncitizens when they are at your border, then on this view you are acting unjustly. For many conservatives, however, citizenship bounds obligations: our government has obligations to our fellow citizens that it does not have to noncitizens. If the government does not extend rights to the people outside the country's border who want to get in, then it is not committing an injustice. There may be a different government that is acting unjustly that is causing people to flee, but this is not the American government's responsibility.

## Moralization of National Solidarity Beliefs

We argued in chapter 4 that Democrats moralize their social justice beliefs and that their social justice worldviews have a pronounced impact on their respect for Republicans. People who hold their beliefs as moral convictions think their beliefs are factual and universal, and these beliefs are intensely felt and not swayed by external forces (Skitka and Morgan 2014). People who agree with these beliefs are good and moral, whereas those who disagree are bad and even evil (see, e.g., Ryan 2014; Ryan 2017; Skitka and Morgan 2014). While Democrats hold their social justice beliefs as moral convictions, we argue in this chapter that Republicans do the same with their national solidarity beliefs. Republicans are more likely than Democrats to believe that being loyal, believing in America's core principles (at least as they understand them), and viewing citizenship as a special status are moral convictions.

We used four items in our Social Justice and Solidarity Survey to measure moral convictions relevant to national solidarity. One item was the extent to which respondents agreed or disagreed with the statement, "It's immoral for Americans to criticize the United States." The other three items came from people's responses to whether they held various issues as core moral beliefs (the same stem question as those used for the social justice moral beliefs): "Whether you support or oppose these issues, we'd like to know the extent to which your stand is a reflection of your core moral beliefs; that is, how much are they connected to your fundamental beliefs about right and wrong? How much of a core moral belief is your stand on . . . ?" The three issues we use for this analysis are loving your country (patriotism), defending religious freedom, and protecting the right of Americans to own guns. Response options ranged from not at all to very much (transformed to range from 0 to 1). Figure 5.4 shows the mean differences between Democrats and Republicans on the extent to which they hold their beliefs as moral convictions.

In contrast to the social justice issues discussed in chapter 4, Republicans are significantly more likely than Democrats to hold their national solidarity beliefs as moral convictions, with means above 0.8 for patriotism and religious freedom and just below 0.8 for gun rights. Democrats are more likely to hold religious freedom as a moral conviction than the other issues, but the mean is still significantly lower than it is for Republicans. Loving one's country is clearly a major concern to Republicans, and the fact that many think it is a core moral belief is important for understanding their reaction to people whom they perceive to be unpatriotic. Liberty, as measured by religious freedom and gun rights, is also highly moralized by Republicans. Although viewing criticisms of the United States as immoral garnered less support than the other issues, Republicans are still significantly more likely than Democrats to view their stand on liberty as a moral conviction (means of 0.56 and 0.30, respectively). Overall, figure 5.4 provides clear evidence that Republicans, much more so than Democrats, hold their national solidarity beliefs as moral convictions.

When people hold their beliefs as moral convictions, they think anyone who holds opposing views is morally wrong. They are bad people. Democrats think Republicans are bad people because of their stand on social justice issues, but Democrats significantly underestimate Republican support for social justice (see chapter 4). We examine here if Republicans similarly underestimate Democratic support for national solidarity. In figure 5.5, we compare where Democrats and Republicans personally stand on patriotism, religious freedom, and gun rights to where they think opposing partisans stand on the same issues. As with figure 4.1, the solid bars are partisans' personal support for each issue, and the bars with patterns are what partisans think opposing partisans' support is for each issue.

Democrats underestimate Republicans' support on all three issues (the dotted bars), although their estimate on gun rights is close to reality. For both

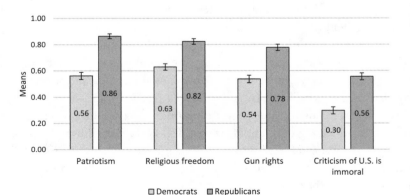

FIGURE 5.4. National Solidarity Beliefs as Moral Convictions
*Source*: 2020 Social Justice and Solidarity Survey

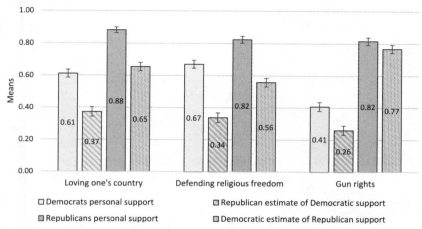

FIGURE 5.5. Partisan Support for National Solidarity Issues and Attributed Support by Opposing Partisans
*Source*: 2020 Social Justice and Solidarity Survey

patriotism and religious freedom, Democrats' underestimation brings Republicans closer to the Democrats' means. Among Republicans, however, their underestimation of Democrats' support for national solidarity (the hatched bars) is pronounced and places Democrats much farther away from them than is reality. On loving one's country, Democrats give Republicans a mean score of 0.65, compared to Republicans' actual mean score of 0.88, but Democrats think Republicans are quite patriotic. Republicans do not think the same of Democrats, giving them a mean patriotism score of only 0.37. Only 13 percent of Republicans said they thought Democrats love the United States very much. Republicans also underestimate Democrats' support for gun rights, but by much less. They most seriously underestimate Democrats' support for religious freedom. These results show that both Democrats and Republicans underestimate the national solidarity support of opposing partisans, but the important point for our argument is that for Republicans, their view of Democrats as unpatriotic and opposed to liberty matters a great deal and casts Democrats as immoral and bad people.

## Who Holds a National Solidarity Worldview?

We created a National Solidarity Worldview scale using responses to the Social Justice and Solidarity Survey questions concerning the valuing of liberty, a personal belief in solidarity issues, moralizing those issues, strength of American identity, group cohesiveness, and promoting a less critical view of American history (see appendix C for the questions used). The National

TABLE 5.2. National solidarity worldview support

|  | Total | Democrats | Republicans |
|---|---|---|---|
| Overall mean | 0.64 | 0.53 | 0.79 |
| Age |  |  |  |
| Young (20–39) | 0.61 | 0.55 | 0.75 |
| Older (40 and older) | 0.65 | 0.51 | 0.80 |
| Sex |  |  |  |
| Male | 0.63 | 0.53 | 0.78 |
| Female | 0.65 | 0.52 | 0.79 |
| Race |  |  |  |
| White | 0.65 | 0.50 | 0.79 |
| People of color | 0.61 | 0.57 | 0.73 |
| Education |  |  |  |
| Less than college | 0.65 | 0.55 | 0.79 |
| College degree | 0.64 | 0.51 | 0.80 |
| Post-baccalaureate degree | 0.57 | 0.45 | 0.75 |
| Place of residence |  |  |  |
| Urban | 0.59 | 0.52 | 0.78 |
| Suburb | 0.64 | 0.52 | 0.77 |
| Rural | 0.70 | 0.54 | 0.81 |
| Ideology |  |  |  |
| Liberal | 0.53 | 0.50 | 0.75 |
| Middle of the road | 0.60 | 0.56 | 0.69 |
| Conservative | 0.80 | 0.70 | 0.81 |
| Voting behavior |  |  |  |
| Plan to vote in 2020 | 0.64 | 0.52 | 0.79 |
| Do not plan to vote in 2020 | 0.69 | 0.67 | 0.70 |

Source: 2020 Social Justice and Solidarity Survey
Note: Cell entries are mean scores on the national solidarity worldview scale (0 = anti–national solidarity worldview, 1 = pro–national solidarity worldview).

Solidarity Worldview scale ranges from 0 to 1, with higher scores signifying a more pronational solidarity view (mean = 0.64, sd = 0.215, alpha = 0.886).

Table 5.2 shows the differences in means of support for the national solidarity worldview by various demographic groups broken down by party identification. Republicans are, as expected, significantly more likely than Democrats to hold the national solidarity worldview (means of 0.79 and 0.53, respectively). These differences hold quite well regardless of demographic group. Younger Republicans are slightly less likely to hold the worldview compared to those over forty, whereas the opposite is true among Democrats. The most highly educated, those with a graduate or professional degree, in both parties are less likely to hold the national solidarity worldview than their less well-educated fellow partisans. The Democrats and Republicans who are most similar in their national solidarity worldview are those who did not plan to vote in 2020. People willing to admit that they weren't planning to vote were small in number, but Democratic nonvoters had higher worldview scores and Republican nonvoters had lower worldview scores than their voting counterparts.

## National Solidarity and Respect for Opposing Partisans

The liberal respect paradox highlights the difficulty liberals have in giving respect to conservatives who, they think, oppose equality and social justice. Democrats believe in equality and the importance of respect, but they have a hard time respecting Republicans. Yet there are many Republicans who have a similarly difficult time respecting Democrats. Republicans, as we have shown, hold a moralized national solidarity worldview that clashes in many ways with Democrats' moralized social justice worldview. Republicans think that focusing on racial, ethnic, and gender groups undermines the cohesion of the American people, yet the social justice agenda does just this by focusing on oppressed groups. Republicans believe that a strong America is one where its citizens are loyal and positive about the country and its history. The social justice agenda is critical of the United States and its past. Republicans believe that loyalty to and identifying with the United States is a moral good and that citizenship is not just a matter of belonging legally to a particular country but is instead a special status. The social justice agenda promotes more open borders and a more globalized view of citizenship. To Republicans, the social justice agenda weakens America, which is a moral wrong. This, we argue, can make it difficult for Republicans to respect Democrats.

We test the impact of the national solidarity worldview on respect using the Social Justice and Solidarity Survey. We use the same recognition respect scale as we did in chapter 4. We also created a respect scale using questions about those who disagree with respondents on national solidarity issues (just as we did with the social justice respect questions). These questions started: "We asked you some questions earlier about various issues. Now we're going to ask you questions about people who strongly disagree with you on these issues. How easy or difficult is it for you to respect someone who strongly disagrees with you on . . ." The national solidarity issues about which we asked were loving your country (patriotism), defending religious freedom, and protecting the right of Americans to own guns. Response options ranged on a 5-point scale from very difficult to respect to very easy to respect. We created a National Solidarity Respect Scale from these three items that ranged from 0 (very difficult to respect) to 1 (very easy to respect) (mean = 0.454, sd = 0.261, alpha = 0.751).We argue that Republicans, who tend to score modestly higher

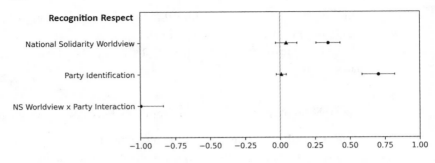

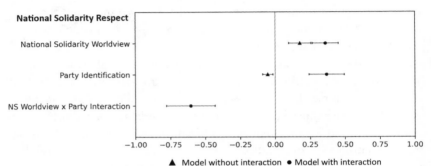

▲ Model without interaction ● Model with interaction

FIGURE 5.6. National Solidarity Worldview, Party Identification, and Respect.

*Source:* Social Justice and Solidarity Survey (2020)

*Note:* Data are unstandardized regression coefficients with 95% confidence interval error bars from OLS regressions. The regression models included control variables for age, sex (male), race (white), rural, and education level (data not shown; see appendix D, table D.2, for the full models). Party identification is coded 0 = Democrats and leaners, 0.5 = pure Independents, 1 = Republicans and leaners. Recognition respect: Model without interaction—Constant = 0.482 (se 0.028), $F$ = 1.84^, Adj. $R^2$ = 0.005, $N$ = 1191; Model with interaction—Constant = 0.290 (se 0.031), $F$ = 20.37***, Adj. $R^2$ = 0.115, $N$ = 1191. National solidarity respect: Model without interaction—Constant = 0.531 (se 0.029), $F$ = 25.42***, Adj. $R^2$ = 0.126, $N$ = 1191; Model with interaction—Constant = 0.414 (se 0.033), $F$ = 28.89***, Adj. $R^2$ = 0.158, $N$ = 1191. ^$p$ < 0.10; ***$p$ < 0.001.

in respect than Democrats, are especially put off by Democrats who they think are actively undermining national solidarity in their pursuit of equality and social justice. The more Republicans believe in the national solidarity worldview, the less likely they are to give respect to Democrats. Figures 5.6 and 5.7 provide evidence that these expectations are right. The top panel in figure 5.6 contains the results for recognition respect and the lower panel for national solidarity respect.[5] In general, national solidarity worldview and party identification have a direct effect on national solidarity respect but not on recognition respect. It is the interaction of worldview and party identification that has the strongest effect. We find that holding a national solidarity worldview leads Republicans to be much less respectful of Democrats. The impact on recognition respect is especially strong, but the finding holds for national solidarity respect as well. Republicans and leaners drop from having a high level of respect for Democrats when they reject the national solidarity worldview to disrespecting Democrats when they hold this worldview as a core belief. We also find that Democrats who support the national solidarity worldview are much more likely to respect Republicans than are Democrats who reject this worldview.

There are many factors that could affect Republicans' respect for Democrats. We contend that Democrats' pursuit of a social justice agenda, which most Democrats believe in strongly because of their emphasis on the value of equality and the way they interpret it, is especially difficult for Republicans to accept because of the way they value national solidarity. Democrats believe that society must work toward achieving equality and justice. It is not good enough for individuals to behave better since racism is deeply embedded in structures and processes. As Republicans see it, though, focusing on racial or ethnic or gender groups undermines the solidarity of the American people and weakens the country. Americans should be color-blind, they argue. They should see themselves as Americans, first and foremost. These social justice efforts also, Republicans believe, diminish their liberty. They should be free to say and do what they want and not have to accept Democrats' views on what are the most important societal problems and how to fix them. The social justice agenda,

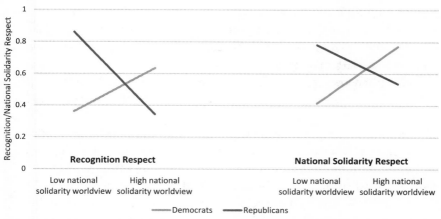

FIGURE 5.7. Respect and the Interaction of Party Identification and National Solidarity Worldview
Source: 2020 Social Justice and Solidarity Survey
Note: The values for "high national solidarity worldview" were calculated using the highest score possible (a score of 1) on the scale. The values for "low national solidarity worldview" were calculated using a score of 0.205, which is 2 standard deviations below the mean of the scale, to more realistically reflect low scores since no one scored 0 on the scale.

in this view, misdiagnoses the problem and introduces new problems into the mix. How can Republicans respect people whose agenda and efforts will undermine their values and weaken America in the process? They can't.

## Conclusion

What contributes to Americans' lack of respect for opposing partisans? In the last chapter and this one, we have argued that Democrats overwhelmingly hold a moralized social justice worldview, whereas Republicans overwhelmingly hold a moralized national solidarity worldview. Respect for those who do not hold the same worldview can be difficult to maintain. The fact that the two worldviews clash in important ways, however, makes it even more difficult to view opposing partisans as worthy of respect. Democrats think Republicans reject social justice as a societal goal, and they can't respect them when social justice so clearly ought to be a top goal for society. Republicans think Democrats reject national solidarity as a societal goal, and they, too, find it difficult to respect Democrats who seem so unpatriotic and divisive.

As we have shown, though, partisans' perceptions of opposing partisans on these fundamental worldviews are misguided. We looked at who fell into the top and bottom quartiles of the social justice worldview and the national solidarity worldview. If partisans' perceptions were correct, we'd see a large number of Democrats in the top quartile of the social justice worldview and the bottom quartile of the national solidarity worldview. Similarly, we'd find a large number of Republicans in the top quartile of the national solidarity worldview and in the bottom quartile of the social justice worldview. We don't find this at all. Only 7 percent of Democrats score high on social justice and low on national solidarity, and only 8 percent of Republicans score high on national solidarity and low on social justice. More partisans score high on both, 10 percent of Democrats and 17 percent of Republicans, than these more divisive options.

While misperceptions of opposing partisans' beliefs can be destructive to respect, there is an additional element of these worldviews that must be explored. In chapters 4 and 5, we have focused on the social justice and national solidarity beliefs individuals hold. Because these worldviews encompass beliefs about how society ought to work, they are prescriptive for everyone in the society. To get rid of social injustices in America, all Americans must work toward this goal. To achieve national solidarity in America, all Americans must come together as loyal Americans. Everyone has a responsibility to achieve the goals of the worldviews. We address this notion of collective responsibility in the next chapter.

# 6

# Collective Responsibility and Judging Others

People could believe wholeheartedly in social justice or in national solidarity, accept that some people hold an opposing view, and be willing to give those opponents respect. It is just one individual's viewpoint against another's. Yet it is much harder for people to respect their political opponents when their beliefs are moralized, as we showed in the last two chapters. In this chapter, we address a further obstacle to respect: if people believe that the goals their society ought to try to achieve can be accomplished only if all people do their part, then it is even more difficult to respect those on the other side. Disagreement is more intensely judged because the other side's actions harm society.

As we argued in chapter 4, the social justice worldview includes beliefs about structural injustice. Ridding society of structural injustice necessarily entails not just individuals behaving better but also structural, systemic change. Yet structural change will only occur if a large proportion of the population presses for this change; that is, people must get on board and work toward justice. In this view, even when people do not actively work against social justice goals and simply don't take necessary action to eradicate structural injustice, they contribute to an unjust society. We argue in this chapter that liberals often think that citizens have both a personal and a collective responsibility to end structural injustice. Collective responsibility includes actions directly aimed at creating social justice as well as symbolic gestures, voting, and consumer choices. There are many ways by which people can fail to fulfill their collective responsibility (for example, by not voting for pro–social justice candidates, by remaining silent when injustices occur, and by buying goods at anti–social justice businesses or those that contribute to injustices), which helps explain why liberal citizens have a hard time respecting conservatives.

Republicans also believe in collective responsibility. While many Republicans view justice as a matter of individual behavior, they believe people have a personal and collective responsibility to be loyal citizens and to keep the nation strong. It might seem odd that we have conservatives believing in both individual and collective responsibility, but we argue that conservatives think a strong nation is the foundation of freedom, and that citizens have a responsibility to maintain national solidarity to keep their nation strong—and free. Certainly, the individualism that runs through conservatives could soften their insistence for collective responsibility. In contrast to liberals, whose social justice goals affect many choices, conservatives are less likely to see one's choices, particularly individual consumer choices, as a matter of collective responsibility.

We are interested in people's beliefs about collective responsibility and how these beliefs affect their judgments of and respect for other people, specifically opposing partisans. We use the term *collective responsibility*, which is rarely studied by social scientists, to capture the idea that people believe that everyone, or almost everyone, in a society must contribute to achieving societal goals.[1] Social scientists have extensively studied collective action problems that explain how each individual's decision to maximize self-interested short-term benefits lead to worse outcomes for the collective (see, e.g., Ostrom 2010).[2] Collective responsibility shifts the focus from the individual decision in an interdependent situation to understanding how individuals judge people who they think are not contributing to the collective outcome. Whether people are opposed to the goals or even when they simply remain inactive, they are contributing to making society worse off. Collective responsibility helps us understand why partisans have a hard time respecting one another. As we will show, individuals who strongly believe in collective responsibility judge others harshly.

We begin by looking at psychologists' understanding of collective responsibility and the arguments for possible differences between liberals and conservatives. We then turn to political theorists' arguments, beginning with the role of responsibility in theories of structural injustice, followed by conservaives' arguments about solidarity and liberty and how the two are intertwined. Using focus group and survey data, we show that Democrats have a strong sense of collective responsibility surrounding social justice goals just as Republicans do concerning national solidarity goals. This sense of collective responsibility increases people's tendency to make harsh judgments of and decrease respect for opposing partisans. As we explain in the conclusion, the liberal respect paradox is in part explained by collective responsibility. Liberals believe both that respect is a cardinal virtue of democratic citizenship and that citizens have a collective responsibility to work against structural injustice. But these two strongly held beliefs easily clash. While many conservative citizens also experience tension between respect and their view of collective responsibility, the tension is not as deep since their view of respect and collective responsibility is less intensely held than it is for liberals.

## The Importance of Collective Responsibility

The well-known moral foundations theory holds that there are five moral foundations on which people intuitively draw: harm/care, fairness/reciprocity, purity/sanctity, authority/respect, and ingroup/loyalty (Haidt 2001; Haidt 2012; Graham, Haidt, and Nosek 2009; Graham et al. 2011). The first two, harm/care and fairness/reciprocity, are individualizing foundations because they focus on protecting the individual. An individual learns to treat fairly or not to harm another individual. Purity, authority, and ingroup are binding foundations because the social order (including religion) binds people to certain roles or duties that constrain immoral behavior. An individual learns not to do something immoral because authorities, social groups, or religious institutions have clear rules regulating such behavior, and people feel a sense of obligation to obey. Haidt and his colleagues suggest that liberals are more likely to focus on the individualizing foundations, whereas conservatives focus on both the individualizing and binding foundations (Haidt and Graham 2007). The two moral foundations of liberals are *"individualizing foundations* because they are (we suggest) the source of the intuitions that make the liberal philosophical tradition, with its emphasis on the rights and welfare of individuals, so learnable and so compelling to so many people"* (Graham, Haidt, and Nosek 2009, 1031).

Our disagreement is with the implication that liberals are motivated by individual-level concerns while conservatives are motivated by both individual and broader societal forces when it comes to moral intuitions.[3] One could interpret fairness/reciprocity through the lens of collective responsibility, making the individuating/binding distinction that Haidt and colleagues make more opaque than they suggest. We argue that *both* liberals and conservatives are motivated by individual and societal forces. Janoff-Bulman and Carnes (2013) make this clear when they discuss the three levels of moral motives: the individual level (doing right in regard to oneself), the interpersonal level (doing right in regard to another person), and the group level (doing right in regard to the group or society). Liberals and conservatives alike experience moral motives on all three levels. Where a major difference occurs, however, is at the group level. Janoff-Bulman and Carnes argue that liberals are motivated by a social justice motive, which means they are motivated to help the oppressed and those less fortunate in their society, whereas conservatives are motivated by a social order and solidarity motive, which means they are motivated to protect people in their society from harm.[4]

Janoff-Bulman and Carnes's research highlights the importance of thinking about moral convictions not only in terms of what individuals should do toward other individuals but also in terms of what is morally right for the society or the group at large. This shift from the individual to society is keenly important. At the self or interpersonal level, people are motivated to control their own behavior: I am going to think and behave in a way that doesn't cause harm to or that helps others. At the group level, though, people's beliefs about morality have implications for everyone else in the group: not only should I think and behave in a moral way but everyone else should as well. That's what makes society function the way it should. And since moral convictions are beliefs about right and wrong, good and bad, people are likely to view those who disagree with them on their group-level moral convictions not just as bad people but as bad for society.

In chapters 4 and 5, we focused on individuals' beliefs about social justice and national solidarity, including people's beliefs about what opposing partisans think about these issues. In this chapter, we address the fact that these worldviews implicate not only individual behavior but societal goals as well. They are about what the United States as a nation should try to achieve.[5] While individual choices and behaviors are important for achieving those goals, the societal level focus means that everyone, or almost everyone, carries some responsibility for dismantling systemic injustices and for keeping the nation united and strong. That is, people have a collective responsibility to further society's, or in this case, the nation's, interests. In this view it is impossible to achieve national solidarity or a socially just society if many Americans refuse to help achieve these goals, making disagreements more salient and intense.

Taking appropriate actions toward achieving collective goals could entail not being socially unjust or anti-American. Some people are actively racist or anti-American, and they take very public actions espousing their views. Most Americans, however, are not actively working to undermine social justice or national solidarity goals. Instead, they do nothing. Inaction can be a positive if the inactive are at least not doing harm. "Rather than as proactively contributing to and expanding the social good, social responsibility in the current American perspective may be understood as not bothering others, as not contributing to social ills, or as not requiring help from other people or organizations" (Markus et al. 2001, 362). According to this view, our responsibility to the collective is fulfilled by not doing anything.

This argument doesn't work, though, when achieving societal goals demands broad action. While most Americans do not actively pursue an anti–social justice or anti–national solidarity agenda, from the collective responsibility perspective this is irrelevant. People not taking action on behalf of social justice or national solidarity is just as morally implicating as those who actively oppose one or the other. By not taking action, people are behaving immorally. In his well-known book, *How to Be an Anti-Racist*, Ibram X. Kendi (2020) argues that one either actively opposes racism in actions and deeds or one is racist—there is no neutral ground. Omissions matter. "In fact, many debates in the moral realm seem to specifically involve our failure to help . . . [M]orality and immorality concern both what we do and what we don't do" (Carnes and Janoff-Bulman 2012, 138). By not acting to achieve social justice or national solidarity, these Americans are behaving immorally through their omissions. By not helping, they are doing harm.

## Responsibility for a Socially Just Society

Janoff-Bulman and Carnes (2016, 3) state that "social justice involves communal responsibility and activates collective efforts to advance the group's welfare," although they do not fully explore what this communal responsibility entails. The social justice motive holds that it is insufficient for any single individual to pursue social justice goals. While social psychologists have not explored in depth what this means, this is an important topic in recent political theory. There has been a turn in political theory and in the attitudes of liberal citizens over the last fifteen years or so that all citizens have a responsibility to work toward creating a just society. Justice only arises when people work toward it, and we all have a responsibility to work toward a better society according to this kind of thinking.

We briefly reviewed in chapter 4 the idea of structural injustice, which took off in earnest in the early 2000s when Iris Marion Young's work on structural injustice spawned a large and growing literature, with many of these arguments echoed in the larger culture, particularly by liberal or progressive citizens.[6] Here we connect structural injustice to responsibility, particularly collective responsibility. Young's argument—and the many that are inspired by her—is that we need structures to change if there will be justice, but structures usually are not created or used on the command of one person. Rather, institutional rules and norms reproduce injustices over and over again, and individuals have a responsibility to act in concert to change the structures so they do not continue reproducing injustice. Young argued that we should focus less on who caused the injustice and more on the responsibility to end it.

Individual agents rarely, on their own, do much to cause structural injustice or know what their role was in causing the injustice.[7]

Young argues for what she calls a social connection model of responsibility; this means that responsibility for justice is shared among all actors who participate in structural processes that create or maintain structural injustices. With the focus on the process, there are many people who are connected, and they are responsible for the outcomes of the processes they participate in, even if the outcomes are unintentional. This means that we do not always look for a victim and a singular culprit when it comes to structural injustice (Young 2011). It means, importantly, that we have a shared responsibility to work toward ending structural injustice. Young argues that her model of "forward-looking responsibility can be discharged only by joining with others in collective action. This feature follows from the essentially shared nature of the responsibility. Thousands or even millions of agents contribute by their actions in particular institutional contexts to the processes that produce unjust outcomes. Our forward-looking responsibility consists in changing the institutions and processes so that their outcomes will be less unjust. No one of us can do this on our own" (Young 2006b, 123). Still, Young does not say that people are wrong to refuse to work to change injustice, perhaps because she says no one is responsible for creating the structural injustice.

Young's influential argument is criticized by sympathetic critics who find her arguments on structural injustice to be convincing but her responsibility argument weak. The most important criticism is of Young's idea that responsibility is only forward looking—on Young's argument, no one is to be blamed for structural injustice since blame is so diffuse. The problem with this argument, as Martha Nussbaum (2011, xxi) explains, is that "time marches on." Someone may be ignorant of structural injustice today, and so escape blame for not doing much about it, but is this still true tomorrow? Or the next day? If you know that structural injustice exists yet do nothing to stop it, then you are blameworthy according to several structural injustice theorists (McKeown 2021; Hayward 2017). Indeed, much of the recent literature on structural injustice focuses on the issue of responsibility and blame. Many theorists argue that individual citizens have a *political* responsibility to end structural injustice (Hayward 2017; Schiff 2014; McKeown 2018; Sardo 2020; Ackerly 2018; Atenasio 2019; Heilinger 2019; Sangiovanni 2018; Neuhäuser 2014). On these arguments, ignorance is not an excuse to escape responsibility to work toward ending the structural injustice, nor is responsibility diffuse as it is in Young's argument. Moreover, while Young says that no one is to blame for the creation of structural injustice, some theorists argue that this is mistaken in some if not many cases (McKeown 2021).

While some theorists argue that certain individuals have a greater responsibility than others to undo structural injustice, since some people (the well-off, for example) have greater latitude in their choices, all think that in general citizens have an obligation to end structural injustice. Treating others fairly is insufficient to fulfill one's responsibility. With the goal being to eradicate social injustice, there is no neutral ground, no way to avoid the imperative to act. *Not* taking individual action or *not* supporting candidates or government efforts to eliminate social injustice is the same as supporting injustice because inaction allows these policies and practices to continue. The meaning of the idea of political responsibility is that we all have an obligation to act politically to change the injustice.

There are three levels of responsibility that structural injustice theorists discuss, but in each the individual is obligated to act. First is the responsibility of the individual to avoid contributing to structural injustice. Some people argue, for example, that someone taking a Sunday afternoon drive contributes such a tiny amount to climate change that it does not matter (Sinnott-Armstrong 2005). Others disagree and argue that even a tiny amount that contributes to climate change matters (Hiller 2011). On this vein Mara Marin (2017, 63) argues: "As the unjust structure is our doing, it follows that our actions contribute to injustice and therefore we have an obligation to modify them in ways that would modify the unjust character of the structure."

Second (and closely related) is the responsibility of the individual as a part of a particular group (Americans, people who fly frequently, people who drive gas-powered automobiles, and so on). I have a responsibility to drive less, but my actions will only affect climate change if it is in concert with others. This means that we all have a responsibility to act. Melany Banks (2013, 43) develops a theory of "collective responsibility that can determine the responsibility of individuals." Similarly, Björnsson (2021) argues that when we have a collective obligation to overcome an injustice, we have a "resulting individual obligation" as well. Schwenkenbecher (2021, 34) argues that "most moral agents will hold a variety of different—individual and collective—obligations to contribute to addressing structural injustice." On these arguments, individuals are obliged to meet the responsibility held by the group.

Third, it is the responsibility of the individual to join or pressure institutions to also combat structural injustice. Since institutional change is needed to change, say, structural racism, people have a responsibility to pressure those institutions to change in the necessary ways. Fahlquist (2009, 121) argues, "Thus, due to the urgency and scale of environmental problems, it appears a good case can be made to include institutions into the discussion on how to distribute responsibility for such problems. Having said that, the fundamental unit in society is the individual citizen and institutions are created and upheld by individuals acting together. Hence, it appears reasonable to expect individuals with capacity, resources, and knowledge to create environmentally friendly institutions. In addition to voting, this also involves creating, supporting, and joining organizations that work to improve the environment" (see also Kortetmäki 2018; Gabrielson et al. 2016; Zheng 2018; Banks 2013; Baatz 2014). Indeed, unsurprisingly, some theorists join Fahlquist and argue that we have an obligation to vote in a way that helps dismantle structural injustice (Sardo 2020; Maltais 2013). If structural injustice is institutional, the institutions will need to change, and that will only happen if the people at the top feel pressure to do so.

## Responsibility for National Solidarity

Janoff-Bulman and Carnes (2013) apply the idea of communal responsibility only to liberals' moral motives for social justice, not to conservatives' moral motives for social order and solidarity, thereby suggesting that conservatives are not motivated by a sense of collective responsibility. Conservative theorists, too, have not focused on collective responsibility, which is surprising given the significant attention liberal egalitarian theorists have paid to the concept. We argue here that conservatives *also* have an ethic of responsibility, but one based on the idea of national solidarity.[8]

Conservative scholars' lack of attention to collective responsibility is, we think, partly because many of them tend toward libertarianism, where national solidarity is not highly valued. Another reason is that conservative thinkers argue that national loyalty is weaker than it used to be not because citizens are failing their collective obligations but because elites have led them astray. Rich Lowry (2019, 189) entitles chapter 10 of his book the "Treason of the Elites" and laments that a "broadly cosmopolitan sensibility infuses our elite in government, academia, and business." Scruton (2004) coins a term, *oikophobia*, which means "the repudiation of inheritance and home." He argues that the "oiks," who are part of the elite, are partly responsible for the attacks on national solidarity that he thinks are occurring in Britain: "The domination of our own national parliament by oiks, as we might call them, is partly responsible for the assaults on our constitution, for the acceptance of subsidised immigration, and for the attacks on customs and institutions associated with traditional and native forms of life" (37).

Still, the idea of collective responsibility is present in conservative thought but in a more muted way than among egalitarian theorists. Hazony (2018, 226–27) argues that "one should be a nationalist." A nationalist should "have his eyes constantly on what must be done to maintain and build up the material well-being of his own nation, its internal cohesiveness and its unique cultural inheritance—all of which must be diligently tended to if the nation is to grow strong." This is not a direct argument for collective responsibility, but it comes close. We argue that the national solidarity worldview supports the notion that it is a collective enterprise: nations are only strong if most of their members view themselves as part of a collective that shares a unifying identity. In this view, strong nations are free, and individuals are free when their nation is strong; therefore, a nation's members have a collective responsibility to ensure national solidarity and strength. Still, it is important to emphasize that the collective responsibility of conservatives is less broad than that of liberals. Freedom might be more likely to flourish in a strong nation, but it also weakens the demands put on the collective outside of the specific realm of national solidarity (see Bellah et al. 1985). We can see this, for example, in expectations concerning consumer choices. Liberals are more likely than conservatives to both boycott (refuse to buy) and buycott (intentionally buy) products for political reasons (Endres and Panagopoulos 2017; Fernandes 2020; Jost, Langer, and Singh 2017). We found a similar difference between Democrats and Republicans in our 2019 Pluralism and Respect Survey. We asked respondents the extent to which they agreed with the statement, "I would join a boycott of a store if the owner held extreme political views." Forty-three percent of Democrats agreed or strongly agreed compared to only 23 percent of Republicans. Conservatives more than liberals are apt to think that these are individual decisions that one takes without having to be responsible to anyone else, beyond perhaps one's family.

The issue of vaccinations also highlights the narrower conservative idea of collective responsibility. Collective responsibility is often used by those who advocate vaccinations (Giubilini 2021; Attwell, Smith, and Ward 2021) since most vaccinations protect not only oneself but others as well. Some conservatives look at vaccinations (and mask wearing during the COVID-19 pandemic) as an individual choice, much like consumer choices. We know that liberals are more likely to favor vaccine mandates than conservatives.[9] Many conservatives use an individual and family framework when they look at vaccines, and not a collective responsibility framework. One study shows that vaccine resisters often "recast vaccination as a purely individual consumption choice . . . vaccine rejecters inhabit a more comfortable and familiar psychic territory of free decision-makers making what they believe are the best choices for their own families" (Attwell, Smith, and Ward 2021, 270–71). To be sure, most conservatives are not vaccine resisters, but most vaccine resisters are conservatives.

We leave aside here the disturbing misinformation about the dangers of vaccines. When it comes to vaccines, one rarely must choose between the individual and society, since vaccines protect both. Nonetheless, many liberals and conservatives often perceive the vaccination issue differently, with most liberals emphasizing collective responsibility and many conservatives emphasizing individual liberty. In the words of one liberal American citizen: "I feel we have a social contract in this country with our neighbors, and people who can get vaccinated and choose not to get vaccinated are breaking it" (Rabin 2021). Conservatives, as we will show, also have a strong sense of collective responsibility, but one more narrowly construed than it is for liberals and focused almost solely on national solidarity.

## Collective Responsibility and Other People's Choices

When people have a strong belief in collective responsibility, the choices other people make matter a great deal. It isn't simply the case that individuals make a bad decision that affects themselves. Rather, the individuals' bad decision has a negative impact on society. Because of these broad implications of individual behavior, we argue that people are less likely to view behaviors they consider bad for society as simply the other person's free choice and more likely to view these behaviors as irresponsible or even immoral. That is, they are likely to judge harshly those who think and behave in ways that undermine the achievement of a good society. We draw on our Social Justice and Solidarity Survey (2020) to examine people's beliefs about collective responsibility and how they judge those who make choices that go against their worldview.

We gave respondents three statements about citizens' responsibility to promote social justice goals and three statements about citizens' responsibility to promote national solidarity goals. The social justice statements were "It is the responsibility of all citizens to help groups worse off in society," "It is the responsibility of all citizens to combat climate change," and "It is the responsibility of all citizens to vote for officials who will work towards ending systemic racism, sexism and other forms of systemic injustice." The national solidarity statements were "It is the responsibility of all citizens to make sure America stays strong," "It is the responsibility of all citizens to vote for officials who will keep America strong," and "It is the responsibility of all citizens to vote for officials who will protect the right of Americans to own guns." Response options for all six statements ranged from strongly disagree (coded 0) to strongly agree (coded 1).

The results in table 6.1 show that Democrats are significantly more likely than Republicans to believe citizens have a collective responsibility to promote social justice concerns. The means for Democrats are consistently above 0.8, and almost two-thirds of Democrats strongly agree that all citizens must

TABLE 6.1. Collective responsibility and party identification

| Responsibility of all citizens to . . . | Democrats | | Republicans | | Difference of means |
|---|---|---|---|---|---|
| | Mean | Percent | Mean | Percent | t value |
| Social justice | | | | | |
| Help groups worse off | 0.81 | 47 | 0.63 | 15 | 13.01*** |
| Combat climate change | 0.84 | 60 | 0.58 | 22 | 15.49*** |
| Vote for officials to end systemic injustice | 0.87 | 65 | 0.65 | 26 | 15.00*** |
| National solidarity | | | | | |
| Make sure America stays strong | 0.80 | 48 | 0.89 | 66 | −7.26*** |
| Vote for officials to keep America strong | 0.79 | 46 | 0.89 | 65 | −8.00*** |
| Vote for officials to protect gun ownership | 0.48 | 21 | 0.80 | 51 | 16.76*** |
| Responsibility scale (all) | 0.77 | | 0.74 | | 2.98** |
| N | 622 | | 491 | | |

Source: 2020 Social Justice and Solidarity Survey
Note: Cell entries under "percent" are the percentage of people who answered "Strongly agree." The t-tests are one-sided. **$p < 0.01$; ***$p < 0.001$.

combat climate change and vote for candidates who will end systemic injustice. Republicans have means above 0.5 on these social justice responsibility items, but they are certainly less enthusiastic in their views. They are much less likely than Democrats to strongly agree that people have a responsibility to fight for social justice. Republicans are more likely than Democrats to believe in collective responsibility on national solidarity concerns, especially on the protection of gun rights. Republicans have means of 0.8 or higher on all three national solidarity items. It is interesting to note, given our argument about liberals having a more encompassing sense of collective responsibility than conservatives, that Democrats agree that everyone has a responsibility to keep America strong, with means at about 0.8 on both items. In contrast, Republicans' support for the social justice responsibility items is only around a mean of 0.6. Overall, though, Democrats—and egalitarian theorists—accept the charge to correct structural injustice, which is a matter of both individual and collective responsibility. For Republicans, citizens must be united in doing what is best for promoting national solidarity.

When fellow citizens make choices that are counter to social justice or national solidarity goals, people can view them as simply exercising their freedom to do what they want, or they can judge them negatively. The idea of collective responsibility arose in many of our liberal focus groups, and when the participants disagreed with someone's actions, they judged the person harshly. We asked both of our second-round liberal and conservative groups the following question: "What do you think of a person who drives a Hummer

or some other big vehicle, and says that emissions of just one car doesn't really
matter for the environment, it's just one car, people should just drive whatever
car they want?" While this may seem like a leading question, the answers from
the liberal and conservative groups were quite different. Many (though not all)
of our liberal participants responded in an almost visceral way.

> They're a dick. I have a bad reaction to it. And I don't think as far as we've got-
> ten like "Oh, like, maybe they work for the EPA and like are actually making
> systemic change," like I'm literally I'm just like "why?" So yeah, that's me. (Bay
> Area Liberals 2, Woman 2)

> Exactly why? Like if they're living in the world with limited resources and
> you're sharing these resources with other people, share the same world with
> you, why do you want to take up so much space? Even if we are not talking
> on an environmental point of view and like recycle or not, or taking a flight
> or not, it's like it's big, it's unnecessary for like the world we live in, like it's
> expensive, it's a lot of noise, there's pollution, there are like so many bad things
> coming with that. Like why is that your choice? Just like, I don't understand,
> just give me one reason. (Bay Area Liberals 2, Woman 3)

> So I know someone that does that, and they live in the East Bay. Like, literally,
> drive the big Hummer around, they live in the East Bay and I asked them and
> so their answer was "I don't give a shit, you know, like my car is not the only
> thing, global warming. Go deal with companies and stuff like that." I think
> they're douchebags, that's—and every time I see a car like that, doesn't matter,
> in the more suburban areas or inside the city, it's the same reaction. I just don't
> think they care. (Bay Area Liberals 2, Man 4)

Not all liberal respondents condemned the Hummer driver, giving more
measured responses like the following:

> Okay, if I'm being honest, my first reaction is "how selfish," but I usually check
> myself. I usually think, you know, wow, I do a lot of things that are not very
> good for the environment too, and should I judge them for doing that when I
> don't recycle as much as I should, my car isn't the most energy efficient, I fly a
> lot. So I usually try to stop myself from holding that position for a long time,
> but my first reaction is that's very selfish and we should all try to do better.
> And I think that they're a selfish person, yeah. (Nebraska Liberals 1, Woman 1)

Conservatives had differing views on the quality of the Hummer driver's argument, but all thought someone who legally buys a product is not to be
condemned or judged.

> It's his personal choice. You know, depending on what you believe in, you
> know? (Sacramento Conservatives, Man 2)

I think they're missing a bigger picture. There's a lot of just one Hummers on the road. But I also think that that's their right and I can't stop them from driving that vehicle. It's very expensive for someone to get a new vehicle, and if that's the one that they have, I mean, drive it until it dies. But, if they're going out and getting another car and just wasting that, that would be more wasteful. I think that we should be moving in that direction, of cars being cleaner and cleaner, but I don't know enough about that person to know . . . well I'm not one to judge their effect on the environment based on the car that they drive. (Tennessee Conservatives, Man 1)

I agree a hundred percent. I mean, if a company's made a product, you've chosen to buy it. Now I think, some of these, Hummers specifically, are way too expensive, and I don't like to put a lot of money into things with wheels because they lose value. But that's their financial decision, they bought a product, and if that's what they want to drive and they want to fill it up with gas, that's their business. (NC Conservatives 5, Man 2)

The different tenor of these answers is quite striking: while many liberals and conservatives agree that buying a Hummer is bad for the environment, it was only among our liberal participants that judgments were made. Our liberal focus group participants thought that people buying the Hummer were harming the common good by unnecessarily causing pollution. They argued that we have a collective responsibility to do what we can to reduce pollution. Conversely, conservatives might think the choice is mistaken but it is up to the individual. Individuals rarely must think of the larger community when they make consumer choices (unless perhaps their choices lead them to be dependent on the state—it is likely that conservatives will moralize and condemn such choices).

We asked respondents three questions in the 2020 Social Justice and Solidarity Survey to gauge their reaction to those who make a choice at odds with social justice or national solidarity goals. The possible responses to the questions included agreeing with the person's choice, thinking the person was free to decide whatever he or she wanted, and disagreeing with the choice by thinking it was irresponsible or immoral. When people care about the societal goal and collective responsibility, we expect they will judge the person as irresponsible for going against an important societal goal or, even more negatively, that the person is immoral. On a social justice issue, then, we expect Democrats to be more likely to say the person is irresponsible or immoral, whereas on a national solidarity issue, we expect Republicans to judge the person as irresponsible or immoral.

Playing off the Hummer question from our focus group discussions, we asked our survey respondents a social justice question, "Which comes closest to your view? When I see someone driving a large, gas-guzzling vehicle, I think . . ." The four response options were as follows: (1) I would love to be driving that kind of vehicle; (2) People's vehicle purchases are their own business and they can drive whatever they want; (3) The person is irresponsible for contributing to climate change; and (4) The person is immoral for contributing to climate change.

We also asked respondents about their views on two national solidarity scenarios that had a similar range of response options. One asked about flying the American flag: "If a person refuses to fly an American flag outside their home, I think . . ." The response options were as follows: (1) I wouldn't fly an American flag outside my home either; (2) Whether people want to fly the flag or not is their own business; (3) The person is irresponsible for refusing to show that they are proud to be an American; and (4) The person is immoral for refusing to show that they are proud to be an American. The second national solidarity scenario is more politically fraught, and therefore more like the question about gas-guzzling vehicles and climate change. We asked respondents, "If a person refuses to stand for the national anthem at a sporting event, I think . . ." The response options were as follows: (1) I wouldn't stand for the national anthem either; (2) Whether people want to stand for the national anthem or not is their own business; (3) The person is irresponsible for refusing to show that they are proud to be an American; and (4) The person is immoral for refusing to show that they are proud to be an American.

The national anthem scenario is particularly important because it pits national solidarity against social justice. Colin Kaepernick, quarterback for the San Francisco 49ers, kneeled during the national anthem to protest racial injustice and police brutality during the 2016 season. People's reactions to Kaepernick's actions were highly polarized, with many praising his social justice stance and others denouncing him as unpatriotic. One conservative writing in the *National Review* explained why he thought Kaepernick's actions were misguided:

> Rather, the flag stands for the American ideal, and while we can all disagree about how well we have lived up to the principles comprising that ideal, only extremists would decry the principles themselves. Kaepernick said he took a knee during the National Anthem as a gesture of solidarity for, and concern about, black Americans mistreated by police. His error was in conflating the actions of a few errant police officers with America itself. His protest was therefore rightly seen by many football fans as outrageous, a slander as indefensible as saying black Americans in general should be disrespected because of the criminal actions of a minority of blacks. (Smith 2017)

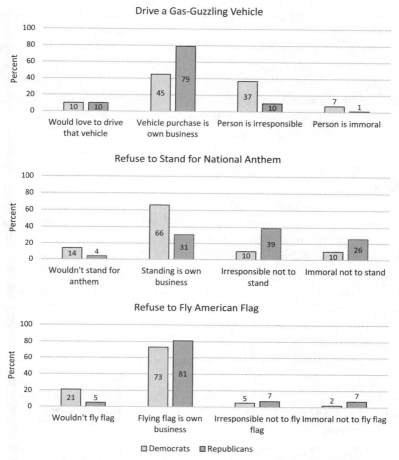

FIGURE 6.1. Reactions to People Who Defy Social Justice or National Solidarity Goals
*Source*: 2020 Social Justice and Solidarity Survey

If one refuses to fly the flag on one's home, this is not necessarily a sign of disloyalty since no one knows why the flag is not flying. In contrast, many conservatives interpreted kneeling during the anthem as an insult to the United States and an act of disloyalty. The issue of refusing to stand during the national anthem therefore pits social justice against solidarity in the eyes of conservatives.

Figure 6.1 shows how people responded to the scenarios. The two issues that are the most polarizing, climate change and taking a knee during the national anthem, are also the most divisive on collective responsibility reactions. Most

Republicans (65 percent) think refusing to stand for the national anthem is irresponsible or immoral, compared to only 20 percent of Democrats who have this reaction. Most Democrats (66 percent) think standing for the national anthem is people's own business. Democrats and Republicans react very differently when asked about someone who drives a gas-guzzling vehicle. In this situation, Democrats are much more likely to think the behavior is irresponsible or immoral (44 percent) than Republicans (11 percent), who overwhelmingly think driving this type of vehicle is people's own business (79 percent).

Democrats and Republicans differ little in their reactions to someone refusing to fly the American flag. While flying the flag can be seen as a national solidarity issue, it differs in important ways from the national anthem issue. When an issue pits social justice against solidarity, as is the case with kneeling during the national anthem, Republicans generally place solidarity over symbolically advocating for social justice. The collective responsibility to be loyal to the nation is not obviously violated when one refuses to fly the flag on one's home, since no one knows the reason why one does not fly the flag. Refusing to stand during the national anthem, however, is to many conservatives a clear symbolic act that focuses on group interests (race) and abandons one's responsibility to keep the nation strong and unified.

We argued earlier that conservatives view collective responsibility in a narrower band than do liberals. While conservatives think that collective responsibility has a strong hold on people, they also leave a wider path for liberty than do liberals. Of course, to the extent that some conservatives lean in a libertarian direction, they will choose individual liberty over collective responsibility. To get at these conservative constraints on collective responsibility, we asked respondents the extent to which they agreed with two statements: "It is the primary responsibility of citizens to help their own families; their responsibility to society at large is secondary," and "It's fine for people to vote for the candidate who will personally benefit them the most." The first statement explicitly says that people's responsibility to their society is not as important as more personal responsibilities. The second statement, which was included in the series of statements on the collective responsibilities of voting, simply says that self-interested voting is fine. While the implication of self-interested voting is that the person isn't voting for societal interests, this isn't explicitly stated. Democrats and Republicans differ significantly when it comes to placing family responsibilities over societal responsibilities. Republicans are much more likely to agree with this statement than Democrats, with means of 0.82 and 0.69, respectively ($p < 0.001$). There is no significant difference when it comes to self-interested voting (means of 0.59 for Demo-crats and 0.61 for Republicans).

When people hold themselves and everyone else responsible for the well-being of society, they judge harshly the behaviors and choices of those who do not do their part. We measured people's tendency to be judgmental toward opposing partisans using three questions: "How often do you quickly judge [Republicans/Democrats] as bad?" "How often do you criticize [Republicans/Democrats] for their views?" and "How often do you think any criticisms you have of [Republicans/Democrats] are simply the truth?" Response op-tions were never, rarely, occasionally, and frequently. We created an additive judgmentalism scale from the responses to these three questions that ranges from 0 (low judgmentalism) to 1 (high judgmentalism) (mean = 0.72, sd = 0.26, alpha = 0.843). Democrats and Republicans are similarly judgmental toward people in the opposing party (Democrats have a mean of 0.73 and Republicans a mean of 0.75). We argue that people will be more judgmental the more they believe in the collective responsibility of everyone to achieve societal goals. Democrats are especially likely to judge Republicans harshly when they think Republicans are not taking actions to reduce social injustice. Republicans, conversely, are likely to be more judgmental about Democrats when they think their opponents are not contributing positively to national solidarity.

The data support these contentions (see figures 6.2 and 6.3). We regressed the judgmentalism scale on the social justice responsibility scale (top of fig-ure 6.2) and on the national solidarity responsibility scale (bottom of fig-ure 6.2), party identification, and the interaction of each responsibility scale with party identification. We included in the models the social justice or na-tional solidarity worldviews to control respondents' worldview beliefs, along with controls for age, race, sex, education, and rural place of residence. While responsibility and party identification do not have a direct effect on judgmen-talism, the interaction of these variables has a large and significant effect. Democrats are much more likely to judge Republicans harshly the more they believe everyone has a responsibility to promote social justice efforts. Repub-licans react the same toward Democrats when it comes to national solidarity responsibility. Those who are much less judgmental toward the other side are Democrats who believe strongly in national solidarity responsibility and Republicans who believe strongly in social justice responsibility.

Unlike beliefs that simply implicate oneself, a belief in collective responsi-bility implicates everyone in one's society. Democrats believe that Republicans oppose social justice, just as Republicans believe Democrats oppose national

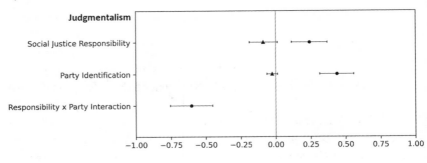

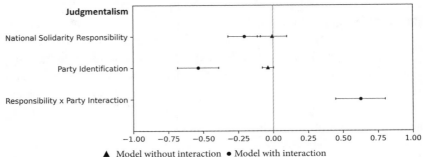

▲ Model without interaction ● Model with interaction

FIGURE 6.2. The Impact of Collective Responsibility on Judgmentalism.

*Source*: Social Justice and Solidarity Survey (2020)

*Note*: Data are unstandardized regression coefficients with 95% confidence interval error bars from OLS regressions. The regression models included control variables for social justice worldview (in the social justice responsibility models), national solidarity worldview (in the national solidarity responsibility models), age, sex (male), race (white), rural, and education level (data not shown; see appendix D, table D.3, for the full models). Party identification is coded 0 = Democrats and leaners, 0.5 = pure Independents, 1 = Republicans and leaners. Judgmentalism toward opposing partisans, social justice responsibility: Model without interaction—Constant = 0.698 (se 0.040), $F$ = 4.52***, Adj. $R^2$ = 0.023, $N$ = 1208; Model with interaction—Constant = 0.413 (se 0.053), $F$ = 10.98***, Adj. $R^2$ = 0.069, $N$ = 1208. Judgmentalism toward opposing partisans, national solidarity responsibility: Model without interaction—Constant = 0.597 (se 0.038), $F$ = 4.24***, Adj. $R^2$ = 0.021, $N$ = 1191; Model with interaction—Constant = 0.749 (se 0.043), $F$ = 9.24***, Adj. $R^2$ = 0.059, $N$ = 1191. ***$p$ < 0.001.

solidarity. If achieving a just or strong nation demands that everyone get on board to help achieve that goal, then those not doing their share are harming the society. People judge others harshly when they believe this is the case. As we show next, they also lose respect for these fellow Americans.

## Collective Responsibility, Judgmentalism, and Respect

People who have a worldview about the good society want to see that vision achieved, and this means everyone needs to contribute to the collective good,

as defined by their particular worldview. While most Americans are not opposed to social justice or national solidarity, it is true that opposing partisans
are weaker supporters of the partisans' worldview than copartisans are. As
we argued earlier, even if people aren't taking action against the preferred
societal goals, their unwillingness to take positive action to promote these
goals can be judged harshly. And when they do take negative actions, such as
by driving a vehicle that contributes to climate change or by not standing for
the national anthem, partisans judge them as irresponsible or even immoral.
People are also more likely to be highly critical and judgmental toward opposing partisans when they have a strong sense of collective responsibility.
We close this chapter by examining the effects of these dynamics on recognition respect.

Psychologists are primarily interested in whether people feel respected
and what their reactions are when they feel disrespected. Research on social
identity provides some insight, though, into how group members react to fellow group members who challenge or go against group morals. When moral
values are shared by a group, people know they can gain respect by following those values (Pagliaro, Ellemers, and Barreto 2011; Ellemers, Pagliaro, and
Barreto 2013). Because groups want to achieve their collective goals, they are
especially harsh against group members who do not share these goals. Going
against the group's morals can lead to rejection, ridicule, and ostracism, and
to the loss of respect (Ellemers and Van der Toorn 2015). People have less respect for fellow group members who hinder the achievement of group goals,
whether through action or inaction.

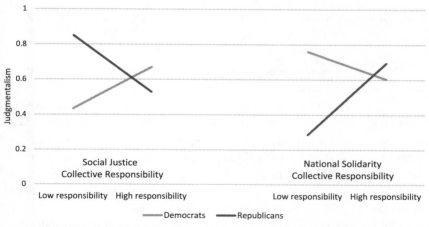

FIGURE 6.3. Judgmentalism and the Interaction of Party Identification and Collective Responsibility
Source: Social Justice and Solidarity Survey (2020)

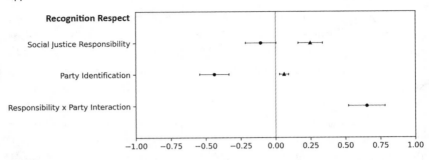

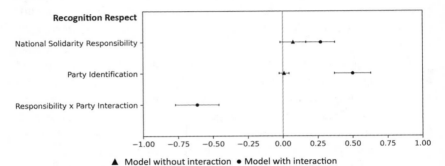

▲ Model without interaction ● Model with interaction

FIGURE 6.4. The Impact of Collective Responsibility on Recognition Respect.
*Source*: Social Justice and Solidarity Survey (2020)
*Note*: Data are unstandardized regression coefficients with 95% confidence interval error bars from OLS regressions. The regression models included control variables for social justice worldview (in social justice responsibility analyses), national solidarity worldview (in national solidarity responsibility models), age, sex (male), race (white), rural, and education level (data not shown; see appendix D, table D.4, for the full models). Party identification is coded 0 = Democrats and leaners, 0.5 = pure Independents, 1 = Republicans and leaners. Recognition respect, social justice responsibility: Model without interaction—Constant = 0.340 (se 0.034), $F = 7.12^{***}$, Adj. $R^2 = 0.039$, $N = 1208$; Model with interaction—Constant = 0.648 (se 0.046), $F = 17.59^{***}$, Adj. $R^2 = 0.110$, $N = 1208$. Recognition respect, national solidarity responsibility: Model without interaction—Constant = 0.453 (se 0.033); $F = 1.92^{\wedge}$; Adj. $R^2 = 0.006$; $N = 1191$; Model with interaction—Constant = 0.304 (se 0.038); $F = 8.43^{***}$; Adj. $R^2 = 0.053$; $N = 1191$. $^{\wedge}p < 0.10$; $^{***}p < 0.001$.

We begin our examination of respect by testing whether collective responsibility affects recognition respect. We argue that Republicans, who think Democrats are insufficiently loyal to the nation, believe that Democrats have failed their collective responsibility and do not deserve respect. Democrats, who usually believe that all people deserve respect, also believe that all people have a responsibility to work toward justice. When people fail this responsibility, and these people are especially likely to be Republicans, Democrats' willingness to respect wavers. To test this argument, we regressed recognition respect on social justice or national solidarity responsibility, party identification, and the responsibility by party identification interaction, controlling either social justice or national solidarity worldview and various demographic variables. We hypothesize that the more partisans hold a belief in collective responsibility, the less they will respect opposing partisans.

Figures 6.4 and 6.5 show the significant impact collective responsibility has on recognition respect for opposing partisans, especially when we look at its interaction with party identification. In general, the more people believe everyone is responsible for helping to create a socially just society, the more they respect opposing partisans, but the more accurate story is told in the interaction. The more Democrats believe they have a collective responsibility to promote social justice goals, the less they respect Republicans. Republicans who reject the idea that they have a responsibility to promote social justice have very little respect for Democrats, as do Republicans who believe that everyone has a collective responsibility to create national solidarity. Moving from a low to a high sense of national solidarity responsibility, Republicans' respect for Democrats drops a third of the recognition respect scale.

Finally, we have argued that this sense of collective responsibility makes people more judgmental about opposing partisans (see figure 6.2). When people do not contribute to the collective good of the society, they deserve heightened criticism and any negative judgments that come their way. Judgmentalism, we argue, is also likely to be highly related to respect. The more critical people are of opposing partisans, the less likely they are to respect them. While being judgmental toward opposing partisans can be caused by many things, it is important to consider the role played by a belief in collective responsibility. Collective responsibility makes people more judgmental about opposing partisans, and judgmentalism, we argue, makes people less respectful of

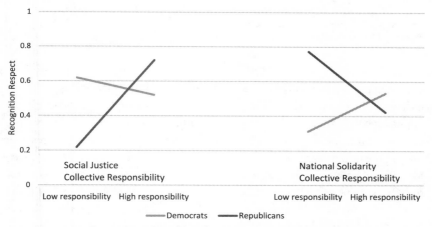

FIGURE 6.5. Recognition Respect and the Interaction of Party Identification and Collective Responsibility
Source: Social Justice and Solidarity Survey (2020)

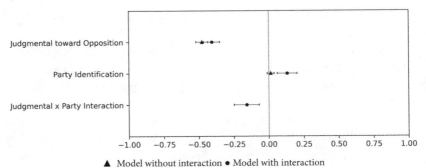

FIGURE 6.6. The Impact of Judgmentalism on Recognition Respect.
*Source*: Social Justice and Solidarity Survey (2020)
*Note*: Data are unstandardized regression coefficients with 95% confidence interval error bars from OLS regressions. The regression models included control variables for age, sex (male), race (white), rural, and education level (data not shown; see appendix D, table D.5, for the full models). Party identification is coded 0 = Democrats and leaners, 0.5 = pure Independents, 1 = Republicans and leaners. Model without interaction—Constant = 0.815 (se 0.020), $F$ = 73.65***, Adj. $R^2$ = 0.293, N = 1227; Model with interaction—Constant = 0.762 (se 0.025), $F$ = 66.55***, Adj. $R^2$ = 0.300, N = 1227. ***$p$ < 0.001.

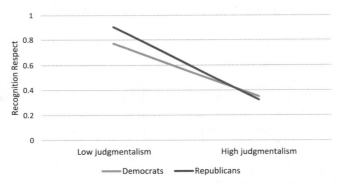

FIGURE 6.7. Recognition Respect and the Interaction of Party Identification and Judgmentalism
*Source*: Social Justice and Solidarity Survey (2020)

opposing partisans. Figures 6.6 and 6.7 show the strong relationship between judgmentalism and respect. Judgmentalism makes people less respectful of opposing partisans, regardless of party identification, but the interaction with party is significant as well. Moving from low to high judgmentalism, respect for opposing partisans drops almost half of the respect scale. When party identification is considered, Democrats have less respect than Republicans for opposing partisans even when they are low on judgmentalism, but both Democrats and Republicans have low respect for opposing partisans when they are highly judgmental. Collective responsibility increases people's judgmentalism, and this judgmentalism is strongly related to respect.

## Conclusion

Many people believe that creating a good society demands more than any one individual's actions. Everyone in the society, or almost everyone, has a responsibility to work to achieve the goal. Democrats and Republicans emphasize different worldviews about what the good society entails, and in many ways, these competing worldviews are at odds. The social justice worldview demands that we as a society raise up the lives of those who are oppressed, acknowledge the bad that has been done historically in the United States, and work toward a future that is more egalitarian and inclusive. The national solidarity worldview demands that Americans be loyal to and appreciative of their country and its history, value liberty, and recognize the special status held by Americans as a united group. Neither set of partisans rejects the opposing party's worldview. The perception, though, that the opposing party either actively or through omission harms the efforts to achieve the goal makes people much more judgmental and much less willing to respect those with whom they disagree.

While we lack data on the matter, we think the COVID-19 pandemic highlights the liberal view of collective responsibility and the liberal respect paradox: we think it likely that many liberals have a hard time respecting those who do not vaccinate themselves or their children from COVID-19 (and other potentially deadly infectious diseases). For many liberals, breaking the social contract includes not just social justice issues but also public health issues.

While both conservatives and liberals believe in collective responsibility, the conservative version is narrower and less pervasive than the liberal version. Standing for the national anthem is a matter of collective responsibility for conservatives, but it is something that most of us have an occasion to do only occasionally. And while conservatives are equally or more likely than liberals to support having the US government buy American-made products and to buy American-made goods themselves (Jackson and Duran 2021; Economic Policy Institute 2009), there is not the same sense that all of one's choices have implications for society. In addition, conservatives' views of collective responsibility clash in some ways with their views of liberty. All people should work to build national solidarity, but there are different ways to do this. Some people might join the military; others might fly the American flag or take care of their families.

The liberal version of responsibility, in contrast, tends to be more encompassing, which is surely one important reason why Democrats find it hard to grant respect to Republicans. It helps explain the liberal respect paradox— liberals believe in both recognition respect *and* the collective responsibility to end structural injustice. In addition, liberals think the responsibility to work against social injustice is a frequent demand. For example, liberals are more likely than conservatives to view consumer choices through the lens of collective responsibility. People should be cognizant of the impact their consumer choices have on society, whether they are buying cars or sandwiches for lunch. They also think that work to eradicate structural inequalities must be taken on frequently in our everyday lives. It is the collective responsibility ethos of liberal citizens that clashes most deeply with their beliefs about respect—a clash mirrored in egalitarian political theory.

# PART III

# Democracy: The Importance of Saving Respect

# 7

# Respect versus Justice?

Many egalitarian theorists assume that respect and justice can sit together readily, but this is not the case. It is the tension between respect and justice that haunts many of our liberal focus group participants. Substantive egalitarianism embraces an egalitarian ethos, the idea that equality and equity should dominate in our social relations and in state policy; it leads many liberals to the idea that we all have a collective responsibility to fight against structural injustice. Many nonliberals do not share this ethos, and some liberals question the focus on collective responsibility, recognizing how challenging an idea it is. We argue here that egalitarian political theory has a troubled relationship with pluralism, and we explain why many theorists need to prioritize respect *or* justice. We also defend pluralism over its rival, monism. Pluralism understands that different values will often have to be balanced against each other and will sometimes conflict; it also understands that even one value may have an internal tension when it comes to a particular policy or issue. We suggest what we call an egalitarian pluralist ethos as an alternative to an egalitarian ethos.

We then discuss the bounds of civic respect that limit when it ought to be granted. The limit, we argue, is tied to a disregard for procedural democracy. We conclude this chapter by explaining why political theorists should care about our empirical findings. One might say that if citizens cannot grant respect to one another, the problem is not with ideas about justice or democratic theory but with the people. We explain why this response is inadequate. In the next chapter, we return to the issue of personal and impersonal civic respect.

Our argument here relies on two ways to think about democratic equality, basic equality and substantive egalitarianism, which we defined in chapter 1.

Basic equality and procedural democracy are closely related. This version of equality focuses on equality before the law and equal rights among all citizens. Substantive egalitarianism views equality as a social ideal that is at the heart of justice and social justice. Substantive equality is not only concerned with procedures; it aspires to ensure that people's life chances are roughly equal and that institutions are not implicitly (or explicitly) biased against certain social groups. Substantive egalitarianism also argues that people need to see each other as equals as well—that for institutions to treat people fairly, citizens must insist that they do so. But fairness does not mean treating everyone the same. Substantive egalitarianism is often concerned with the status of social groups, viewing some social groups as having advantages that other groups lack; when this occurs, substantive egalitarians expect institutions to change the privilege that some groups enjoy. And citizens have a responsibility to pressure these institutions to change. The challenge for substantive egalitarians arises with the question of respect for the many citizens who do not share their views. Indeed, egalitarian theory in general (which we use interchangeably with substantive egalitarianism) takes for granted agreement on the idea that we want to live in a just society, but even that assumption is mistaken.

Before we delve into the tension between respect and justice within egalitarian political theory, we want to note that conservative citizens are not better than liberal citizens when it comes to civic respect. Both sets of citizens find it hard to grant that their political opponents have anything worthwhile to say about politics; both sets think the other side is ignorant, misinformed, and misled. We focus here on egalitarian political theory and not conservative political theory for two reasons. First, few conservative political theorists discuss respect. Second, conservative political theorists in the academy are often libertarian (or "bleeding-heart libertarian") and have views that are at some distance from conservative citizens. Liberal citizens and egalitarian political theorists, by contrast, have overlapping and often parallel views. Our argument is not that liberal citizens or egalitarian political theorists are less respectful than their conservative counterparts (though some of our empirical evidence on recognition respect suggests this is so); rather, our argument is that the *tensions* about respect that liberals and egalitarians face are not shared by conservatives. Our focus on egalitarian political theory and liberal citizens should not be interpreted as suggesting that conservatives are better in some way. Indeed, conservative citizens and theorists perhaps *should* care about respect more than they do. Some conservative citizens ought to have a reckoning—about the mistaken and dangerous view of stolen elections; the January 6, 2021, insurrection; misinformation about vaccines; and so on.

There is good reason to think that these beliefs are often based in disrespect, as they refuse to accept legitimate political differences among citizens, but that is not the main subject of this chapter.

## The Tension between Respect and Justice

One argument we have made repeatedly is that respect is harder to grant than many theorists admit. (Since this is the case for both civic and recognition respect, we simply discuss respect in this section, encompassing both kinds of respect.) Our research shows empirically that giving respect to people with whom one heartily disagrees is simply difficult for many. Sometimes there may be simple reasons for this. As Teresa Bejan (2017, 159) argues, based on her interpretation of Roger Williams, "Our natural partiality and pride as human beings mean that we invariably judge the rightness of others' reasoning . . . with reference to our own." As Thomas Hobbes said long ago, when we compare our own views with those with whom we disagree, we often look down upon those with the "wrong" ideas.[1]

Much of our argument in this book, however, is not merely that people think more highly of their own opinions than those of others, but that their view of justice is narrowly construed. Weaving respect into egalitarian justice is what many liberal citizens think they ought to do but cannot, which is why so many of our liberal focus group participants felt anguish when we asked them about respecting opposing partisans. They were torn between two strongly felt values—respect and justice—that they wanted to be intertwined. To be sure, many chose one or the other, but many struggled because they did not want to have to choose.

Egalitarian theorists ignore the struggle between respect and justice. They assume a consensus on substantive egalitarianism, even though this widespread agreement only holds among egalitarian theorists and liberal citizens. This assumed agreement allows theorists to escape asking two fundamental questions. First, can you respect the many, many citizens who do not believe that substantive egalitarianism is something that the state should actively support? Second, what does it mean to develop a theory of justice that makes it difficult to respect a large percentage of citizens? Egalitarian political theories argue that both justice and democracy are foundational values of the good society. If you say that respect is a cardinal feature of democracy, but that there are other cardinal features or values of democracy as well, what happens when some people deeply disagree with these latter features or values?

Theorists should ask how the value of respect works with the other values they see as paramount. Respect is hard to grant when values conflict, our surveys and focus groups suggest; theorists should not assume that respect is easy to grant. If there is a tension between respect and other values, or if other values trump respect, then theorists should acknowledge this. If substantive equality is at the top of the pyramid, theorists should make the case that other values may be nice to have but not always possible. Perhaps some will argue that respect is less important than justice. We will not, however, make that argument, since we think there is good reason to worry about the loss of respect—recognition and civic.

The tension between respect and equality in egalitarian theory arises in John Rawls. In the dominant book in political philosophy in the last seventy-five years, *A Theory of Justice*, Rawls (1999 [1971], 3) states in the second paragraph that "justice is the first virtue of social institutions, as truth is of systems of thought." Rawls states this as if it were obviously true, and to liberal egalitarians, the idea that we want to live in a just society with just institutions is clearly true. Who *wouldn't* want to live in a just society? Rawls's argument about the ability of a plural society to reach agreement on justice—which he argues is necessary for a stable society (Abbey and Spinner-Halev 2013)—assumes that people want justice to be the first virtue of their institutions. Rawls, of course, is writing ideal theory. He sketches out what justice would look like in an ideal society, but many conservative citizens think that the path is inevitably scorched with insurmountable obstacles.

Justice, for Rawls, is intertwined with equality. Rawls's question—"What kind of justice would equal people choose if they did not know who they were?"—sets equality as the springboard of justice.[2] Echoing Rawls, Jonathan Quong (2022) says, "Justice is widely agreed to be an important value, arguably 'the first virtue of social institutions.'" Yet many conservatives, both theorists and citizens, do not view egalitarian justice as a goal or a virtue of social institutions.

Egalitarians argue that respect is part of justice, but they narrow the grounds of acceptable views by assuming the importance of egalitarian justice.[3] As Teresa Bejan (2017) so poignantly argues, egalitarians who argue for respect within the confines of egalitarianism simply assume away or ignore those who do not share this basic worldview. But many ordinary citizens do not believe that justice, at least the way that Rawls and other egalitarians define it, is the first virtue of social institutions. Our survey evidence shows that many conservative citizens shy away from the ideal of justice—they worry that an ideal of justice will trump liberty, or that government's attempts to ensure justice will not merely fail but make matters worse. When Quong, following Rawls, says that justice is widely agreed to be an important value, he simply ignores the widespread disagreement on the issue.

Relational equality similarly ignores what to do if many citizens do not agree with theorists' premise about justice and equality. Relational egalitarians argue that what matters is that citizens see each other as equals—if citizens do not grant each other equal respect, those that do not receive respect will be ignored, their voices discounted, their interests invisible. The central policy proposal of relational egalitarians is to reduce income inequality to ensure that the wealthy do not ignore or scorn the poor (Anderson 2008, 263; Scheffler 2005, 23–31).[4] The focus on income allows relational egalitarians to evade any possible conflicts between respect and their version of egalitarianism. Relational egalitarians posit the main source of disrespect, without any attempt to think about other possible sources. What if a major cause of disrespect is not income but disagreement over the meaning and value of egalitarian justice? Relational egalitarianism—like most kinds of substantive egalitarianism—does not try to navigate the challenging issue of respect among citizens who hold a range of values. Rather, the relational (and substantive) egalitarian expectation is that citizens will embrace an egalitarian ethos—by this we mean that substantive egalitarianism is the guiding light of how citizens view each other, and that it informs public policy. Justice and substantive equality are intertwined, and the implicit assumption made by many substantive egalitarians is that everyone is an advocate for substantive equality. Of course, if citizens are guided by an egalitarian ethos, then respect between citizens is relatively easy to grant.[5] But this will never be the case in a modern democracy.

The assumption that citizens should converge on a similar view of justice goes one step further in the structural injustice literature. Social justice advocates not only moralize their views on justice but also believe that all citizens have an obligation to fight injustice. Once you add collective responsibility and obligation to (social) justice, then respect for those who disagree with you becomes quite difficult. If we are to achieve a just society, structural injustice theorists argue, we all must work together toward ending injustice. This means that those who do not actively commit to undermine injustice are themselves unjust and actively abet injustice. There is no neutral ground—"silence is complicity" is the slogan, but the idea behind it fits the structural injustice theorists and the idea that everyone has a responsibility to work toward justice. Indeed, our evidence in the previous chapter shows that many liberal citizens think that people do have a responsibility to end social injustice. (And of course, conservatives believe that people have a responsibility to enact their vision of national solidarity.)

If this is the case, if we have a *responsibility* to work toward social justice, how can those who do not do so be respected? It is very difficult to grant

respect to those whom one thinks are irresponsibly undermining social justice. If you think that social justice is a crucial value, perhaps the preeminent
one, then those who block it are not performing a key human duty. And if
someone fails in this basic human duty, how does the person deserve respect?

We believe that one can interpret our survey results in light of the structural injustice literature, whose ideas have clearly influenced many liberal
citizens. When you have a moralized framework and a strong belief in collective responsibility, reasonable disagreement is not the most plausible explanation for why people have different views than you do. It is not surprising that
liberal citizens think that those who think differently from them are ignorant
or misled (a view echoed by conservative citizens) or racist or sexist. Once
you settle into the social justice worldview, and you think that people have a
responsibility to act to further social justice, those who choose not to do so
are readily seen as failing their civic duty.

## Pluralism and Monism

Another way to think of our argument is through the lens of pluralism, the
idea that there are multiple reasonable ways to see the social and political
world. We argued in earlier chapters that moralizing certain values undermines the ability of opposing partisans to respect one another. One reply to
this argument is that if people have views about justice, as many understand-
ably do, they will of course moralize these values. Yet even Rawls places liberty as the first principle of justice: Rawls attempts to combine a vision of
substantive equality with liberty, albeit not as successfully as he had hoped.
In other words, even an ideal of justice can hold several values within it—it
can be a plural view.

When a moralized worldview is attached to collective responsibility, respect becomes harder to grant. A worldview is the combination of several
overlapping or complementary moralized views that creates a lens or framework through which people view most or all issues. The worldview of many
liberal citizens rests on substantive equality, which feeds into the social justice
worldview. The worldview of many conservatives is based on loyalty and liberty, which feeds into a solidarity worldview. The problem is that worldviews
lean toward monism, not pluralism. By monism we mean that one value
dominates—monists believe that society should be organized around one
value (say, equality or liberty) or virtue or a particular religion. An egalitarian monist might see national solidarity as a value but not one to be balanced
against equality—it would be subordinate to equality. A liberty monist might
view equality as a subordinate value.

By contrast, a pluralist view allows different values to be balanced against each other. Isaiah Berlin (1969), often considered the founder of modern pluralism, argued that pluralism means accepting that several ideas have value: justice, but also love, loyalty, identity, liberty, equality, order, and so on. There is a large debate on pluralism (and on the content of Berlin's pluralism), with much discussion focused on the relationship between pluralism and liberalism (Crowder 2002; Galston 1999; Galston 2002; Galston 2009; Gray 2020; Myers 2010; Zakaras 2013; Riley 2001). We want to reorient this debate to a discussion about pluralism, democracy, and respect. To do so, we focus on two aspects of pluralism.

First, pluralism means that values may conflict. This does not mean they cannot be ranked—people will have to make decisions in their personal lives, at work, and when they vote. It means that some choices are difficult to make, and that one can recognize that others will reasonably choose to rank these values differently. Pluralism encourages us to see that there are "many personal and public policy decisions that require trade-offs" (Crowder 2002, 63). People will differ on which value should dominate—and some people will think different values should predominate depending on the situation. What, for example, does it mean for a state to grant recognition to a group that discriminates against those who do not share the dominant religion? Or against women? Some argue that toleration means allowing the group to live by its own rules (Kukathas 2003); others argue that the state should insist that groups treat their members equally (Okin 2002; Brettschneider 2010). Even if one thinks that equality should be the dominant value, one might think that there are times when other values—liberty or toleration, for example—should come to the fore.

Second, pluralism means that even if one has one predominant value, there will be times when that value tugs in different directions (Myers 2010, 601–2). Many people think that liberty means the right to earn money and accumulate wealth, but one can also argue that the liberty of the poor is constrained in many ways if they lack sufficient income. That liberty is important does not mean that it (like equality) will always point to a clear policy. It is also the case that pluralists often have a "moral minimum": that people have, for example, "minimal freedoms that we must not trade off against other goods" (Galston 2009, 96). In a democracy, this moral minimum will include basic rights: the right to vote, the right to be treated fairly by the courts, the right to be treated without prejudice by state institutions. Some pluralists argue that we should respect the values between societies; Berlin argued, for example, that pagan and Christian societies had different values (Zakaras 2004, 502). This argument is something we avoid here—our setting is a democracy, and our argument is aimed at citizens and scholars who think that democracy is a good that should not be traded off against other goods.

Many people find it challenging to be pluralists. One might ask: How can justice compete with other values? Is it not obvious that justice is the most important value? This includes the justice of climate change, which is surely in our view (as well as many others') one of the most urgent issues of our day. But it is true that what is the most urgent issue of the day will differ among people: if we are to accept the diversity of people, we must acknowledge the differences in the way people see political and social issues, and which issues they will find the most important. Moreover, to think that climate change is the most important issue of our times does not lead to an obvious political or personal agenda. What to do about climate change is a complicated issue, and as we suggest below, the personal actions of many liberals do not match their political beliefs about the importance of climate change. This is not a criticism of how liberals act but rather support for the idea of pluralism— that our values conflict and often pull us in different directions. People with highly moralized worldviews with strong expectations of collective responsibility should beware since they will often fail their own standards of behavior.

Moralized worldviews block the ability of many people to accept pluralism, but to be a pluralist is to have some humility that one may not always be correct and that even when one differs from others, the disagreement may be reasonable (Rauch 2021). Since pluralism grants reasonableness to a variety of different views, it overlaps with respect. You do not have to be a pluralist to understand that your political opponents may not always be mistaken, or if they are, they may have good reasons for their beliefs, but it is easier to believe this if you are a pluralist than if you are a monist. A pluralist may be sure of her beliefs, but she will also recognize and accept as legitimate that others will prioritize values differently than she will. Moreover, a pluralist will recognize that her own values will often pull in different directions.

Pluralists do not have to be relativists or argue that all values are equal. One could have an *egalitarian pluralist* ethos (or a liberty pluralist ethos or some other kind of ethos). Egalitarian pluralism means to privilege egalitarianism but to recognize that there may be times when equality should defer to other values. On this view one's belief in egalitarianism leads one to often view issues and behavior through an egalitarian lens, but one would treasure other values as well: liberty, respect, tolerance, love, loyalty, and so on. An egalitarian pluralist would usually privilege egalitarianism, but this could be overridden, depending on the context.[6] That I have my ranking of values, and that I understand this ranking may change depending on the context, means that I can readily recognize that others will have a different ranking. Since it is often hard to decide which value should predominate in a situation, I understand that others will come to different conclusions than I do. Even as different pluralists emphasize different values, they recognize the diversity of humans and their ideals. An egalitarian pluralist will also recognize that equality will not direct our personal lives all the time.

One way to fill in our view of egalitarian pluralism is by looking at the COVID-19 pandemic. An egalitarian lens does not necessarily help answer all the hard questions that arose during the pandemic. While the COVID-19 rules in the spring of 2020 at first may have made sense, after the first few months, the path forward was not clear. For example, when schools should have reopened or what mask rules should have been in place were hard questions without obvious answers. The deaths and severe illness caused by COVID-19 hit the poor and communities of color the hardest, which would seem to favor an egalitarian stand to keep schools closed or open them up with many restrictions. Yet we also know that school closings had a predictably disproportionately adverse effect on poor children, who tend to be African American and Latino, and so egalitarianism can lead one to think that schools should be open, particularly once vaccines were available. An egalitarian pluralist must obviously choose which path to take, but egalitarianism does not necessarily tell one what to think in this situation, and so other values must be considered.

A pluralist (egalitarian or liberty) approach recognizes that the initial restrictions that many countries put in place in the beginning of the pandemic were a violation of liberty, but the value of liberty had to be balanced against the saving of lives. Still, how much liberty should have been restricted was an open question—severe limits on outdoor gatherings, for example, were questionable. An egalitarian pluralist recognizes that liberty is an important value, and that society cannot perpetually restrict liberty. Once vaccinations were widely available, the balance between restrictions and liberty changed. Egalitarian pluralists will recognize that whatever their own views on the balance between restrictions and liberty, there will be disagreement among reasonable people about where this balance lies.

The idea of collective responsibility is one way in which moralization of issues leads to people judging the behavior of others as wrong or unjust, which is what egalitarian pluralists are reluctant to do in many instances. We can see the value of egalitarian pluralism by looking at the idea that all citizens have a responsibility to end structural injustice. This argument is both too directive and underdetermined—it is both too much and too little. The idea that we all are responsible for undoing structural injustice is too directive in the sense that there are too many injustices in the world for any one person to take on. The directive can be limitless and, indeed, more than a full-time job. If every decision is fraught with world implications that one must weigh, and every nondecision must be scrutinized as well, then one will have a hard time acting in the world. Stylized examples that theorists sometimes provide (Marin 2017) do not help one navigate how often one should act against social injustice. Time spent combating one injustice is time not spent on another one, or with one's family, or with friends, or at one's mosque or church or synagogue, or watching soccer. An egalitarian pluralist recognizes that the drive for equality should be one important motivation in one's life but that it is not the only motivation. Sometimes these other values will pull egalitarians away from combating injustice.

We also think that many liberals ignore how living a life combating injustice is not merely extraordinarily difficult but can blind us to our own behavior. One thoughtful liberal focus group participant said the following:

> I also have probably, maybe, an unpopular opinion on this, but that person driving the Hummer probably takes zero international flights. And like if you think about liberals, how many international flights do we often take, like all of my friends fly everywhere all the time, which releases way more carbon dioxide into the atmosphere than a Hummer does . . . we like to drive around in our Prius and kind of think we're morally better or righteous, but then we're probably taking all these flights. (Bay Area Liberals 2, Man 3)

Philosophers can argue whether taking a Sunday drive is ethically wrong because of its effects on climate change, but one airplane trip is much worse for the environment than the Sunday drive. In other words, stylized examples that philosophers and theorists conjure do not match the complex decisions that people must make in their everyday lives, so they don't really help navigate our ethical and political choices. Indeed, giving examples like the Sunday drive to illustrate an argument may obscure the decisions that people actually face in their everyday lives. Our argument is that many liberals should be wary of condemning others for unjust attitudes and behaviors since liberals will often violate and perhaps even routinely violate their ideals. Of course, we are not suggesting one must never be judgmental or condemn others for unjust or irresponsible behavior, but we are suggesting that people think twice before doing so. Liberals may believe that we have a collective responsibility to slow down or reverse climate change, but few liberals act in a decisive and clear way to do so.

It is easy to condemn the person driving the Hummer—it is large and readily seen as symbolic—but taking several trips abroad or across the country several times a year will also have destructive environmental effects, one's

Prius or electronic vehicle notwithstanding (Bows-Larkin et al. 2016). One might recycle (and condemn those who do not), but buying wool or cotton clothes has quite negative environmental effects that are not undone by recycling, as does eating most kinds of meat. What choices someone should make to combat climate injustice is hardly clear or obvious.

While consumer choices are particularly difficult to navigate morally since so many products are ethically fraught, fighting systemic racism can also be hard. We asked our liberal focus group participants what they thought about white parents who pulled their children from inner-city schools to attend private or suburban schools. We received divergent answers. Some thought that this continued racism:

> It doesn't matter what reason you have for taking your kids out of that school, bottom line is, it still propagates racism, no matter what. (Chicago 5, Man 4)

Yet others have a different view:

> So, we moved to Chicago and I think when we got here we thought we would put our kids in the Chicago public schools. . . . Our kids do go to public schools but they go to selective-admission schools and I realized that I can't make my kids, when they're so little, fight a civil rights fight for me. Even if I should be braver than that, even if it would do my kid no harm, but I, I can't take that risk. (Chicago 4, Woman 3)

We are agnostic on which person is correct (like good pluralists, we see the power of both arguments), but the insistence that we have a responsibility to fight systemic injustice does not provide clear guidance on how to deal with the difficult choices people must make when confronted with many issues. Another difficult issue is housing: dense housing is something that will help lower-income people but is often (though not always) opposed by middle- and upper-income people, liberals and conservatives alike. Many people want to live in suburbs with large yards and open spaces, or in urban areas with good views, but doing so has consequences for those who find housing hard to afford. We bring these issues up because social justice theorists and many of our liberal focus group participants are ready to moralize and condemn those who do not fight injustice, yet many liberals also participate in injustices of various kinds.

A substantive egalitarian approach might insist that one's children should attend urban schools, but an egalitarian pluralist approach recognizes these are hard choices; an egalitarian pluralist approach understands that fighting systemic racism and doing the best for one's children are both important values. We are not here to establish what an egalitarian pluralist will do in any particular situation but rather to suggest that an egalitarian pluralist ethos recognizes that people will have different values and weigh issues differently. The egalitarian pluralist will want to work to make underperforming schools better, but the egalitarian pluralist will also recognize the importance of doing well by one's children, as one of our focus group participants said:

> My folks went to, went to Chicago public school and they vowed that I would never set foot in a Chicago public school and I didn't. There was no ambiguity about that, there was no guilt, that was just the way it was going to be. So it was Catholic school for 12 years . . . I interview people who want to go to Stanford, I'm one of the alumni . . . I don't begrudge anyone for making the educational decisions they have to make for the children, because from the black community's point of view, we would make those same decisions if we could. (Chicago 4, Man 3)

Since pluralists do not boil our political and social choices down to one value, pluralists find it easier than monists to respect those with whom they disagree. Pluralists recognize the hard choices that many people often must make. A pluralist approach will indeed look at various arguments respectfully, and not simply assume that those on a different side in the debate are terrible people with immoral ideas. When one approaches issues with humility, with the knowledge that there is no one obvious answer that all will choose, it is easier to be respectful.

Our argument for egalitarian pluralism is aimed at both scholars and ordinary citizens. Our argument to egalitarian theorists is that they either need to explicitly prioritize justice over respect or say how their argument enables respect—and doing the latter may very well mean changing some of their arguments in a more pluralistic direction. Our argument to citizens is to be more pluralistic, to embrace civic respect, and to understand the complexity of our social and political lives. One might say these two statements point in different directions: If theorists can prioritize justice over respect, why should not citizens do the same? While egalitarian theorists must choose either to prioritize justice over respect or have a more pluralistic understanding of egalitarianism, we think the latter choice is the better one. In a democracy, we must work hard to persuade others of our views, which will often be frustrating and full of failures since people will always hold a diversity of ideas in a free society. If theorists explicitly prioritize a version of justice over respect, they need to ask if they are downgrading democracy by doing so. Perhaps, one might say, the issues of the day are so urgent that democracy is less important than it once was. We will not give a full defense of democracy here, except to say that when democracies die, they are rarely replaced with something better.

"Politics," Bernard Crick (1993, 54) says, is "a messy, mundane, inconclusive, tangled business, far removed from the passion for certainty . . . the only basic agreement in a political regime is to use political means. Politics is an activity and so cannot be reduced to a system of precise beliefs or a set of fixed goals." Politics is inevitable in a democracy because disagreement is inevitable; civic respect is important because it enables democratic citizens to work together across these disagreements. As we noted in chapter 2, when people feel respected, they are more likely to cooperate with others. When people respect each other, they are more likely to listen to each other. Granting civic respect is hard but it is important for democracy. Civic respect is not limitless, however.

## Democratic Procedures and the Boundaries of Civic Respect

If democratic theorists want to place civic and recognition respect as central values, they should accept pluralism and think of democracy in procedural terms. We assume here that democracy is a good, and not merely one good among others but a preeminent good. We place our boundary for civic respect within this context and argue that civic respect should be given willingly and widely but not necessarily for views that undermine democracy. Procedural democracy refers only to the procedure and not the outcomes it may achieve—"the only relevant traits of these outcomes are their compliance with procedural rules" (Saffon and Urbinati 2013, 460). Democracy understood as procedure does not necessarily lead to justice or to any other particular outcomes. Indeed, if one argues that democratic procedures will lead to a true or correct outcome, one is not contributing to "accommodation and compromise" and denies pluralism (448). This is because there is not a truth that democracy will or should work toward: "the political process is not tied to any particular doctrine" (Crick 1993, 22). Indeed, "politics represents at least some tolerance of different truths" (18). We of course think that citizens should aim for more than tolerance, but the general point that Bernard Crick makes is the same, that different people will hold onto different truths, and democratic citizens should understand this.

There are several features of procedural democracy; we highlight four of them.[7] First, *all* members of the state have equal political liberty. People have the same rights of expression and association and the right to vote. Notably, equal political liberty is compatible with considerable income inequality—the more you restrict income inequality as a necessary feature of democracy, the more you define outcomes and leave procedures behind.[8] (Of course, the voters may decide to limit income equality, but that is different from a theorist insisting on income inequality limits for democracy to be legitimate.) Second, people are going to disagree, making peaceful political participation, including voting, important; institutions should exist that allow dissenting voices. Third, citizens and candidates alike must accept uncertainty and the possibility of losing an election: political competitors can never be confident of what the outcome of an election will be.[9] Fourth, proceduralist democracy requires that there be competitive elections in a country, and that each candidate in two-candidate elections has a viable chance of winning. Democracy must have meaningful opposition and a meaningful pluralism of proposals.

Views that reject procedural democracy rarely deserve civic respect (recognition respect is a different matter). Accepting procedural democracy means accepting the peaceful participation of other citizens, which includes voting and the right to register dissent through peaceful protest. Denying the rightful votes of other citizens is a rejection of procedural democracy, as is refusing to accept that their side lost an election that was clearly free and fair. One danger of populism is one side's insistence that they "truly" represent the people, and so they cannot lose an election. Similarly, attempts to give state legislatures the power to overturn legitimate election results are outside of the bounds of what democracy allows. Civic respect is not warranted when people insist on undermining procedural democracy.

Even if we are unable to grant some citizens civic respect sometimes, we can still try to understand why they think differently than we do. What are the forces that lead them to hold views we find so outrageous? Why do they think our beliefs and political views are so dangerous? While we reject the idea that most citizens are ignorant or misled, sometimes that is in fact the case. Many citizens only pay some or little attention to politics or get their information from biased sources and in a selective way. As we mentioned in chapter 3, civic respect does not demand attentiveness to conspiracy theories or to ideas unmoored in reality. Still, it is rare that someone will be misled about all issues. Just as important, because someone is misled does not mean they are wrong about everything. Someone might be wrong about the efficacy of COVID vaccines, but this does not mean the person is necessarily wrong to want children to learn in schools without masks. Our argument that civic respect is often nuanced does have limits: if someone espouses clearly racist or anti-Semitic views, we need not spend time searching for reasonable views the person might hold.

Our argument for procedural democracy as the basis of civic respect is *not* an argument that procedural democracy is the only acceptable or the best form of democracy. What our argument suggests is that a belief in procedural democracy is necessary for civic respect. But this says little about the policies one wants or thinks are central to a just society. One can believe that procedural democracy is a necessary condition for respect but an insufficient condition for justice. One can grant respect to those fellow citizens who agree on the importance of procedural democracy but argue with them about justice (or liberty or solidarity).

Our argument leaves one important issue hanging: What if someone believes in procedural democracy but votes for a candidate who explicitly does not? After all, it is rare that we believe in everything a particular candidate stands for, yet a belief in procedural democracy is fundamental to democracy. All democratic citizens have an obligation to avoid undermining democracy. This is the minimum of what we should expect from our fellow citizens. Voting for a candidate who will try to undermine democracy is not outweighed by one's preferred economic policies, for example. A populist leader with authoritarian tendencies should not be elected, and those who vote for such a candidate endanger democracy.

## Racism and Respect

Yet not every candidate with worrisome views will be an authoritarian populist. We want to deepen our argument by responding to an important challenge about the importance of granting respect. Someone might say the following: "People who vote for a candidate tagged as racist are casting votes that support racism, even if they are not themselves racist. Because of their vote, they are blameworthy. That one is not racist in one's personal life is of course good, but one's actions matter as well. And one duty of citizens is to work toward a world in which all citizens are equally respected; if people vote in a way that undermines this goal, then they do not deserve civic respect, regardless of their personal beliefs."[10] On this argument, granting civic respect to those who vote for a candidate who will or does pursue racist policies is not required.

We do think that civic respect is not warranted if people's votes are motivated by the goal of undermining the democratic rights of racial, gender, or religious minorities, but we do not believe that people's motivations can be discerned just by knowing for whom they voted (unless one votes for a party that actively promotes racial hierarchy).[11] If you know that someone's vote is motivated by racism, then withholding civic respect is called for because of the procedural democracy boundary. But barring explicitly racist political parties, one should generally not assume that voters for the opposing political party are motivated by racism. Our argument complements Julia Maskivker's (2019) argument that citizens have a duty to vote for care, which she interprets as voting for what they perceive to be the common good. Maskivker's argument focuses on people's motivation for their vote. Voters should be at least partly motivated by a conception of the common good when they vote, but we should also expect that voters will have different views of what that means (ch. 3).[12] (Maskivker also believes that self-interest can legitimately be part of why someone votes, in combination with a view of the common good, which we agree with.) We believe that this expectation extends to the notion that different conceptions of the common good will lead to different ideas about how best to end racism.

Civic respect means accepting the idea that people will have legitimate differences about how to end racism. More controversially, we think that civic respect means understanding that people define racism differently, as we argued in chapter 4. Some people, for example, see racism as only or mostly a matter of individual behavior, as one person treating others wrongly or badly because of the color of their skin. Many liberals also view racism as a structural matter. Yet the lens of structural racism readily leads to what conservatives think of as identity politics, which they criticize as wrongheaded and even un-American. If one claims that categorizing people in subgroup identities is divisive, then it is hard to see structural racism. Even if one thinks it is wrong to be dismissive of group identities as politically and socially important (our study here takes the idea of groups for granted),[13] we think the conservative idea that we should focus on individuals should not be dismissed out of hand, and that in some contexts it may certainly be appropriate. In other words, while we agree that structural racism is important to tackle, we think it is mistaken to think that those who view racism as mostly a personal matter should be dismissed as racists.

Moreover, the best way to tackle racism is clearly debatable. One of our conservative focus group participants noted that Black unemployment declined under former president Trump, and that this was the most important way to help African Americans. Indeed, in 2019 the unemployment rate for both African Americans and Hispanics was at a historic low (Fitzgerald 2019). While African Americans' support for the Democratic presidential candidate was as strong in 2020 as it was in 2016, the Hispanic vote for Trump increased by ten percentage points (Igielnik, Keeter, and Hartig 2021). The 2022 midterms saw declines in support for the Democratic congressional candidates among both African Americans (four to seven percentage points) and Latinos (nine to ten percentage points) compared to the 2018 midterms (Foster-Frau and Rodriguez 2022). Liberals should not quickly dismiss the fact that Trump did better among Latinos in 2020 and that the Republican Party did better with Black and Latino voters in 2022.

One could argue whether Trump should get credit for the record low unemployment for African Americans, but presidents always get too much credit for good economic news and too much blame for bad economic news (Kane 2016; Kinder 1981; Fiorina 1981). Our general point is that many conservatives have views on race and racism that are not rooted in a belief that some people are inferior to others. Sure, there are some conservatives who are racist, who believe that some or all people of color are inferior to white people and should be treated unequally, but there are many conservatives who do not believe this. Indeed, some of our conservative participants' comments were quite thoughtful:

> I've been involved in a lot of these racial reconciliation things, involved through my church. The XX Church in North Carolina is into racial reconciliation, it's a big deal. And I have sat through meetings involving the concept of white privilege. I have a terrible problem with that . . . And I mean, I understand it in a sense, what white privilege means. But they pick the wrong term. Because it, it negates my personal struggle to get where I got. It negates it and they should have said "Black disadvantages." Because I think that's real, that is real. I don't have a problem with that. (NC Conservatives 2, Man 1)

Whether this man is correct or not is beside the matter: our point is that he is clearly a thoughtful person who thinks that racism is a problem in the United States, but who might not believe that structural racism is a matter for the government to solve.

Many of our liberal participants thought that limiting immigration into the United States is rooted in racism. Our conservative participants mostly thought that illegal immigration should be stopped, but they were split on legal immigration: some wanted it reduced but others thought the main problem with legal immigration was the long number of years it took for immigrants to gain citizenship.

> I think our legal immigration system has gotten to a point where you know, we're seeing years and years' worth of backlogs for people who are going through the process legally who want to become citizens but you know they're waiting for ten years before they can actually, you know, legally come to the country and so, you know, the failings in our legal immigration system have created a way where somebody says "You know, I could do it the right way and maybe, maybe get to the U.S. in ten years, or I could just, you know, cross the border today" and, and so I think there are reforms that we need to make. (Nebraska Conservatives 1, Man 2)

> I'll even go as far as to say we need more legal, we need to increase the number of legal immigrants that come to this country. (Alabama Conservatives, Man 2)

We point out these comments to suggest what should be obvious but is often overlooked: conservatives hold a variety of views, and not all of them are offensive by mainstream liberal standards. While a few of our conservative participants said comments that bordered on xenophobia when we asked about immigrants, a significant portion expressed openness to more immigrants through legal channels. What unites conservatives when it comes to immigration is their desire to stop or slow down illegal immigration, but not all of this is fueled by xenophobia or racism.

Many liberals ascribe racism to most conservatives, but many conservatives do not think of themselves as racist. And the issue is not one of ignorance about racism. For many conservatives, the government should treat everyone similarly, but after that, they think that racism will only change with individual attitudes. While we disagree with this position, our point is that the argument that Republicans who may not be racist but who vote for seemingly racist candidates are blameworthy proves too much: these voters may not like someone like Donald Trump but find the solutions to racism that the Democrats offer to be even worse. Sometimes people vote for a candidate, but often they vote against candidates. And many voters do not like what the Democrats offer.

Moreover, we know from public opinion surveys that the issues Republicans find important are different from those of Democrats (Dunn 2020). Even if some Republicans think that structural racism exists and should be dealt with, as some do, it may simply be less important to them than other issues. This is not only true for racism but for a host of issues (including climate change): the issue priorities for Democrats and Republicans are very different. Practicing civic respect means accepting the legitimacy and reasonableness of these differences even as we continue to disagree.

### Should Political Theorists Care What the People Think about Respect?

One might ask why theorists should care if it is hard for democratic citizens to practice respect. Some theorists and philosophers are uninterested if many people are unable to fulfill the demands of their arguments (Estlund 2019). If theorists are building a utopia, they do not expect it to come to fruition. If they set up utopian ideals, most people will fall short, but the ideals need not waver. We think this is a plausible argument for those interested in creating a utopia, but few respect theorists are interested in creating a utopian theory.

Most egalitarian theorists care about the empirics. They want their theory to be grounded in human psychology and behavior. What our study shows is that respect is hard for many people to practice. About 50 percent of Americans say they practice civic respect, but they also think that opposing partisans are ignorant and misled by the media, and Democrats overwhelmingly think that Republicans are racist. In other words, civic respect is practiced by considerably less than half of Americans, as our experiment in chapter 3 showed. Most Americans sneer at one another when it comes to politics, not because they think their occupation or wealth gives them more status (as relational egalitarians assume) but because opposing partisans are on the wrong political team. To base egalitarian theory in empirics, theorists could readily acknowledge that civic respect is not easy, that being a good democratic citizen is no walk in the park.

We do not think, however, that merely acknowledging the difficulty of granting respect is sufficient. For many theorists the empirics of respect is inherent in their argument. Rawls argues that securing the social basis of self-respect is a primary good. While self-respect may seem like a personal matter, Rawls argues that to secure self-respect is not just an internal matter, but means that *others* respect us, which is why Rawls is interested in the *social* basis of self-respect. This is obviously an empirical matter because what the social basis is will depend on the grounds that citizens use as a basis for respect. If some people do not respect me because I am Black or Jewish or disabled, then the social basis of self-respect is absent. While Rawls says little about the conditions that will lead to the self-respect of all citizens, some have criticized him for downplaying the role that income inequality has on self-respect (Zaino 1998; Miller 1978). These arguments assume that income inequality leads to a loss of self-respect, but the social basis of self-respect cannot be settled theoretically. Rawls says a theory like his should rely on the "laws of psychology." Yet the basis of self-respect is not a universal truth. The social basis of self-respect will depend on whether people respect others, and this will be contingent on the particular facts of a society and how people are actually esteemed or scorned. If many citizens do not practice civic respect, then the issue for a theory like that of Rawls is to explore why this is the case. And if conservatives or liberals do not respect each other, then the social basis of self-respect is diminished.

Rawls's conception of self-respect is not the same as how we conceive of respect in this book, but it shares one crucial element: the kinds of respect that we and Rawls discuss depend on how citizens view and respect each other. For the two sets of theorists we discuss in this book, relational egalitarians and structural injustice theorists, respect as an empirical matter is at the heart of their arguments. Relational egalitarians, for example, assume that democratic equality means that citizens relate to each other as equals. While the principles behind relational egalitarianism are theoretical, the challenges to respect are empirical. One can guess what hinders respect—either recognition or civic—but one cannot know without undertaking an empirical analysis, like we have done here. A key mistake made by relational egalitarians is to assume that large income differences translate into respect differences. This *may* be the case, but it is ultimately an empirical matter. Indeed, in our focus groups, income differences rarely arose, though there was plenty of disdain for opposing partisans.

Surely some wealthy people ignore the poor, but this does not necessarily mean that they do so because they look down upon the poor. Wealthy liberals often scorn poor conservatives, but what is driving their scorn is not poverty but rather conservatism. These quotations from our focus groups suggest as much:

> I think all that is true and probably more important than the insult that I'm about to throw out about rural people, but I do think that there's a level of ignorance going on in rural America and distinguishing that from stupidity, but you've got Sinclair News and you've got Fox and you've got the little newspapers and the pastors in very religious churches and the television ads that come from the NRA and they're presenting a picture of a world in which the liberals are out to get your guns, they're out to commit abortions, they're out to take your money and give it to, I don't know. (NC Liberals 3, Man 2)

> I think there's also an education factor here and I'm not right now saying that everybody that voted for Trump was stupid or ignorant or whatever. I might say that sometime, but I'm not saying that right now. But I think with education comes thinking analytically, thinking in gray, not just black and white, thinking in, you know, what did he just say, is there anything to back that up? Thinking in terms of scientific process where there's—you do certain things and you get certain answers and you believe because of the process that—and I think if you don't have the kind of educational rootage, you're more vulnerable to the stuff that's made up or that's based solely on emotion or some of the things that led people who voted for Trump, I think not to analyze what they were doing as closely as I wished they would've. (NC Liberals 5, Man 2)

Similarly, conservatives look down upon liberals, but not for the reasons that social egalitarians put at the heart of their arguments.

> I was just going to say, I also think, I swear, I believe it with all my heart, that many, many liberals, it's just like junior high: you do what your friends do. And you don't want to be shunned, and you don't want to be looked down on because you are an idiot conservative. And they don't really know why they voted for Hillary. (Conservatives 1, Woman 3)

> I really believe that a lot of our constituents are uninformed, they do not do a good job of self-educating, so they are taking the media perspective. They're taking what information they're decisioning on at face value, from what they

see, visually, you know and aesthetically, from the media. And so I agree with you, I think "I'm a Democrat, and she's our Democrat. I'm going with it, that's it. I'm not going deeper, I'm not going to look at policy, I'm not going to look at her past decisioning, what she's done, her record, I'm just going Democrat." (Conservatives 3, Woman 1)

While focus group quotations offer only a glimpse into how people view one another, our surveys provide more evidence that many people disdain opposing partisans because they think they are ignorant and misled by the media.[14]

More important for our purposes, our data show that partisan differences drive respect differences. If you think that the reason why relational equality is important is because democratic citizens should listen to one another respectfully and without disdain or scorn, then our findings should be disturbing. Relational egalitarians argue that we should decrease income differences to ensure respect among citizens, an argument that rests on the idea that actual conditions affect relational equality. If it is partisan differences, not income differences, that drive lack of respect, then egalitarian theorists are missing an important part of the picture. If most democratic citizens are unable to respect opposing partisans, then we are far from reaching relational equality.

Similarly, what drives structural injustice theorists is, in part, the idea that society does not show certain groups of citizens sufficient respect. Structural injustice theorists are moved by the injustice that exists today in our society— one of their starting points is the current conditions in Western democracies. Here, too, the importance of respect is a normative ideal, but the lack of respect and how to ensure it are partly (or mostly) empirical matters. As we explained in chapter 1, Iris Marion Young's vision is one where citizens respect one another, and where the institutions of the state respect all citizens. Moreover, Young aspires for a society where people respect one another across differences, not where differences are a source of disdain or scorn, or a reason why one is ignored. We doubt that we need near universal respect to have sufficient societal respect, but a society where most think that opposing partisans are misled by the media or ignorant is far from any reasonable respect threshold.

One might say that while egalitarian theorists are interested in ensuring respect, their focus is on oppressed groups, and we normally do not think of partisans as oppressed. Yet what drives part of egalitarian theory is the importance of respect, and there is no reason to think that the theoretical importance of respect should be restricted to just some groups. If respect is a cardinal feature of democratic citizenship, the lack of respect should be a concern of egalitarian theorists, regardless of who is not being respected. Our

research shows that in at least one important respect egalitarians misunder-
stand the respect problem: to the degree that citizens refuse to listen to one
another, refuse to look each other in the eye, and show one another disdain
instead of respect, it is the partisan divide that must be bridged. Egalitarians
are right to worry that citizens scorn one another, but they do not locate the
problem correctly. What is true is that partisanship is the foundation of lack
of respect among American citizens, and if theorists think that respect is central to democratic citizenship, then they should consider why partisanship is
a source of disrespect, and what might be done about it.

# 8

## Struggling toward Respect

Democracy is worse off without respect than with it. It is likely that citizens who respect one another are more likely to discuss, bargain, negotiate, and work together than those who do not. They are more likely to see the viewpoint of those with whom they disagree than when respect is lacking. Moreover, citizens who respect one another can work together in good faith—it is likely that they are more willing to trust one another and to maintain norms that sustain democracy. There is also a large personal cost when respect is lost, which came through several sad stories in our focus groups.

We begin this chapter with what is lost when there is little respect, both civic and recognition, and when civic respect is not practiced. While some of this discussion is speculative, we think the consequences we raise align with common sense and with our findings that many people are not interested in listening to or engaging with opposing partisans. We then discuss the strategy of some of our focus group participants to toss civic respect aside to retain recognition respect, a strategy we endorse as a second-best strategy but only for interpersonal relations. We then discuss the importance of recognition respect and argue that its loss undermines democracy. As many of our liberal focus group participants suggested, respect is a core value of democracy. Of course, our book invites the question: If respect is hard to grant but so important to democracy, what can be done to get more citizens to be more respectful? Simply appealing to the democratic conscience within each of us will not get us very far. We offer a few suggestions on how to increase respect, though there is no silver bullet. We end with a sketch of future research on respect, an underexplored topic in political science and political theory.

## Democracy without Civic Respect?

As we showed in chapter 3, our focus groups and surveys provide evidence that many people cut friends and family out of their lives because of divergent political views. The hardest moments in our focus groups were hearing stories of people's vote choices ruining close relationships. Without our prompting, many liberal focus group participants talked about the problem of maintaining relationships:

> It's a hard thing for me, 'cause I'll tell you something, most of my conversations with the people that I'm having a problem with, up until about a year and a half ago, were about sports, were about your family, were about stuff that you just normally would talk about, we could kind of relate to each other. . . . When the election started happening and it started being more political, a lot of the people that I'm sitting there having a great time with on a Sunday afternoon watching football, I'm now arguing politics with them. . . . Next thing you know I know he's a Trump supporter and I'm now having this, you know, really hard time relating to him. And do I socialize with him? And so it's, it's a tough one for me. (Chicago Liberals 5, Man 3)

> Oh I've cut her out, a lot. But now she's not, she did not vote for Trump, but there are certain, I more look at the issues, like, if you voted for Trump it really pisses me off but now it's coming down to like what you said, it's a human rights thing. And I told both of my parents that if you even give me a hint of the fact that you agree with any of these, any issues that violate somebody's human rights, you will never see your grandson again. I'm not kidding. . . . Oh, it's horrible. I'm very close to my parents. (Chicago Liberals 5, Woman 1)

Our conservative focus group participants most often shared how their liberal friends and relatives cut them out of their lives.

> And in fact, I've been very quiet with my friends, you know, I started moving to the right when I was still in college, and I kept my mouth shut about it. And my friends started to understand that I was a little bit further to right than they were, and I think they considered me their token, you know, conservative friend. But I was, I behaved myself. . . . During the election, you know, I, I sort of came out, if you will, of how far to the right I actually am. *And I literally lost every single friend.* One, there was one friend who did not, there was one friend who said to me "I know your heart, you know, I've known you for many years." People who I knew for 35 years, who have loved me for 35 years. (NC Conservatives 1, Woman 1)

> And every single conservative you talk to will tell you that they have people in their lives, including family, who have ended relationships with them. (NC Conservatives 1, Woman 1)

While our focus group discussions highlighted liberals ending relationships with their conservative friends and family, our surveys did not show such a discrepancy.[1] What our surveys show is that both liberals and conservatives are cutting off friends and relatives because of their political views. This is an obvious loss for people on a personal level.

In these cases, both civic and recognition respect are tossed asunder. We treat their loss separately, however. Civic respect is important for democracy, while recognition respect is fundamental. We understand that it can be hard to grant civic respect to our fellow citizens. Still, even in cases when our political opponents have views that we think are without foundation or even dangerous, it is important to understand the bases of their beliefs. It is easy to tar Trump voters as racist, and some surely are, but there are other factors that explain why people do not vote for the Democratic Party. A few of our focus groups respondents said as much:

> I think of lot of it was economic. I think they, a lot of people were abandoned by the Democrats long ago and were riding on just the tail wind of "once upon a time" there were labor unions and etc. . . . So I think a lot of it was, "you know, I don't hear anyone telling me that they care about me anymore, and I'm hurting, and here's this pie-in-the-sky maniac, let's try him." (NC Liberals 3, Woman 1)

> So the main thing that drove the election of Trump as far as I'm concerned was people's response to a fear in their lives. They felt threatened, they were very angry. They wanted solutions and the solutions were not coming to their normal or traditional parties. The Republican Party was not giving them the answer or the leadership they wanted, the Democratic Party of course was not, the Independent Party was ineffectual. People were angry. (NC Liberals 6 , Man 3)

The comments suggest respect for those who voted differently, a respect grounded in understanding. This understanding is perhaps important for its own sake, but it also has a practical grounding. As we noted earlier, if people want their political party to increase its vote share, then understanding why some people won't vote for it becomes politically important. To be sure, some people will never vote for the opposing political party, but many people are not strong partisans willing only to listen to and vote for their own party. Understanding why some people aren't voting for one's party is important information. But we want to push beyond pragmatics. While one can understand the party switchers *only* for pragmatic reasons, we think understanding is best gained when it is also propelled by moral reasons—respect for one's fellow citizens and the acceptance that disagreement is often rooted in different and legitimate ideas about society, not necessarily ignorance or misunderstanding.

There are additional practical gains that follow from practicing civic respect aside from understanding people's votes and party identification. To grant civic respect allows the space for possible political agreement, or at least for places where differences with some political opponents are not as clear and wide. Pluralist countries harbor diverse political and social views. People will rarely disagree with their political opponents on every issue, and not all people align perfectly on issues with their party. By refusing to listen to the other side, the opportunity will be lost to find where people actually stand on these disparate and sometimes shared views. One practical outcome of civic respect, then, is the potential saving of some relationships as people gain a more nuanced understanding of others' views. A second practical outcome is that civic respect increases the likelihood that people will find areas of possible compromise. Assuming that the other side is immoral, unjust, disloyal, or racist (or some combination) makes it hard to justify working together to find solutions to society's problems. We assume the other side is always wrong and that our side is always correct, leaving problems unaddressed and possible compromise solutions completely ignored. Even if some views are clearly misguided, it does not mean that civic respect should be tossed aside. Just because someone denies climate change, for example, does not mean that you close down conversations with other opposing partisans on the issue or refuse to read what opposing partisans say about other issues. Finding possible paths to solving problems is hard work but potentially invaluable. Democratic citizens should hold onto as much of civic respect as they can.

## Saving Recognition Respect

While some of our focus group participants decided they could not practice either civic respect or recognition respect with the opposing partisans they knew, others drew a line between civic and recognition respect, though they did not use that language. Several of our focus group participants, liberals and conservatives alike, said that avoiding political discussions was an important way to save their relationships. In other words, saving recognition respect meant tossing civic respect aside:

> Total Trump supporters. But we just don't discuss it when they're here, and they're very good people in so many ways, and you know, we love them, but it's been really difficult. My husband if anything is more out-there, I mean, he voted for Bernie in the primary and stuff, more socialist even than I am, and so it's difficult but we have respect and certainly we can retain love for people who are, but there have to be clear boundaries as to what you're not going to beat up on each other about. (NC Liberals 1, Woman 1)

So, I have these sort of feelings and conversations with them but we back away from them. To your question, do I respect them? I respect them as people, I respect my father as my father—we can get along. I just don't talk about it. I can't. (Chicago Liberals 5, Man 2)

I have a number of friends that are, I'm sorry to say I learned were Trump supporters or Trump voters and I hold them and a lot of parts of their lives in great respect but the fact that they voted for Trump diminishes that respect for me. I don't, I certainly respect their right to choose a, a, to make a choice in an election. I have great respect for the system and the way it works and their exercising that. I agree with X, I think their choice is just grossly wrong, but that doesn't mean that I think they're awful people in all parts of their lives. So what does that mean about respect? Yes, no? (NC Liberals 5, Man 3)

Other respondents argued that avoiding politics was simply a way to remain civil with acquaintances.

I'm pretty cautious about getting into conversations with people that voted for Hillary. As a matter of fact, I usually don't get into conversations, so I guess that goes to the point of my very serious concern about the divisiveness in our country, it's terrible. It's not helpful for anybody. (NC Conservatives 2, Man 1)

I do have friends, sort of, I'm not sure that's the right term. I have acquaintances who have voted, who voted for Hillary. And I'm, you know, mostly we don't talk about that. I—certainly they don't bring it up. They certainly do bring up zingers about Trump all the time, and I normally respond to it. And that usually puts an end to any further discussion about most of anything. (NC Conservatives 2, Woman 1)

Many people avoid discussions about politics because partisans on each side are so sure that they are correct and they find it difficult to listen to views with which they disagree. While in the abstract they think listening to others is the right thing to do, in practice many citizens find this to be challenging.

We do not think that casting civic respect aside is ideal, but we do think that forgoing civic respect is sometimes an understandable approach for *interpersonal engagement*. We argued before that one does not have to continually engage with those one disagrees with on the same issue repeatedly, but that does not mean disengagement on all issues. Yet if one has reason to believe that interpersonal engagement on certain political and social issues will lead to such anger that one will cut off (or be cut off from) relations with one's friends and family (Webster, Connors, and Sinclair 2022), then this engagement is not helpful. Since so many people partly or mostly define others by their partisan choices, avoiding political discussions is often the right choice if it means saving recognition respect. Still, even as withholding civic respect

to retain recognition respect can be a reasonable strategy, we want to emphasize that this is true for interpersonal civic respect, not impersonal civic respect. Avoiding political discussions to retain relationships with friends and
family is sensible if it is necessary, but that does not excuse one from trying to
understand opposing partisans in impersonal ways—through news sources,
magazines, books, and so on. Practicing impersonal civic respect is much
better than not practicing it at all. Indeed, impersonal civic respect has another advantage. We have suggested in this book that civic respect can be in-
termittent: it does not expect us to listen respectfully to all views of opposing
partisans all the time. It will certainly try the patience of many (including us)
if Aunt Frances or Uncle Joe keeps repeating at our dinner table the fiction
that President Biden was illegally elected or that COVID vaccines will rewrite
our DNA. Indeed, listening to these kinds of lies and falsehoods might make
listening to the other things that Frances and Joe have to say quite challenging. Yet when we practice impersonal civic respect, we can do so selectively:
we can ignore the falsehoods and conspiracy theories and focus on the policy
ideas of the other side. We can choose to read thoughtful conservatives and
liberals, those that do not engage in lies, conspiracies, or racism. Impersonal
civic respect has advantages over interpersonal civic respect because it allows
us to practice civic respect in a partial but meaningful way.

Casting interpersonal civic respect aside is sometimes necessary to save
recognition respect, but we argue that it is never an appropriate solution to
cast recognition respect aside. Saving recognition respect is important because seeing our fellow citizens as people with dignity and as fellow humans
is a cornerstone of democratic equality. If we stop respecting opposing partisans as people, then democratic equality—and democracy—may begin to
fray. If we do not recognize our fellow citizens as equal people with dignity
who deserve respect as humans, then it does not seem like a far leap to deny
these others the right to vote or to have a voice in our polity. If we do not
grant recognition respect to our fellow citizens, then it is not far from not caring what happens to them. The loss of recognition respect is a real possibility,
which became apparent in some of our focus group discussions:

> I have a hard time respecting Trump supporters. I feel like you have to be
> really disabled mentally not to see that he's not stable and it was just so clear
> that he, you know, I wonder who his mother was? (NC Liberals 6, Woman 1)

> I'm totally unforgiving. . . . I have, I have no respect for somebody who didn't
> pay enough attention to see what the man is, and he put it out there front and
> center [crosstalk] there was nothing hidden. (NC Liberals 6, Man 2)

When recognition respect is missing, dehumanization is likely to raise its worrisome head. There is strong evidence that the more affectively polarized people are, the more they dehumanize opposing partisans (Cassese 2021; Martherus et al. 2019). Moral disengagement happens with dehumanization, which is when one decides that another person or group is less than human and so deserves less moral consideration than others (Bandura 2017; Bandura 2015). Dehumanized groups are often seen as dangerous and not in control of their own behavior (Bastian et al. 2011; Leach, Ellemers, and Barreto 2007). If people are dangerous and hard to control, it justifies the use of force, instead of reason, against them. This is why the loss of recognition respect is so worrisome: when partisans dehumanize their political opponents, the moral recognition of their opponents—as people who deserve rights and to be heard—is endangered. Dehumanization is the opposite of recognition respect, and it is dangerous to the idea of rights, equality, and democracy. If democratic equality is to be sustained, dehumanization must be avoided and recognition respect sustained.

## Is There a Remedy for Disrespect?

We have argued that respect is fundamental to equality, which is at the heart of democratic political systems. Liberals and conservatives find it difficult to respect those with whom they disagree, and it is especially liberals who struggle with this respect gap. They believe in the need for respect, and they find it hard to give it to opposing partisans. In this section, we address possible solutions designed to increase respect for opposing partisans. There is no silver bullet answer to the challenge of respect. Since people who are stronger partisans and who negatively characterize opposing partisans are much less willing to give them respect, we begin by looking at the remedies offered for decreasing affective polarization. We then focus specifically on respect. Our proposed solutions work for both civic and recognition respect (unless we note otherwise).

Decreasing the animosity people feel for opposing partisans would, we think, increase the respect people have for one another. Affective polarization leads to negative consequences, such as an unwillingness to compromise and legislative deadlock among elected representatives (Hetherington and Rudolph 2015) and a turning away from democratic norms (Kalmoe and Mason 2022; Kingzette et al. 2021; McCoy and Somer 2019; Voelkel et al. 2021). Various proposals address ways to decrease affective polarization, though unfortunately there is reason to be skeptical of many of these ideas. Hartman and her colleagues (2022) offer a useful typology of the proposed interventions. The most common solutions fall into the "thoughts" category, which involves correcting the misperceptions people hold of opposing partisans (see, e.g., Voelkel et al. 2021). People often think opposing partisans disagree with them more than they actually do (as we showed in chapters 4 and 5; see also Ahler 2014; Ahler and Sood 2018; Moore-Berg et al. 2020). One way to decrease affective polarization, then, is to give people correct information about opposing partisans. Doing so decreases the tendency of people to stereotype and to feel animosity toward those in the opposing party (Lees and Cikara 2020; Lees and Cikara 2021; Ruggeri et al. 2021).

Another way to get people to better understand that opposing partisans are not so different from themselves is to highlight a common ingroup identity (Gaertner et al. 1993). For example, instead of thinking of fellow citizens as Democrats or Republicans, people can think of them as fellow Americans, and this common ingroup identity decreases affective polarization. This effect holds whether people have their national identity primed in an experiment or they are surveyed near the Fourth of July (Levendusky 2018).The common ingroup identity solution, however, appears to have a negative side effect. When American identity becomes more salient, people can become more hostile toward people who are not Americans, such as immigrants (Wojcieszak and Garrett 2018).

The second type of solution focuses on relationships (Hartman et al. 2022). When people are put into situations in which they interact cooperatively with someone from a group they dislike, they are less likely to be prejudiced toward and hate people from that group (Pettigrew and Tropp 2006). When people are made to interact with opposing partisans, they are less likely to stereotype them, especially when the topic of conversation is not about politics (Santoro and Broockman 2022). Unfortunately, it is difficult to see how this solution would work in the real world. People increasingly have social networks that include few people from the opposing party (see chapter 3; Butters and Hare 2020; Stroud and Collier 2021), they tend to date or marry copartisans (Alford et al. 2011; Huber and Malhotra 2017), and they cut short holidays spent with extended family when family members disagree about politics (Chen and Rohla 2018). They also gain much of their information from mass and social media sources that reinforce their point of view (Choi 2022; Stroud and Collier 2021). Even more important than the self-selection problem, though, is that the findings on the success of this type of intervention are mixed. These interventions work best under the watchful eye of a good moderator and rules that guide the discussion (Kubin et al. 2021; Tuller et al. 2015; Bond, Shulman, and Gilbert 2018; Warner and Villamil 2017; Warner, Horstman, and Kearney 2020; Wojcieszak and Warner 2020), but neither moderators nor rules exist in everyday discussions.

We can also consider institutional changes (Hartman et al. 2022). There is some evidence that the way the United States practices its politics exacerbates affective polarization, including using single-member plurality districts, primary elections, and minority-empowering institutions like the US Senate (Horne, Adams, and Gidron 2022; McCoy and Somer 2019). The more people view politics as a zero-sum game, the more threatened they feel having the opposing party win elections (McCoy and Somer 2021). In proportional representation systems, political parties often must form coalitions to govern, and people have positive feelings about coalition parties for a long time, even after the parties are no longer in a coalition together (Horne, Adams, and Gidron 2022).

Increasing the support for moderate candidates within each party can also help with polarization: center-right and center-left candidates are more likely than more extreme candidates to work across the political aisle and less likely to demonize their political opponents. In the US system, there appears to be some evidence that using ranked-choice voting decreases partisan animosity, perhaps because candidates running for office feel the need to moderate their stances to gain more votes but also because people start to look at other parties as viable alternatives (McCoy and Somer 2021). It is also possible that compulsory voting pushes the parties toward moderation (Oprea, Martin, and Brennan, unpublished).

We are reluctant to put forward as a remedy for civic respect the idea that people simply need more contact with opposing partisans or better information about them. People who have more heterogeneous discussion networks are indeed more respectful of opposing partisans, as we showed in chapter 3, but it is unclear whether heterogeneous networks drive respect or if respect leads people to have more diverse networks. In either case, the bottom line is that most people don't want to have contact with opposing partisans. Our focus group discussions made this very clear, especially among the liberals. The experiment discussed in chapter 3 provides direct evidence that people are not eager to talk politics even with those with whom they agree, and they absolutely do not want to talk politics with those with whom they disagree. In fact, they even refuse to read about the ideas of those with whom they disagree. Many of the remedies used to address affective polarization are put into place in contrived research settings, such as a lab where contact is forced. When people have a choice, as our experiment showed, people refuse.

We can also look to education as a partial solution to the challenge of how to increase respect. The more strongly people believe in the abstract principles associated with democratic rights and the rule of law in a pluralist system, the more tolerant they are of groups they strongly dislike (Prothro and Grigg 1960). As with respect, tolerance does not expect that people will like each other. In fact, by definition, tolerance occurs when people strongly dislike an outgroup, but the more strongly people believe in abstract democratic principles, the more tolerant they are toward groups they strongly dislike (Sullivan, Piereson, and Marcus 1982). Targeting the enhancement of people's adherence to democratic principles is therefore a possible remedy for intolerance. Tolerance curricula that focus on people's understanding of basic rights and the rule of law, along with getting people to accept that there are diverse points of view in any democratic system, has a strong impact on tolerance (Avery, Sullivan, and Wood 1997; Avery 2002). Education and early socialization also increase people's understanding of and support for compromise, highlighting the importance of teaching people this basic democratic principle (Wolak 2020). Given this work on tolerance and compromise, we think it likely that teaching people to accept pluralism and political diversity could have a positive impact on both recognition and civic respect (Hjerm et al. 2020; Warner, Colaner, and Park 2021). If young people are taught that people hold a variety of different views about politics and that these different views are legitimate, we could see an increase in respect.

We can also offer advice to citizens about how to increase respect. First, be aware of motivated reasoning (Redlawsk 2002). Motivated reasoning is when people's biases influence their thinking and reasoning: if we dislike the views of opposing partisans because they are unreasonable, we will find reasons to find all (or most) of their views unreasonable, whether they are or not. When motivated reasoning kicks in, new information doesn't soften our views of opposing partisans because we interpret the new information to fit our biases. It is certainly easy to demonize opposing partisans, but one can try to put aside one's biases and stereotypes to listen. Find writers on the other side who show some humility and respect for a diversity of views. One could also find writers on one's own side who have some heterodox views. Second, watch more sports! That seems facile, but when people are with friends and relatives, and cannot talk about politics, they find common ground elsewhere: sports, television shows, and other forms of entertainment can bring people together.

We also think part of retaining recognition respect is up to our elected officials. When political leaders question election results without evidence, for example, they undermine recognition respect. Questioning election results simply because one does not like the other side undermines democracy, as many have noted. But part of why it undermines democracy is because it leads many people—who trust certain political leaders—to wrongly believe that the other side "stole" the election. And if they believe that, then they (mistakenly) believe that *their* votes are not counted; it means they believe that they are not granted recognition respect by opposing partisans. Moreover, those on the side that won fairly will believe that they are not granted recognition respect, since they will believe that opposing partisans are suggesting that *their* votes should not count as much as those on the opposing side. Of course, neither side uses the language of recognition respect, but we believe that it is nonetheless one of the things at stake in false claims about election fraud. Part of what democracy is founded on is the idea that we have a moral and a political equality, that we all count equally, particularly when it comes to voting. When our political leaders question election results for their own crass and dangerous political purposes, they undermine recognition respect—and democracy.

But the best option to increase respect, ironically perhaps, is for people to put politics aside sometimes, and to resist the temptation to organize their social lives according to their political views. When people pay attention to politics, they often do so through social media and the news, not by engaging in political discussions and certainly not by spending time with people with whom they disagree. In the 1990s about a third of Americans (35 percent) said they enjoyed political discussions (Ulbig and Funk 1999). Twenty years later, that percentage dropped to 26 percent (Carlson and Settle 2022). Robert Talisse (2019) argues that too many of us are too focused on politics and political citizenship. If citizens spent less time following politics on social media and polarizing news outlets, they could use that time to take up nonpolitical activities, particularly with people who have different political values (160). We should often put politics aside in our relationships with others to see them as civic friends. If we spend time with others on nonpolitical activities, by reducing the role of politics in our lives, we can recognize them as real human beings. The challenge is that politics is so pervasive these days, and people's political views and social circles overlap (see, e.g., Mason 2018). Talisse challenges people to end this overlap, a challenge we hope some people can meet. It is ironic that paying less attention to politics may lead to a better politics, but that is a strong possibility.

We wish we had a silver bullet that would increase respect among American citizens, but the lack of respect is not an easy problem to solve. As long as many American citizens view each other as enemies, our democracy stands on a weakened foundation.

## Where Do We Go from Here?

Respect is central to political theorists who are interested in equality and justice, but the concept had not been clearly defined nor interrogated fully, especially in terms of the difficulties people face trying to respect those with whom they disagree. We have tried to provide a clearer conceptualization of respect by addressing both recognition and civic respect and by acknowledging the difficulties people face trying to give respect in a pluralist society. Monism makes it hard, if not impossible, to respect those who prioritize a different value. By pointing out these issues, we hope to encourage political theorists to dig deeper into the idea of respect and its implications.

In contrast to political theorists who have been writing about respect for quite some time, empirical political scientists have ignored the concept. As such, our in-depth examination offers a first stab at answering fundamental questions about respect, including what respect is, who gives or does not give respect, and what explains people's lack of respect for opposing partisans. There remain many questions about respect that we have not attempted to answer. We end our book by laying out possible research ideas that address these unasked questions.

We chose to focus our book on understanding what explains respect. We could not look at everything in this regard, nor did we examine the consequences of refusing to give respect to fellow citizens, aside from the loss of friendships and relations with family members. We propose here some areas for future research on respect based on our speculations about what some of the alternative explanations and consequences might be.

- When people refuse to grant civic respect, they assume they are right about most things and that opposing partisans are wrong about most things, but this is unlikely the case. Refusing to grant civic respect therefore can lead to worse political decisions because people are unwilling to entertain ideas from the other side that might well be right. They are also likely to refuse to compromise with opposing partisans because of this lack of respect. Future research should test the impact of refusing to give civic respect to opposing partisans on support for basic democratic processes like debate and compromise and on the quality of people's decisions.
- We ignore in our book a fundamental feature of the current political environment, the existence of information silos. People gain their political information from social media and media sources that reinforce their viewpoints. Given the astonishing unwillingness of people to give even impersonal civic respect by refusing to read a couple of articles from the opposing viewpoint, we think it likely that people's choice of the source of their political information will further undermine civic respect. People who rely on social media and on biased media sources are, we think, less likely to give civic respect, and it is likely they will be less willing to give

recognition respect as well. Research on political information sources could provide further understanding about the causes and consequences of respect.

- Recognition respect is fundamental to democracy and democratic equality. We have argued that a lack of recognition respect undermines democracy by making people more likely to dehumanize their opponents and therefore to deny them agency in the democratic system. This process, we suggest, makes it easier for people to embrace unfair and undemocratic procedures, such as attempts to keep certain people from voting and efforts to have election outcomes not reflect the will of the voters. The notion of equality that is at the heart of procedural democracy is undermined. Research into these consequences of a lack of recognition respect is essential.

- We focused in our book on two worldviews that help explain why people have such a hard time respecting opposing partisans. We think these two worldviews, the social justice worldview and the national solidarity worldview, are key to understanding the lack of respect between Democrats and Republicans because they are so fundamentally tied to how these partisans think society ought to be. As such, they implicate not just people's personal beliefs but their beliefs about collective responsibility. A question that naturally arises is whether other issues or worldviews exist that have a similar impact on respect. There are likely individual differences in what these issues or worldviews might be, since people differ in the issues they moralize, but it would be useful to know if other issues or worldviews drive respect.

- We showed in chapters 3 and 4 that people make a lot of assumptions about their fellow citizens based on their vote choices. Voting for particular candidates—wanting to put certain people into positions of power that will then affect policy outcomes—carries a lot of meaning for many people. A vote choice distills into a simple message all the negative things opposing partisans associate with that candidate. People don't just stereotype opposing partisans. They also stereotype people by their vote choice, and this contributes to less respect. A possible area for future research is trying to disentangle vote choice and partisanship in terms of their impact on respect.

- Finally, while political theorists continue to be interested in pluralism as a concept, quantitative political scientists have, as far as we can tell, stopped examining pluralism as a key part of democracy. Political scientists used to invoke pluralism frequently, and we think it should come back. Acceptance of pluralism, as we have shown, is related to civic respect. We think it likely that a belief in pluralism increases people's sense of humility or, to use Jonathan Rauch's (2021) term, fallibilism. Understanding people's belief in pluralism not only helps us understand respect but could also contribute to our understanding of populism and democracy.

Democracy is in trouble, not only in the United States but around the world. While we do not have a simple solution to the problem, we believe that respect is at the heart of a well-functioning democracy. We therefore need to understand both the causes and consequences of why so many people cannot respect their fellow citizens—and why some people are able to do so. Accepting fellow citizens as equal participants in the political system is crucial to a healthy democracy, and this means respecting fellow citizens as equal moral agents. When people refuse to give this respect to people with whom they disagree, the democratic system is diminished.

*Acknowledgments*

We have incurred many debts while writing this book. Perhaps our largest debt is to our focus group participants, who generously gave up their time to perfect strangers and spoke to us freely and frankly. We also must thank several audiences who heard or read parts of the book at Duke University, Nuffield College at Oxford University, the London School of Economics, the University of Pennsylvania, the University of Wisconsin, the University of North Carolina at Chapel Hill, the University of Nebraska-Lincoln, the Southern Political Science Association, the Midwest Political Science Association, and the International Society of Political Psychology. Warm thanks to those who commented on parts of the manuscript: Cameron Ballard-Rosa, Mark Crescenzi, Jeff Howard, Mollie Gerver, Emily McTernan, Santiago Olivella, Alex Oprea, Jason Roberts, Kevin Smith, Sarah Truel, and Jonathan Weiler. Especially warm thanks to Hana Ali, John Hibbing, Marc Hetherington, and Tim Ryan, who gave us comments on all or most of the manuscript. We owe a tremendous thanks to Matthew Young for transcribing all the focus groups. Thanks to Michael Greenberg and Alison O'Toole for their coding expertise; to Chris Morse for his help with figures; and to Libby Kellmanson, Hana Ali, and Joseph Maestas for superb research assistance. Thanks to the two reviewers of the press who gave us thoughtful and helpful comments that made the book better. Finally, working on this book took a long time, and many weekends—we dedicate this book to our spouses, Elyza Halev and Randy Morse, for their patience with us and for their many conversations about this book. We were heartened both by their enthusiasm for the project and by their pushing back against some of our ideas, which was always done with respect.

# Appendix A: Focus Groups

We conducted two rounds of focus groups, the first primarily in 2018 and the second in late 2019 and early 2020. Focus group recruitment for liberal groups was by word of mouth. We asked friends if they had friends who had a circle of friends who would be interested in forming a group to meet with us. We also contacted liberal churches and bookstores, the latter to make connections to book clubs. We asked contacts, once we had them, if they would be able to get a group of people together who were liberal, college educated, and knew one another. (This was our first screen to establish that people thought of themselves as liberal.) We wanted groups of people who were accustomed to speaking with one another, to free them to speak their minds and to lessen the chance that one person would dominate a group. Once a group was identified, each person in the group received a consent form, where we screened again for liberal participants in the following way: "You are being asked to be in the study because you have a college degree, you live in a city or suburb, and you politically lean liberal or progressive."

We found that liberals were more open to participating in the focus groups than conservatives, who were more suspicious of being part of an academic study. To recruit conservatives, we contacted people we knew to see if they knew people who would be interested in participating in a focus group. As was the case with the liberal groups, we specifically asked for people who self-identified as conservative and who had college degrees. We also wanted people who knew one another. Once a group was identified, we sent each participant a consent form, again spelling out that we wanted participants who had college degrees and who politically leaned conservative.

The first round of thirteen liberal focus groups took place in Chicago and North Carolina (drawing people mostly from Raleigh, Durham, and

Chapel Hill) between February and May 2018. The first round of six conservative groups took place in North Carolina (four groups), Nebraska, and Alabama between July 2018 and January 2019. We donated $50 to a charity of each group's choice for its participation. Most participants in each focus group knew one another and often met regularly, as part of a church group or book club or just as friends. Groups ranged in size from four to thirteen, with liberal groups having an average of 7.3 participants and conservative groups an average of 5.8 participants. Nearly all participants had college degrees and their mean age was sixty (a couple of participants indicated in the pre-focus group survey that they had attended college, but did not graduate). Most participants were white, but there were Black and Latino/Latina participants in both the conservative and liberal groups. Fifty-eight percent of the liberal participants and 46 percent of the conservative participants were women. Altogether, we spoke with ninety-five liberals and thirty-five conservatives in the first round. The focus group sessions lasted approximately one and a half hours and were audio recorded. A graduate student transcribed the recordings, and we hired two graduate students to code the transcriptions.

In the pre–focus group survey, 80 percent of the liberal participants called themselves liberal, while 20 percent called themselves moderate. None self-identified as conservative. Of those calling themselves moderate, all but one said they were closer to liberals than to conservatives (one person said neither). Similarly, 80 percent of all liberal focus group participants said they were Democrats, while 20 percent said they were Independent. Of the latter group, all but two said they were closer to the Democratic Party than to the Republican Party (two people said neither). In other words, almost all participants in the liberal groups viewed themselves as liberal and Democratic or leaned in that direction. Similarly, 79 percent of the conservative participants called themselves conservative, while 18 percent said moderate and 3 percent (one person) said liberal. Of those calling themselves moderate, all but one person said they were closer to conservatives than to liberals (one person said neither). Most of the conservative participants, 85 percent, said they were Republican, 12 percent said they were Independent or other, while 3 percent (one person) said they were Democrat. Of the Independent/other group, all but one person said they were closer to the Republican Party than to the Democratic Party (one person said neither). In other words, almost all participants in the conservative focus groups viewed themselves as conservative and Republican or leaned in that direction.

We used a similar process to recruit our second round of focus group participants. We had five liberal groups (two in Nebraska, one in North Carolina, and two in the San Francisco Bay Area) and three conservative groups (one in California, one in Tennessee, and one in North Carolina). The liberal focus groups were held between October 2019 and February 2020. The conservative focus groups were held from February to April 2020 (the groups in Tennessee and North Carolina via Zoom because of COVID). We talked to a total of thirty-six liberals and fourteen conservatives in the second round. As with the round one focus groups, these sessions lasted approximately one and a half hours and were audio recorded. We hired a graduate student to transcribe the recordings.

## Focus Group Protocols

### FIRST ROUND—LIBERALS

1. I'm going to start with just a general question and then I'm going to move into the first of the three topical areas. I'd like to get a sense of what you mean by "equality." When you hear the word *equality*, what does that mean to you?
2. The first topic is rural conservative Americans. If we look at political maps in the United States, the big thing that we see is that there are red states and there are blue states, and the red states are outnumbering the blue states.
   2.a. A lot of people living in rural America voted for Donald Trump. I'd like to get your view of rural, conservative, religious Americans. Why do you think a lot of them voted for Trump?
   2.b. What did you think when Hillary Clinton referred to Trump supporters as the "deplorables"?
   2.c. There are some people who argue that equal respect is at the core of democratic citizenship. Do you have respect for Trump supporters?
3. The second topic is on racial inequality.
   3.a. Some people have argued that a way to reduce racial inequality is to focus on education, but we know that inner-city schools tend to be under-resourced. A lot of white people who live in inner cities prefer to take their children out of public schools and put them into better-resourced private schools or suburban schools, although these schools are also racially less diverse. What are your thoughts about white parents pulling their kids out of inner-city schools to attend better-resourced, less diverse schools?
   3.b. Moving from the education system to the workplace, what do you think about affirmative action in the workplace?
   3.c. Have you done anything yourself, personally, to try to combat racial inequality? If so, what did you do?
4. The last topic I want to talk about is income inequality. There have been several arguments made about what can be done to try to diminish the

income inequality that we have currently in our country. I will throw out some of the options that have been put out there as possible solutions.

4.a.  The first one is that some people argue that immigration leads to lower wages for low-skilled workers. Are you in favor of limiting immigration to reduce income inequality?

4.b.  Some people have argued that free trade leads to more income inequality by reducing the number of well-paid, low-skilled, and blue-collar jobs in the United States. Are you in favor of restricting free trade to reduce income inequality?

4.c.  Another possible solution for reducing income inequality is strengthening unions. Do you think strengthening unions is a solution for reducing income inequality?

5.  The last question is, What is the one thing you think needs to be done to increase social equality?

### FIRST ROUND—CONSERVATIVES

1.  I'm going to start with just a general question and then I'm going to move into the first of the three topical areas. I'd like to get a sense of what you mean by "equality." When you hear the word *equality*, what does that mean to you?

2.  The first topic is urban liberal Americans. If we look at political maps in the United States, the big thing that we see is that there are red states and there are blue states, and there are big circles of blue around urban areas.

2.a.  A lot of people living in urban America voted for Hillary Clinton. Why do you think a lot of them voted for Clinton?

2.b.  There are some people who argue that equal respect is at the core of democratic citizenship. Do you have respect for Hillary Clinton supporters?

2.c.  Do you feel like your fellow citizens with very different political views from you, like Hillary Clinton supporters, respect you?

2.d.  Have any of your friends or family members ended their relationship with you over a vote or has your vote damaged any of these relationships?

2.e.  Have any of you ended a friendship or a relationship with a family member, or become more distant to a friend or relative, because of how they voted?

3.  I want to ask about income inequality.

3.a.  Unemployment in America is actually very low by historical standards, but unemployment and underemployment rates in rural areas are higher. What do you think is going on? What's happening?

3.b.  Let me ask a parallel question about inner cities. Unemployment generally is very low, but in many inner cities there are higher underemployment and unemployment rates. Why? What do you think is happening?

3.c. Some people argue that immigration leads to lower wages for low-skilled workers. Are you in favor of limiting immigration? Should we limit the number of people coming into the United States, to protect jobs or wages, or is that not a good idea?

3.d. Some people argue that higher tariffs are better for America because they protect jobs and so on. Other people argue that lower tariffs are better for America. What do you think?

4. If there were one or two things you could do in America to increase equality—equality of opportunity or however you think of equality—what would it be?

### SECOND ROUND—LIBERALS

1. We'd like to start this part of the focus group by getting a sense of what you mean by justice.

1.a. What do you mean by justice?

1.b. When you hear the phrase *social justice*, what do you think?

1.c. Many people argue that antidiscrimination laws are a basic element of justice, and this means that discrimination against gay couples is wrong. Others argue that small business owners should be allowed to discriminate if doing so means following their religious conscience, that this is a matter of religious liberty. What do you think is required given your view of justice?

1.d. Some people say that it is time for catcalls directed toward women to stop, as well as off-color jokes in the office, and that the perpetrators should be penalized or at least called out. In this view, justice demands that everyone be treated with equal respect. Others say that while real sexual harassment should be stopped, we all need to be less touchy and sensitive and not let the small stuff bother us. What do you think is required given your view of justice?

1.e. If someone were to say the following, what would you think? "I think if we subsidize something, we will get more of it. If we subsidize corn, we get more corn. If we subsidize people not working, we get more people who will decide not to work, which is why we need to limit welfare spending."

2. Thinking about your life in general, how important is being an American to how you think of yourself? Do you feel strongly connected to fellow Americans?

2.a. Do you get upset when people are negative or critical about being American?

2.b. Some people say that the United States is a great country, and we should celebrate its achievements. Others say that America's promise is far from fulfilled and we should focus on all the many things we need to reach our promise of equality and justice for all. Which of these two views comes closest to what you think?

3. I am now going to ask you about your attitudes about people who do or say certain things. I would like you to focus on what you think of the person in each scenario.

   3.a. What do you think of a person who drives a Hummer and says that the emissions of just one car does not really matter for the environment, and so people should just drive any car they like?

   3.b. What do you think of a person who says that racial inequality is unfortunate, but America is the land of opportunity, and everyone can get ahead if they hard work.

   3.c. What do you think of a person who says that some schools will just always be terrible, and trying to fix them with more money is just throwing money away?

### SECOND ROUND—CONSERVATIVES

1. We'd like to start this part of the focus group by getting a sense of what you mean by justice.

   1.a. What do you mean by *justice*?

   1.b. Many people argue that antidiscrimination laws are a basic element of justice, and this means that discrimination against gay couples is wrong. Others argue that small business owners should have the liberty to refuse service to certain people if doing so means following their religious conscience. What do you think is required by justice?

   1.c. Some people say that it is time for catcalls directed toward women to stop, as well as off-color jokes in the office, and that the perpetrators should be penalized or at least called out. In this view, justice demands that everyone be treated with equal respect. Others say that while real sexual harassment should be stopped, we all need to be less touchy and sensitive and not let the small stuff bother us. What do you think is required by justice?

   1.d. When you hear the phrase *social justice*, what do you think?

2. Thinking about your life in general, how important is being an American to how you think of yourself? Do you feel strongly connected to fellow Americans?

   2.a. What do you think when you hear people who are negative or critical about being American?

2.b.    Some people say that the United States is a great country, and we
        should celebrate its achievements. Others say that America's promise
        is far from fulfilled and we should focus on all the many things we
        need to reach our promise of equality and justice for all. Which of
        these two views comes closest to what you think?

3.   I am now going to ask you about your attitudes about people who do or
     say certain things. I would like you to focus on what you think of the per-
     son in each scenario.

3.a.    What do you think of a person who drives a Hummer and says that
        the emissions of just one car does not really matter for the environ-
        ment, and so people should just drive any car they like?

3.b.    What do you think of a person who says that racial inequality is un-
        fortunate, but America is the land of opportunity, and everyone can
        get ahead if they work hard? *(Follow up: What is racism? What do
        you think of the idea of structural racism?)*

3.c.    What do you think of a person who says that some schools will just
        always be terrible, and trying to fix them with more money is just
        throwing money away?

## Focus Group Coding

In chapter 2, we include data based on coding the focus group transcripts.
Focus groups are not representative samples of the population of all American adults and therefore coding the percentage of focus group participants
who gave responses of X or Y would not be very meaningful. We would not
know if the participants' responses are representative of the population of
all American adults because the sample could be, and likely is, skewed in
some way. If, however, relevant the population is all of the statements made
in the focus group discussions, then coding to determine the proportion of
*statements* about X or Y (not the proportion of participants) makes perfect
sense. For example, we showed in table 2.2 that over half (56 percent) of all
conservative focus group statements on equality focused on equality of opportunity and that none of the statements mentioned equity and fairness.
These percentages differ from liberal statements on the meaning of equality.
This analysis provides important information on how liberals and conservative think about equality.

To do the coding of the focus group transcripts, the researchers devel-
oped the codes both via their knowledge of the literature and using an itera-
tive process using the transcripts. We then hired two graduate students to
code the transcripts. The graduate students were trained on the codes for
equality before the law and equality of opportunity before coding the rest of

TABLE A.1. Intercoder reliability (kappa) for focus group statements on the meaning of equality

| The meaning of equality | Liberals | Conservatives |
|---|---|---|
| Equal before the law (law, rights) | 1.0 | 0.92 |
| Equal opportunity | 0.93 | 0.79 |
| Moral worth or value | 0.81 | 0.41 |
| Equal under God | 1.0 | 1.0 |
| Fairness (affirmative action, fairness, equity) | 0.90 | — |
| Equal voice or access | 0.84 | 0.69 |

Source: Equality Attitudes Focus Groups 2018
Note: Cell entries are kappas. No conservative statements mentioned Fairness, a result corroborated by both coders.

TABLE A.2. Intercoder reliability (kappa) for focus group statements on the struggle to respect

| Respect and no respect | Liberals | Conservatives |
|---|---|---|
| No struggle | 0.73 | 0.71 |
| No struggle—no respect | 0.68 | — |
| No struggle—respect | 0.54 | 0.72 |
| No struggle—ambiguous | 0.51 | 0.66 |
| Struggle | 0.76 | — |
| Struggle—no respect | 0.82 | — |
| Struggle—respect | 0.50 | — |
| Struggle—ambiguous | 0.67 | — |

Source: Equality Attitudes Focus Groups 2018
Note: Cell entries are kappas. There were no conservative statements in the parent category Struggle or on "no struggle—no respect."

the transcripts. The Cohen's kappa statistic, which is a measure of agreement among the coders, ranges from 0 (no agreement) to 1 (perfect agreement). Above 0.8 is considered excellent; between 0.6 and 0.8 good; between 0.4 and 0.6 fair. Table A.1 lists the intercoder reliabilities for statements on the meaning of equality. Some kappas are high if a simple word search ("God," "law," "rights") is used because it is easy to reach agreement. A small number of mentions can lead to a low kappa if there is any variation in coding. For example, moral worth or value had very few conservative mentions (three), which explains the relatively low kappa. Coding differences were reconciled with a meeting between the two graduate student coders and one of the authors.

We also coded statements on respect in our liberal and conservative focus groups. Respect and no respect had parent codes and child codes, as shown in table A.2. Many participants had ambiguous responses, which led to some reasonable disagreement among the coders for the child codes. The parent codes have a much higher kappa, since the distinction between struggle and no struggle was easier to determine than between ambiguous and unambiguous responses. There were no conservative statements reflecting struggle or no struggle, no respect.

## Appendix B: Surveys

We fielded three surveys between 2018 and 2020. We used the Internet survey company ResearchNow SSI, which then became Dynata. Dynata recruits participants to be part of their online community and then, after screening, invites them onto the panel. Participants are randomly selected from the panel to participate in a particular study. We asked ResearchNow SSI/Dynata to recruit a sample of 1,600 respondents for each of our three surveys. We set the population of our sample as American citizens twenty years old or older, and oversampled college-educated respondents. We set a quota of 60 percent college-educated respondents and 40 percent less than a college degree. The US Census in 2017 showed that just over 34 percent of the American population had a college degree or higher (https://www.census.gov/data /tables/2017/demo/education-attainment/cps-detailed-tables.html). We also set quotas on ideology: 40 percent liberal or moderate liberal, 40 percent conservative or moderate conservative, and 20 percent middle of the road. We weighted the data to reflect US Census data on respondent sex, education, and race/ethnicity. The weights were as follows: sex—0.49 male, 0.51 female; race—0.75 white, 0.25 people of color; education—0.03 less than high school, 0.28 high school graduate, 0.09 technical/trade school, 0.21 some college, 0.21 college graduate, 0.04 some graduate school, 0.10 master's degree, 0.04 doctorate or advanced degree.

### Equality Attitudes Survey (2018)

The Equality Attitudes Survey took place between December 3 and 9, 2018. We included an attention test question ("To ensure that responses are being recorded accurately, please choose the Strongly agree response") and those who failed the test (13 percent of the total sample) were dropped from the analyses. The median duration of the survey was 7.8 minutes.

We embedded an experiment in the Equality Attitudes Survey. The experimental design was a 2 (ideology: liberal, conservative) x 3 (label: control, party, vote choice) between-subjects design. Respondents were randomly assigned to read a vignette about a fictitious person, Bob, that laid out his liberal or conservative policy stands (the ideology condition). Everyone read Bob's policy positions. People assigned to the control label condition read only about Bob's policy stands. Those assigned to the party label condition were given Bob's policy stands and were told with which party Bob identified (in italics below). Those assigned to the vote choice label condition were given Bob's policy stands and were told for whom Bob voted in the presidential election (in boldface below). The conservative version of the vignette was:

> Bob believes that large government means wasteful spending and too much regulation, which can hurt small businesses. He thinks unions often protect lazy and bad workers. He favors charter schools because he believes that competition will improve education and help all children, especially poor children. He thinks affirmative action is reverse discrimination. He believes that raising the minimum wage will lead to job losses, mainly among the poorest citizens. If labor costs too much money, he says, employers will turn to automation. Indeed, he favors restrictions on immigration because he thinks too many immigrants will depress wages for many American citizens, particularly the poorest, or leave them unemployed. *[Party Label condition: Bob is a Republican.]* **[Vote Choice condition: Bob voted for Donald Trump in the 2016 presidential election.]**

The liberal version of the vignette was:

> Bob believes in the positive role of government in people's lives and that government regulation often protects many citizens, especially the most vulnerable. He thinks unions are important to protect the wages of many middle- and lower-income people. He is against charter schools because he thinks they undermine support for public schools, which are important for nearly all children but particularly the poor. He thinks affirmative action is important for certain groups of people to be treated fairly. He believes that raising the minimum wage is important so the poorest citizens can earn enough to live decent lives. Without a minimum wage, there will be a "race to the bottom" among employers to pay employees less and less. With a good minimum wage set in place, he thinks many immigrants can be allowed into the US because

they add so much socially and economically to the country. *[Party Label condition: Bob is a Democrat.]* **[Vote Choice condition: Bob voted for Hillary Clinton in the 2016 presidential election.]**

Following the vignette, respondents were asked the extent to which they agreed with Bob, how they would characterize Bob using a series of polar adjectives (such as racist/not racist and misled by the media/well informed by the media), and how much respect they have for Bob.

## Pluralism and Respect Survey (2019)

The Pluralism and Respect Survey took place between October 23 and 29, 2019. We included the same attention test question ("To ensure that responses are being recorded accurately, please choose the Strongly agree response") and again had 13 percent of the total sample who failed the test. We dropped these respondents from the analyses. The median duration of the survey was 11.2 minutes.

## Social Justice and Solidarity Survey (2020)

The Social Justice and Solidarity Survey was in the field from July 30 to August 3, 2020. We included the same attention test question ("To ensure that responses are being recorded accurately, please choose the Strongly agree response") and had 10 percent of the total sample who failed the test. We dropped these respondents from the analyses. The median duration of the survey was 11.4 minutes.

## Civic Respect Experiment (2021)

We also hired Dynata to recruit eight hundred participants for an online experiment we fielded between May 13 and 20, 2021. The population of our sample was US citizens nineteen years and older. We set quotas on age (50 percent nineteen to forty-four, 50 percent forty-five and older) and ideology (35 percent liberal, 30 percent moderate, 35 percent conservative).

We began the online experiment with survey questions on demographics and beliefs about social justice and national solidarity. Participants were then randomly assigned to one of five conditions: control, pro–social justice, anti–social justice, pro–national solidarity, and anti–national solidarity. Participants in each condition were asked to read a series of statements on their randomly assigned topic and then answer some questions specific to the task.

Now we would like you to read five statements that reflect what some people believe about hiking. Please read them carefully. Once you have done that, rank order the statements from 1 = the strongest statement reflecting this point of view, 2 = the second strongest statement reflecting this point of view, to 5 = the weakest statement reflecting this point of view. You can't have two statements with the same number.

- Whether hiking a new trail or repeating a trail already hiked, people always see new and interesting things.
- A positive thing about hiking is that it promotes fellowship rather than competition, which makes it great for families.
- Hiking has been shown to burn fat, increase cardiovascular health, and help people relax, making it a good option for maintaining one's health.
- Hiking allows people to spend time outdoors and with nature, and we don't get to do that enough in our fast-paced lives.
- Unlike many sports, hiking is inexpensive; it just takes a good pair of shoes or boots.

Now we would like you to read five statements that reflect what some people believe about social justice. Please read them carefully. Once you have done that, rank order the statements from 1 = the strongest statement reflecting this point of view, 2 = the second strongest statement reflecting this point of view, to 5 = the weakest statement reflecting this point of view. You can't have two statements with the same number.

- Studies show that most Americans support efforts to reduce racial, gender identity, and economic injustice.
- The Black Lives Matter movement is one of the most important social and political movements of our day.
- Universities and businesses that have a diverse workforce often are more successful than when the workforce is homogeneous.

- Conducting regular diversity training sessions for employees at all medium and large organizations increases awareness of and activism against racism and sexism.
- Progress on social justice issues will happen much faster if majority groups—such as white people, straight people, and wealthy people—are social justice allies.

### ANTI–SOCIAL JUSTICE CONDITION

Now we would like you to read five statements that reflect what some people believe about social justice. Please read them carefully. Once you have done that, rank order the statements from 1 = the strongest statement reflecting this point of view, 2 = the second strongest statement reflecting this point of view, to 5 = the weakest statement reflecting this point of view. You can't have two statements with the same number.

- The focus on social justice is misguided because the fact that there are a few racist individuals does not mean the whole system is broken.
- Social justice efforts often cause more problems, such as allowing illegal immigrants to take jobs from Americans.
- Inequalities occur because of the choices people make. Anyone can succeed if they try hard enough.
- So-called social justice warriors are elitists who do not care about the white working class.
- Affirmative action is reverse racism, leading to innocent white and Asian Americans getting hurt.

### PRO–NATIONAL SOLIDARITY CONDITION

Now we would like you to read five statements that reflect what some people believe about American identity. Please read them carefully. Once you have done that, rank order the statements from 1 = the strongest statement reflecting this point of view, 2 = the second strongest statement reflecting this point of view, to 5 = the weakest statement reflecting this point of view. You can't have two statements with the same number.

- Americans have a responsibility to take care of each other, and other countries can take care of their own citizens.
- America is stronger if its citizens share the same basic values and are loyal.

- Criticizing America is only acceptable if it is done from a place of appreciation and respect.
- Our identity as Americans is far more important than any other identity we may have.
- It is important that everyone sees America as a strong country.

## ANTI—NATIONAL SOLIDARITY CONDITION

Now we would like you to read five statements that reflect what some people believe about American identity. Please read them carefully. Once you have done that, rank order the statements from 1 = the strongest statement reflecting this point of view, 2 = the second strongest statement reflecting this point of view, to 5 = the weakest statement reflecting this point of view. You can't have two statements with the same number.

- The right thing for the United States to do is to let in as many refugees and immigrants as possible, regardless of race or religion.
- When people are critical of America, they are trying to make it a better place.
- The United States is a diverse country made up of many races, religions, and ethnic groups.
- Everyone should understand that we live in a globalized interconnected world, and that Americans have an obligation to help everyone, not just fellow citizens.
- The rights of Americans are not any more important than the rights of others.

After reading the statements, all participants, regardless of the condition they were in, were asked to respond to the following questions.

[On the same page as the statements] Please type out the main idea of the statement you chose as 1 = the strongest statement.

[On the next page] Which statement did you choose as having the strongest argument? [The statements were listed and participants could choose one of the statements.]

To what extent do you, personally, agree with the point of view on [hiking/social justice/American identity] reflected in the five statements listed above? 1 = Strongly agree, 2 = Agree, 3 = Neither agree nor disagree, 4 = Disagree, 5 = Strongly disagree.

After reading the statements and responding to these questions, half of the participants were randomly assigned to one of two civic respect conditions, impersonal respect or interpersonal respect.

*Impersonal Respect Condition*: Participants in the impersonal respect condition read: "After reading the statements you just read, some people are interested in learning more about the point of view taken in those statements. We have chosen a couple of articles that more fully lay out that point of view. You'll have an opportunity to read the articles immediately after you have finished the survey. Are you interested in reading the articles after the survey?" Response options were yes or no. Those who answered yes then read: "You have indicated that you are interested in reading a couple of articles on this point of view. We will provide you with a link to those articles at the end of the survey." At the end of the survey, participants who had responded yes were told: "Thank you for completing the survey. You indicated earlier that you were interested in reading a couple of articles on the position taken in the five statements you read. Please click on the Link to Articles button if you are still interested in looking at these articles. If you are not interested in reading the articles, please click on the Not Interested button." Response options were link to articles or not interested.

*Interpersonal Respect Condition*: Participants in the interpersonal respect condition read: "After reading the statements you just read, some people are interested in learning more about the point of view taken in those statements. We have put together a panel of people willing to talk or text with our survey participants and therefore have someone available who strongly holds this point of view. You'll have an opportunity to talk or text with this person immediately after you have finished the survey. Are you interested in talking or texting with this person after the survey?" Response options were yes or no. Those who answered yes then read: "You have indicated that you are interested in talking or texting with this person. We will provide you with a link to talk or text with this person at the end of the survey." At the end of the survey, participants who had responded yes were told: "Thank you for completing the survey. You indicated earlier that you were interested in talking or texting with someone who strongly holds the position taken in the five statements you read. Please click on the Link to Person button if you are still interested in talking or texting with this person. If you are no longer interested, please click on the Not Interested button." Response options were link to person or not interested.

All participants in this civic respect experiment were debriefed: Thank you for participating in this study. Your responses will be helpful in better understanding how people think about politics and various political issues. After reading about the true meaning of the study below, please mark the appropriate choice in the proceeding question to tell us if you would prefer to withdraw your data from being used in our study. This study was designed to help advance understandings of how people respond to information that disagrees with their point of view on a set of political issues. In particular, we were interested in whether people are willing to listen to and engage with those who disagree with them. Importantly, some participants, including you, were randomly chosen to participate in a second study. These participants were divided into two different conditions. Some of you were asked if you would be willing to read some articles that more fully explained the position taken in the statement-ranking task; others were asked if you would be willing to speak with someone who holds the views reflected in the statement-ranking task. If you said no, you simply continued with the survey questions. If you said yes, you were asked at the end of the survey to select the Link button if you were still interested in reading the articles or talking to the person. There were no articles nor was there a person waiting to talk with you. We were simply interested in whether people would be willing to read articles or talk to someone that espoused a particular issue stand. We apologize for the degree to which the experimental manipulations were misleading.

Please mark below whether you would prefer to withdraw your data from being used in our analyses of the second study now that you know the details of this study.

Are you still okay with your data being used in our analyses?

Yes, I have read about the purpose of the study and still consent to having my data used in analyses.

No, now that I know the purpose of the study, I would prefer to withdraw my data from being used in analyses.

# Appendix C: Survey Questions and Scales

The following acronyms are used for the following surveys:

EAS—Equality Attitudes Survey (2018)
PRS—Pluralism and Respect Survey (2019)
SJSS—Social Justice and Solidarity Survey (2020)

If a survey is not specified, the question was asked in the same way in all the surveys.

## Demographics

**Age**: In what year were you born? Transformed to age in years and to range from 0 (20 years old) to 1 (oldest age of survey respondents).

**Education**: What is the highest level of formal education you have completed? 1 = 0 to 11 years, 2 = High school graduate, 3 = Technical/trade school, 4 = Some college, 5 = College graduate, 6 = Some graduate school, 7 = Master's degree, 8 = Doctorate or advanced degree (JD, MD, PhD, etc.). Transformed to range from 0 (0–11 years) to 1 (doctorate or advanced degree).

**Gender**: EAS—Are you male, female, or something else? PRS/SJSS—Are you male, female, or do you not identify as male or female? Responses coded 1 = Male, 2 = Female, 3 = Something else/Do not identify as male or female. Coded 1 = Male, 0 = Female/Something else/Do not identify as male or female.

**Ideology**: When it comes to politics, do you think of yourself as liberal, conservative, or somewhere in between? Response options 1 = Liberal, 2 = Somewhat liberal, 3 = Moderate/middle of the road, 4 = Somewhat

TABLE C.1. Descriptive statistics for demographic variables preweighted

| | EAS | | PRS | | SJSS | |
|---|---|---|---|---|---|---|
| | Mean | SD | Mean | SD | Mean | SD |
| Age | 0.440 | 0.240 | 0.480 | 0.237 | 0.445 | 0.216 |
| Gender (1 = Male) | 0.438 | 0.496 | 0.419 | 0.494 | 0.522 | 0.500 |
| Race/ethnicity (1 = White) | 0.862 | 0.345 | 0.853 | 0.354 | 0.842 | 0.364 |
| Education | 0.544 | 0.237 | 0.539 | 0.240 | 0.551 | 0.250 |
| Place (1 = Rural) | 0.185 | 0.388 | 0.203 | 0.403 | 0.205 | 0.404 |
| Party identification | 0.502 | 0.403 | 0.490 | 0.418 | 0.481 | 0.419 |
| Ideology | 0.500 | 0.367 | 0.499 | 0.396 | 0.495 | 0.384 |
| N[a] | 1,417 | | 1,474 | | 1,358 | |

[a] The cases include only those who passed the attention check question.

conservative, 5 = Conservative. Recoded to range from 0 = Liberal to 1 = Conservative.

**Party Identification**: Generally speaking, do you think of yourself as a Democrat, a Republican, an Independent, or something else? [If Democrat or Republican] Would you call yourself a strong Democrat/Republican or a not very strong Democrat/Republican? [If Independent or Something else] Do you think of yourself as closer to the Democratic or the Republican Party? Responses were coded so 1 = Strong Democrat, 2 = Not so strong Democrat, 3 = Independent leaning toward the Democratic Party, 4 = Independent, 5 = Independent leaning toward the Republican Party, 6 = Not so strong Republican, 7 = Strong Republican. Party identification was recoded to range from 0 = Strong Democrat to 1 = Strong Republican. When comparing Democrats to Republicans, leaners were included with the partisans unless otherwise specified.

**Place**: Which of the following best describes the area in which you live? 1 = Urban, 2 = Suburban, 3 = Rural. Coded 1 = Rural, 0 = Urban/Suburban.

**Race/Ethnicity**: EAS only—Are you of Hispanic origin or descent, such as Mexican, Puerto Rican, Cuban, or other Spanish background? 1 = Yes, 0 = No. What race or races do you consider yourself? 1 = American Indian/Native American, 2 = Asian/Pacific Islander, 3 = African American/Black, 4 = White/Caucasian, 5 = Hispanic/Latino/Latina/Chicano/Chicana, 6 = Other.

### Equality Attitudes Survey (2018)

**Characterizations of Opposing Voters**: Thinking of people in general, what comes to mind when you think of the people who voted for [Hillary Clinton/Donald Trump] in the 2016 presidential election? Educated . . .

Uneducated; Racist . . . Not racist; Sexist . . . Not sexist; Closed to new ideas . . . Open to new ideas; Misled by the media . . . Well informed by the media; Tolerant . . . Intolerant; Willing to compromise . . . Unwilling to compromise; Intelligent . . . Unintelligent; Follows others without thinking . . . Acts and thinks independently; Not condescending . . . Condescending. The first term anchored 1 and the second term anchored 7, with all options in between. Responses were recoded to 0 = most negative characterization and 1 = most positive characterization.

**Clinton/Trump Supporters**: Did you vote in the 2016 presidential election? Yes or no. [If yes] For whom did you vote in the 2016 presidential election? 1 = Donald Trump, 2 = Hillary Clinton, 3 = Gary Johnson, 4 = Jill Stein, 5 = Evan McMullin, 6 = Other. [If no] For whom would you have voted in the 2016 presidential election if you had been able to vote? 1 = Donald Trump, 2 = Hillary Clinton, 3 = Gary Johnson, 4 = Jill Stein, 5 = Evan McMullin. Trump supporters are those who answered Donald Trump for either question. Clinton supporters are those who answered Hillary Clinton for either question.

**Equality Means . . .** : People disagree about what equality means. Please indicate to what extent each of the following reflects your understanding of equality . . . . Everyone deserves equal respect . . . Equal opportunity . . . Equal under the law . . . Equal rights . . . Everyone's voice should be heard equally . . . Equal moral worth or value . . . Equal under God . . . Equal political influence . . . Equal outcome . . . Equal income. 1 = Does not at all reflect my understanding, 4 = To some extent, 7 = Completely reflects my understanding. Transformed to range from 0 to 1. Mean = 0.88, standard deviation = 0.20.

**Friends and Family Opposing Voters**: We want you now to think about the people you are close to and with whom you work (your family, friends, and co-workers). What is your best guess about how many of them voted for [Donald Trump/Hillary Clinton] in the 2016 election? 1 = Very few or none, 2 = About one-quarter, 3 = About half, 4 = About three-quarters, 5 = All or just about all.

Continuing to focus on the presidential election of 2016, did the election of Donald Trump have a negative impact on any of your relationships with close friends or family members? 1 = Yes, 2 = No. [If Yes, respondents were asked the following two sets of questions] We'd like to start by asking about *your* actions after the 2016 presidential election. Did the election of Donald Trump lead *you* to . . . Argue with a family member or close friend? . . . Stop talking to a family member or close friend? . . . Block a family member or close friend on social media? . . . End a relationship with a family member or close friend? 1 = Yes, 2 = No. Now we'd like to know about the actions of your close friends or family members after the 2016 presidential election. Did the election of Donald Trump lead *a close friend or family member* to . . . Argue with you? . . . Stop talking to you? . . . Block you on social media? . . . End a relationship with you? 1 = Yes, 2 = No.

**How would you characterize Bob (experiment)**: Educated . . . Uneducated; Racist . . . Not racist; Sexist . . . Not sexist; Closed to new ideas . . . Open to new ideas; Misled by the media . . . Well informed by the media; Tolerant . . . Intolerant; Willing to compromise . . . Unwilling to compromise; Intelligent . . . Unintelligent; Follows others without thinking . . . Acts and thinks independently; Not condescending . . . Condescending. The first term anchored 1 and the second term anchored 7, with all options in between. Responses were recoded to 0 = most negative characterization and 1 = most positive characterization.

**Respect Opposing Voters Scale**: I struggle a great deal when it comes to respecting people who voted for [Donald Trump/Hillary Clinton]. I might disagree with [Donald Trump/Hillary Clinton] voters but I still respect them as people (reverse coded). (1 = Strongly agree, 2 = Agree, 3 = Neither agree nor disagree, 4 = Disagree, 5 = Strongly disagree) Transformed to range from 0 to 1.

**Respect for Bob (experiment)**: How much respect would you say you have for Bob? 1 = No respect, 2 = Very little respect, 3 = Some respect, 4 = A lot of respect, 5 = Total respect.

## Pluralism and Respect Survey (2019)

**Characterizations of Opposing Voters**: [Asked of Hillary Clinton voters] We are interested now in your thoughts about people who voted for Donald Trump for president in 2016. Please let us know the extent to which you agree or disagree with these characterizations. People who voted for Donald Trump in the 2016 presidential election are . . . Immoral . . . Intolerant . . . Racist . . . Sexist. [Asked of Donald Trump voters] We are interested now in your thoughts about people who voted for Hillary Clinton for president in 2016. Please let us know the extent to which you agree or disagree with these characterizations. People who voted for Hillary Clinton in the 2016 presidential election are . . . Immoral . . . Intolerant . . . Dishonest . . . Condescending. 1 = Strongly agree, 2 = Agree, 3 = Neither agree nor disagree, 4 = Disagree, 5 = Strongly disagree.

Do you think a vote for [Donald Trump/Hillary Clinton] was more a vote based on ignorance, a vote that was immoral, or a vote that was neither? 1 = Ignorance, 2 = Immoral, 3 = Neither.

**Civic Respect**: *Abstract*—Respecting others means being willing to listen to what they have to say, even if one disagrees with them. 1 = Strongly disagree, 2 = Disagree, 3 = Neither agree nor disagree, 4 = Agree, 5 = Strongly agree. Transformed to range from 0 to 1 (mean 0.802, sd 0.194).

*Listen*—I can't listen to someone when I disagree with their political views. Respect is impossible to give to someone whose political views are different from my own. Honestly, I don't really listen to what people say about politics if they belong to a different political party than I do. I sometimes feel it would be better if people in different political groups didn't try to mix together. The Civic Respect-Listen Scale is an additive scale of these four items and ranges from 0 = Low civic respect-listen to 1 = High civic respect-listen (mean 0.632, sd 0.247, alpha 0.849).

*Engage*—I like meeting and getting to know people with political beliefs different from my own. I often spend time with people who have political beliefs different from my own. (1 = Strongly disagree, 2 = Disagree, 3 = Neither agree nor disagree, 4 = Agree, 5 = Strongly agree) How often do you talk about politics with people who belong to a different political party than you? (1 = Never, 2 = Occasionally, 3 = Sometimes, 4 = Often). These three items were transformed to range from 0 to 1. The Civic Respect-Engage Scale is an additive scale of these three items and ranges from 0 = Low civic respect-engage to 1 = High civic respect-engage (mean 0.529, sd 0.205, alpha 0.608).

**Clinton/Trump Supporters**: Did you vote in the 2016 presidential election? Yes or no. [If yes] For whom did you vote in the 2016 presidential election? 1 = Donald Trump, 2 = Hillary Clinton, 3 = Other. [If no] For whom would you have voted in the 2016 presidential election if you had been able to vote? 1 = Donald Trump, 2 = Hillary Clinton, 3 = Other. Trump supporters are those who answered Donald Trump for either question. Clinton supporters are those who answered Hillary Clinton for either question.

**Moralization**: *Social Justice Issues*—Now we'd like to ask you some questions about various issues. People view most political issues simply as policy preferences. However, there are a few issues that people view as core moral beliefs. We'd like to know which of the following issues are to you policy preferences and which are core moral beliefs . . . Climate change . . . Racial equality . . . Gender equality . . . Income inequality . . . LGBTQ+ rights. 1 = Policy preference, 2 = Core moral belief.

*Vote Choice*—The following questions ask about whether you judge people by the way they voted in the last presidential election. We're going to ask you some questions about people who voted for Donald Trump and people who voted for Hillary Clinton . . . To what extent is your attitude toward people who voted for Donald Trump a reflection of *your* core moral beliefs and convictions? . . . To what extent is your attitude toward people who voted for Donald Trump deeply connected to *your* fundamental beliefs about right and wrong? . . . To what extent is your attitude toward people who voted for Hillary Clinton a reflection of *your* core moral beliefs and convictions? . . . To what extent is your attitude toward people who voted for Hillary Clinton deeply connected to *your* fundamental beliefs about right and wrong? 1 = Very much, 2 = Much, 3 = Moderately, 4 = Slightly, 5 = Not at all.

**Recognition Respect**: I believe all people should be given respect simply because they are fellow human beings. All people deserve respect no matter what they have said or done. People who do or say bad things shouldn't be given respect (reverse coded). All people have moral worth. We ought to treat everyone with respect, no matter who they are or what they have done. People need to earn respect, not simply be given it (reverse coded). 1 = Strongly disagree, 2 = Disagree, 3 = Neither agree nor disagree, 4 = Agree, 5 = Strongly agree. The Recognition Respect Scale (PRS) is an additive scale of these six items, ranging from 0 = Low recognition respect to 1 = High recognition respect (mean 0.547, sd 0.178, alpha 0.719).

**Support for Pluralism**: Having at least two political parties that compete in close elections is a good thing. Our country would be better off if the [Republican/Democratic] Party won very few elections. I can't think of any good reasons why someone would vote for the [Republican/Democratic] Party. Our country would be better off if everyone voted for my party. 1 = Strongly agree, 2 = Agree, 3 = Neither agree nor disagree, 4 = Disagree, 5 = Strongly disagree.

## Social Justice and Solidarity Survey (2020)

**National Solidarity Respect**: An additive scale created from the following questions: We asked you some questions earlier about various issues. Now we're going to ask you questions about people who strongly disagree with you on these issues. How easy or difficult is it for you to respect someone who strongly disagrees with you on . . . Loving the United States (patriotism) . . . Defending religious freedom . . . Gun rights. Response options were very easy to respect, somewhat easy, neither easy nor difficult,

somewhat difficult, and very difficult to respect. The scale ranges from
0 = Low national solidarity respect to 1 = High national solidarity respect
(mean = 0.454, sd = 0.261, alpha = 0.751).

**National Solidarity Worldview**: The national solidarity worldview is an additive scale made up of ten variables. Each of the variables was recoded
so higher scores reflected greater support for national solidarity. The National Solidarity Worldview scale ranges from 0 = Low national solidarity
worldview to 1 = High national solidarity worldview (mean 0.636, sd 0.215,
alpha 0.886).

*Liberty*: If society tries too hard to become a just society, it will undermine liberty. 1 = Strongly agree, 2 = Agree, 3 = Neither agree nor disagree,
4 = Disagree, 5 = Strongly disagree.

One of the most important values we have as Americans is the freedom to do what we want. 1 = Strongly agree, 2 = Agree, 3 = Neither agree
nor disagree, 4 = Disagree, 5 = Strongly disagree.

Americans tend to value both equality and freedom but often value
one somewhat more than the other. What do you think? Where would
you place yourself in terms of valuing equality and freedom? 1 = Value
equality much more than freedom, 2 = Value equality somewhat more
than freedom, 3 = Value freedom somewhat more than equality, 4 = Value
freedom much more than equality.

*History and Criticism*: While our country has some flaws, overall the
United States is a great country. 1 = Strongly agree, 2 = Agree, 3 = Neither
agree nor disagree, 4 = Disagree, 5 = Strongly disagree.

Which comes closer to your view? 1 = The United States has made considerable progress on racial equality since the 1960s, and people should be
patient as progress continues, 2 = The United States has not made nearly
enough progress on racial equality since the 1960s, and our society should
prioritize racial justice.

It's immoral for Americans to criticize the United States. 1 = Strongly
agree, 2 = Agree, 3 = Neither agree nor disagree, 4 = Disagree, 5 = Strongly
disagree.

When people criticize America without recognizing its greatness, they
make us weaker. 1 = Strongly agree, 2 = Agree, 3 = Neither agree nor disagree, 4 = Disagree, 5 = Strongly disagree.

*American identity*: How important is being an American to your identity? 1 = Extremely important, 2 = Very important, 3 = Moderately important, 4 = A little important, 5 = Not at all important.

*National Solidarity Issue Stand and Moralization*[1]: We'd like to know
where you stand on the following issues. How much do you personally

support: Loving the United States (patriotism). 1 = Not at all, 2 = Slightly, 3 = Moderately, 4 = Much, 5 = Very much.

Whether you support or oppose these issues, we'd like to know the extent to which your stand is a reflection of your core moral beliefs; that is, how much are they connected to your fundamental beliefs about right and wrong. How much of a core moral belief is your stand on: Loving the United States (patriotism). 1 = Not at all, 2 = Slightly, 3 = Moderately, 4 = Much, 5 = Very much.

**Recognition Respect**: This is an additive scale created from the following questions: I think we need to do more than tolerate [Democrats/Republicans], we need to respect them. [Democrats/Republicans] should be given respect simply because they are fellow human beings. I struggle a great deal when it comes to respecting [Democrats/Republicans]. [Democrats'/Republicans'] political views make it impossible for me to respect them as people. Response options were strongly agree, agree, neither agree nor disagree, disagree, and strongly disagree. The scale ranges from 0 = Low recognition respect to 1 = High recognition respect (mean = 0.508, sd = 0.224, alpha = 0.761).

**Social Justice Respect**: An additive scale created from the following questions: We asked you some questions earlier about various issues. Now we're going to ask you questions about people who strongly disagree with you on these issues. How easy or difficult is it for you to respect someone who strongly disagrees with you on . . . Combating climate change . . . Ensuring equal access to voting . . . Prioritizing social justice. Response options were very easy to respect, somewhat easy, neither easy nor difficult, somewhat difficult, and very difficult to respect. The scale ranges from 0 = Low social justice respect to 1 = High social justice respect (mean = 0.444, sd = 0.277, alpha = 0.865).

**Social Justice Worldview**: The social justice worldview is an additive scale made up of nine variables. Each of the variables was recoded so higher scores reflected greater support for social justice. The Social Justice Worldview scale ranges from 0 = Low social justice worldview to 1 = High social justice worldview (mean 0.714, sd 0.235, alpha 0.912).

*Social Justice Beliefs*: To what extent do you think the following are important for having justice in a society? . . . Government efforts targeted to improve the lives of groups that are oppressed. 1 = Not at all important, 2 = A little important, 3 = Moderately important, 4 = Very important, 5 = Extremely important.

We're going to ask you some questions about social justice. We use the term *systemic injustice*, which refers to systems and structures that unfairly disadvantage oppressed groups. To achieve a truly just society, society must dismantle systemic racism, sexism, and other forms of systemic injustice. 1 = Strongly agree, 2 = Agree, 3 = Neither agree nor disagree, 4 = Disagree, 5 = Strongly disagree

Achieving a truly just society is not only about individual behavior; it's also about structures and institutions. 1 = Strongly agree, 2 = Agree, 3 = Neither agree nor disagree, 4 = Disagree, 5 = Strongly disagree

*Social Justice Issue Stands*: We'd like to know where you stand on the following issues. How much do you personally support: Combating climate change . . . Ensuring equal access to voting . . . Prioritizing social justice. 1 = Not at all, 2 = Slightly, 3 = Moderately, 4 = Much, 5 = Very much.

*Moralization of Social Justice Issues*: Whether you support or oppose these issues, we'd like to know the extent to which your stand is a reflection of your core moral beliefs; that is, how much are they connected to your fundamental beliefs about right and wrong. How much of a core moral belief is your stand on: Combating climate change . . . Ensuring equal access to voting . . . Prioritizing social justice. 1 = Not at all, 2 = Slightly, 3 = Moderately, 4 = Much, 5 = Very much.

**Tolerance**: [Republicans/Democrats/Republicans and Democrats] should not be allowed to make a public speech in my community. The police should have better opportunities for tapping [Republicans'/Democrats'/Democrats' and Republicans'] phones. [Republicans/Democrats/Democrats and Republicans] should not be allowed to teach in colleges or universities. (1 = Strongly agree, 2 = Agree, 3 = Neither agree nor disagree, 4 = Disagree, 5 = Strongly disagree).

# Appendix D: Regression Results

We provide here the OLS regression results for the figures in chapters 4, 5, and 6, including the main independent variables, interactions, and control variables.

TABLE D.1. Social justice worldview, party identification, and respect (figure 4.4)

|  | Recognition respect | | Social justice respect | |
|---|---|---|---|---|
| Social justice worldview | 0.122*** | −0.324*** | −0.061^ | −0.324*** |
|  | (0.033) | (0.051) | (0.035) | (0.057) |
| Party identification | 0.048** | −0.514*** | 0.106*** | −0.219*** |
|  | (0.017) | (0.053) | (0.018) | (0.058) |
| Social justice worldview × party interaction | — | 0.756*** | — | 0.436*** |
|  |  | (0.067) |  | (0.075) |
| Age | −0.038 | 0.001 | −0.235*** | −0.212*** |
|  | (0.029) | (0.028) | (0.030) | (0.030) |
| Sex (Male) | −0.007 | −0.006 | −0.018 | −0.017 |
|  | (0.014) | (0.013) | (0.014) | (0.014) |
| Race (White) | −0.020 | −0.004 | −0.106*** | −0.099*** |
|  | (0.017) | (0.016) | (0.018) | (0.018) |
| Rural | −0.027 | −0.022 | 0.003 | 0.005 |
|  | (0.017) | (0.016) | (0.017) | (0.017) |
| Education | 0.057* | 0.066* | −0.061* | −0.053^ |
|  | (0.028) | (0.027) | (0.029) | (0.029) |
| Constant | 0.404*** | 0.741*** | 0.674*** | 0.873*** |
|  | (0.032) | (0.043) | (0.035) | (0.048) |
| F | 3.63*** | 19.25*** | 31.63*** | 32.63*** |
| Adj. $R^2$ | 0.015 | 0.106 | 0.136 | 0.157 |
| N | 1,227 | 1,227 | 1,358 | 1,358 |

Source: 2020 Social Justice and Solidarity Survey

Note: Cell entries are unstandardized regression coefficients; standard errors are in parentheses. Party identification is coded 0 = Democrats and leaners, 0.5 = pure Independents, 1 = Republicans and leaners.
$^\wedge p < 0.10$, $^* p < 0.05$, $^{**} p < 0.01$, $^{***} p < 0.001$.

TABLE D.2. National solidarity worldview, party identification, and respect (figure 5.6)

| | Recognition respect | | National solidarity respect | |
|---|---|---|---|---|
| Party identification | 0.010 | 0.704*** | −0.052** | 0.368*** |
| | (0.018) | (0.059) | (0.019) | (0.064) |
| National solidarity worldview | 0.045 | 0.345*** | 0.177*** | 0.359*** |
| | (0.039) | (0.044) | (0.041) | (0.048) |
| National solidarity worldview by party identification interaction | | −0.997*** | | −0.604*** |
| | | (0.082) | | (0.089) |
| Age | −0.037 | 0.000 | −0.285*** | −0.263*** |
| | (0.030) | (0.028) | (0.031) | (0.031) |
| Sex (Male) | −0.007 | −0.003 | 0.006 | 0.007 |
| | (0.014) | (0.013) | (0.014) | (0.014) |
| Race (White) | −0.016 | 0.001 | −0.052** | −0.041* |
| | (0.017) | (0.016) | (0.018) | (0.017) |
| Rural | −0.040* | −0.028^ | −0.004 | 0.003 |
| | (0.017) | (0.016) | (0.018) | (0.017) |
| Education | 0.051^ | 0.053^ | 0.007 | 0.009 |
| | (0.029) | (0.027) | (0.030) | (0.030) |
| Constant | 0.482*** | 0.290*** | 0.531*** | 0.414*** |
| | (0.028) | (0.031) | (0.029) | (0.033) |
| $F$ | 1.84^ | 20.37*** | 25.42*** | 28.89*** |
| Adj. $R^2$ | 0.005 | 0.115 | 0.126 | 0.158 |
| $N$ | 1,191 | 1,191 | 1,191 | 1,191 |

Source: 2020 Social Justice and Solidarity Survey
Note: Cell entries are unstandardized regression coefficients; standard errors are in parentheses. Party identification is coded 0 = Democrats and leaners, 0.5 = pure Independents, 1 = Republicans and leaners.
^$p < 0.10$, *$p < 0.05$, **$p < 0.01$, ***$p < 0.001$.

TABLE D.3. The impact of collective responsibility on judgmentalism (figure 6.2)

| | Judgmentalism toward opposing partisans | | | |
|---|---|---|---|---|
| | Social justice | | National solidarity | |
| Collective responsibility | | | | |
| Social justice responsibility | −0.088^ | 0.241*** | — | — |
| | (0.051) | (0.065) | | |
| National solidarity responsibility | — | — | −0.005 | −0.205*** |
| | | | (0.053) | (0.060) |
| Party identification | −0.024 | 0.438*** | −0.036^ | −0.535*** |
| | (0.019) | (0.062) | (0.020) | (0.075) |
| Collective responsibility × party identification | — | −0.603*** | — | 0.625*** |
| | | (0.077) | | (0.090) |
| Social justice worldview | 0.028 | 0.064 | — | — |
| | (0.052) | (0.051) | | |
| National solidarity worldview | — | — | 0.094^ | 0.106^ |
| | | | (0.057) | (0.056) |
| Age | 0.119*** | 0.091** | 0.109** | 0.093** |
| | (0.033) | (0.033) | (0.034) | (0.033) |
| Race (1 = White) | 0.029 | 0.018 | 0.032^ | 0.020 |
| | (0.019) | (0.019) | (0.019) | (0.019) |
| Sex (1 = Male) | 0.034* | 0.032* | 0.032* | 0.030^ |
| | (0.016) | (0.015) | (0.016) | (0.015) |
| Education | −0.022 | −0.025 | −0.006 | −0.010 |
| | (0.032) | (0.031) | (0.033) | (0.033) |
| Rural | 0.001 | 0.001 | 0.003 | −0.006 |
| | (0.019) | (0.019) | (0.019) | (0.019) |
| Constant | 0.698*** | 0.413*** | 0.597*** | 0.749*** |
| | (0.040) | (0.053) | (0.038) | (0.043) |
| Adj. $R^2$ | 0.023 | 0.069 | 0.021 | 0.059 |
| F | 4.52*** | 10.98*** | 4.24*** | 9.24*** |
| N | 1,208 | | 1,191 | |

Source: 2020 Social Justice and Solidarity Survey

Note: Cell entries are unstandardized regression coefficients; standard errors are in parentheses. Party identification is coded 0 = Democrats and leaners, 1 = Republicans and leaners. ^$p < 0.10$, *$p < 0.05$, **$p < 0.01$, ***$p < 0.001$.

TABLE D.4. The impact of responsibility on recognition respect (figure 6.4)

| | Recognition respect | | | |
| --- | --- | --- | --- | --- |
| | Social justice | | National solidarity | |
| Collective responsibility | | | | |
| Social justice responsibility | 0.249*** | −0.106^ | — | — |
| | (0.045) | (0.056) | | |
| National solidarity responsibility | — | — | 0.074 | 0.270*** |
| | | | (0.047) | (0.052) |
| Party identification | 0.062*** | −0.438*** | 0.009 | 0.500*** |
| | (0.017) | (0.053) | (0.018) | (0.066) |
| Collective responsibility × party identification | — | 0.652*** | — | −0.613*** |
| | | (0.066) | | (0.079) |
| Social justice worldview | −0.056 | −0.096* | — | — |
| | (0.045) | (0.044) | | |
| National solidarity worldview | — | — | −0.004 | −0.016 |
| | | | (0.050) | (0.049) |
| Age | −0.030 | 0.000 | −0.040 | −0.025 |
| | (0.029) | (0.028) | (0.030) | (0.029) |
| Race (1 = White) | −0.019 | −0.007 | −0.013 | 0.000 |
| | (0.017) | (0.016) | (0.017) | (0.017) |
| Sex (1 = Male) | −0.010 | −0.008 | −0.007 | −0.005 |
| | (0.014) | (0.013) | (0.014) | (0.014) |
| Education | 0.053^ | 0.056** | 0.058* | 0.062* |
| | (0.028) | (0.027) | (0.029) | (0.029) |
| Rural | −0.026 | −0.027^ | −0.039* | −0.031^ |
| | (0.017) | (0.016) | (0.017) | (0.017) |
| Constant | 0.340*** | 0.648*** | 0.453*** | 0.304*** |
| | (0.034) | (0.046) | (0.033) | (0.038) |
| $F$ | 7.12*** | 17.59*** | 1.92^ | 8.43*** |
| Adj. $R^2$ | 0.039 | 0.110 | 0.006 | 0.053 |
| $N$ | 1,208 | | 1,191 | |

Source: 2020 Social Justice and Solidarity Survey

Note: Cell entries are unstandardized regression coefficients; standard errors are in parentheses. Party identification is coded 0 = Democrats and leaners, 0.5 = pure Independents, 1 = Republicans and leaners.
^$p < 0.10$, *$p < 0.05$, **$p < 0.01$, ***$p < 0.001$.

TABLE D.5. The impact of judgmentalism on recognition respect (figure 6.6)

|  | Recognition respect | |
| --- | --- | --- |
| Judgmentalism toward opponents | −0.477*** | −0.407*** |
|  | (0.021) | (0.029) |
| Party identification | 0.014 | 0.131*** |
|  | (0.012) | (0.036) |
| Judgmentalism × party identification | — | −0.159*** |
|  |  | (0.046) |
| Age | 0.021 | 0.024 |
|  | (0.025) | (0.025) |
| Race (1 = White) | −0.003 | −0.003 |
|  | (0.014) | (0.014) |
| Sex (1 = Male) | 0.007 | 0.007 |
|  | (0.012) | (0.011) |
| Education | 0.042^ | 0.043^ |
|  | (0.024) | (0.023) |
| Rural | −0.031* | −0.029* |
|  | (0.014) | (0.014) |
| Constant | 0.815*** | 0.762*** |
|  | (0.020) | (0.025) |
| $F$ | 73.65*** | 66.55*** |
| Adj. $R^2$ | 0.293 | 0.300 |
| $N$ | 1,227 | |

Source: 2020 Social Justice and Solidarity Survey
Note: Cell entries are unstandardized regression coefficients; standard errors are in parentheses. Party identification is coded 0 = Democrats and leaners, 1 = Republicans and leaners. ^$p < 0.10$, *$p < 0.05$, **$p < 0.01$, ***$p < 0.001$.

# Notes

## Chapter One

1. There are studies from years ago about how status worked on juries, with white men having the most status and the most influence (Strodtbeck, James, and Hawkins 1957), yet we cannot transpose from a small setting several decades ago to impersonal political settings today. Several decades ago many people preferred their child to marry a person of their own race more than a member of the same political party, but now that is reversed (Alford et al. 2011; Golebiowska 2007; Herman and Campbell 2012; Iyengar, Sood, and Lelkes 2012; Iyengar and Westwood 2015). There is obviously considerable racial stereotyping and discrimination, but there is also considerable political stereotyping and discrimination (Ahler and Sood 2018). We know, for example, that conservatives like and are more tolerant of Black conservatives than of white liberals (Brandt et al. 2014; Chambers, Schlenker, and Collisson 2013).

2. Some political theorists have argued that if toleration means putting up with disliked groups, it is insufficient for liberalism (Forst 2018; Galeotti 2015). We do not dispute that normatively respect has much to recommend it over toleration. We, too, think that racial groups and religious groups should be treated with respect. However, we argue that there is conceptual importance in maintaining a difference between respect and toleration. For the importance of maintaining the commonly accepted (among theorists) conceptual distinction between respect and toleration, see Horton (2011).

3. We say little here about neorepublicanism as espoused by Philip Pettit and others (not the American political party, but a set of ideas inspired by ancient Rome), but there is overlap between republicanism and relational equality, as Pettit (2013, 91) notes. Both theories are interested in the social nature of equality. Pettit argues that one must be treated fairly by the state and by one's fellow citizens: "To enjoy the relevant freedom of non-domination is to be someone who commands a certain standing amongst your fellow citizens."

4. Some structural injustice theorists that do discuss respect include Ypi (2017) and Maboloc (2019).

5. Recognition respect is different from what Darwall (1977) calls "appraisal respect." One might say, for example, that I respect my friend's tennis abilities or my doctor's medical abilities. In this case, I respect someone because of her excellence in a particular pursuit. We are mostly uninterested in appraisal respect in this book.

## Chapter Two

1. Since we do not focus on appraisal respect in this book, we do not explore the difference between philosophers and psychologists on this matter.

2. We hope that all our focus group participants will see that we both praise and criticize our liberal and conservative participants, to whom we are incredibly grateful. While focus groups are not a representative sample, it is certainly possible that our conservative focus group members were less representative of better-educated conservatives as a whole than our liberal focus group members were of better-educated liberals. We note in the text where there is a divergence between our focus group results and our survey results; this divergence occurs a couple of times with conservatives, not with liberals.

3. To be part of a focus group, participants had to self-identify as a liberal/progressive or conservative. We provide the number of participants fully understanding that focus group results cannot be generalized to the population. Later we provide the percentages of coded comments that fall within certain categories, a common approach to analyzing focus group data.

4. We set a quota of 60 percent college-educated respondents and 40 percent holding less than a college degree. The US Census in 2017 showed that just over 34 percent of the American population had a college degree or higher (https://www.census.gov/data/tables/2017/demo/education-attainment/cps-detailed-tables.html).

5. We used the standard 7-point party identification measure (see appendix C). "Democrats" are those who said they were strong or not strong Democrats or that they were Independents but leaned toward the Democratic Party. "Republicans" include strong, not strong, and leaning Republicans.

6. The meaning of equality was asked in all conservative groups (thirty-five people) and eleven out of thirteen liberal groups (eighty-four people). In one liberal group (eight people), the meaning of equality question was answered by one person, and everyone else agreed. This was coded as one person speaking. See appendix A for information on coding the focus group transcripts.

7. To test if this is just an artifact of the liberal groups having more respondents, and potentially a longer conversation about equality that would bring in more concepts, we looked at the four smallest liberal groups (an average of 5.75 participants, compared to 5.83 for the conservative groups). The results are very similar to the liberal groups listed in table 2.1, with all categories increasing 1 or 2 points except for equal opportunity, which decreased 6 points.

8. We are deeply grateful to Marc Hetherington and Tim Ryan for allowing us to put some questions on their PFUNC survey. PFUNC is a rolling panel study. The surveys were fielded by Qualtrics to respondents selected to match census benchmarks. We used data from Wave 6, which was fielded in August 2021.

9. The American National Election Studies (www.electionstudies.org); these materials are based on work supported by the National Science Foundation under grant numbers SES 1444721, 2014–2017, the University of Michigan, and Stanford University.

## Chapter Three

1. The two political issues were social justice and national solidarity. See Appendix B for a full description of the experiment.

2. The difference in responses for the willingness to read between those who agree and those who disagree is highly significant ($t = -4.4$, $p < .001$ for a one-sided t-test). The difference is within the more lenient $p < .10$ range for the willingness to talk ($t = -1.31$, p=.096).

3. These results mirror those of a Pew Research Center poll (Gramlich 2016).

4. The question wording was "We are interested now in your thoughts about people who voted for [Donald Trump/Hillary Clinton] for president in 2016. Please let us know the extent to which you agree or disagree with these characterizations. People who voted for [Donald Trump/Hillary Clinton] in the 2016 presidential election are" followed by the term. Response options were Strongly agree, Agree, Neither agree nor disagree, Disagree, Strongly disagree.

5. The question was "Continuing to focus on the presidential election of 2016, did the election of Donald Trump have a negative impact on any of your relationships with close friends or family members?" Response options were Yes or No. The percentages answering yes were: 20–39 year old Clinton voters 48 percent; 40 or older Clinton voters 30 percent; 20–39 year old Trump voters 45 percent; 40 and older Trump voters 16 percent.

## Chapter Four

1. Throughout this chapter and the next, we often assert that Democrats believe this and Republicans believe that. Of course, not *all* Democrats or Republicans believe anything. Rather than tempering our assertions with "most" or "tend to," we simply make the assertions with the understanding that some partisans disagree with their copartisans. Indeed, one of our findings is that the more partisans agree with the outparty, the more respect they have for opposing partisans.

2. Good criticisms of Hayek's view of social justice include Dworkin (1981); Lukes (1997); Tebble (2009). A similar view to Hayek is Burke (2011).

3. The work of Sally Haslanger (2012, ch. 11) on structural injustice was also pioneering.

4. This critique misses out on the radicalism of Rawls's (2001) later arguments, but we will let others explain and defend Rawls (Freeman 2009). Still, the idea of structural injustice is not present in Rawls in an obvious way.

5. People also seriously underestimate the diversity of opinion within their own group and within the outgroup (Dias, Pearl, and Lelkes n.d.). We did not ask about diversity of opinions within opposing partisan groups, but our focus group and survey results suggest that people perceive opposing partisans to be homogeneous in their views when they are not.

6. This is contrary to Jonathan Haidt's (2012) moral foundations theory, which shows large differences in liberals' and conservatives' moralization of issues.

7. Where significant differences do arise is in strength of partisanship: people who identify strongly as Democrats or Republicans are much more likely than weak partisans or Independents to hold issues with moral conviction (Ryan 2014; Skitka, Bauman, and Sargis 2005).

8. All the regression models include age, race, gender, rural, and education as control variables. See appendix D for the full results.

9. For the purposes of making figure 4.5, we set "high social justice worldview" at 1 and "low social justice worldview" at 0.244, which is 2 standard deviations below the mean. We did this to give a more realistic picture of the impact of the interaction on respect since no one scored 0 on social justice worldview.

## Chapter Five

1. It is important to note that these views are contested by Americans (Citrin, Wong, and Duff 2001; Schildkraut 2005).

2. When forced to acknowledge a criticism, strong identifiers are more likely to defend the group and rationalize its actions and to feel less guilt about their group's bad behavior, preferring to focus on the positive and downplay the negative (Doosje et al. 1998). Part of the motivation for this is that people want to be members of highly esteemed groups, since they gain a sense of reflected esteem from being a member of such a group; national groups are especially potent in this regard (Spinner-Halev and Theiss-Morse 2003). In the United States, children are taught to view the country's founders as revered heroes and, since histories are written by the winners, textbooks give a positive spin on historical events. National successes are highlighted and celebrated, whereas national failures are often ignored (Doosje, Ellemers, and Spears 1999; Branscombe et al. 1999).

3. Libertarians often favor open borders (Hidalgo 2015; Sager 2020; Kukathas 2021).

4. The exact question wording was as follows: "Many conservatives argue that a key task of a sovereign state is to protect its border and that the US government should therefore work to prevent people from illegally overstaying their visas or crossing into the United States illegally. This does not necessarily mean building a wall, but there are several ways in which we can do more to protect our border. Should we do so?"

5. All the models included control variables for age, race, gender, rural, and education. See appendix D, table D.2 for the full results. For the purposes of making figure 5.7, we set "high national solidarity worldview" at 1 and "low national solidarity worldview" at 0.205, which is 2 standard deviations below the mean. We did this to give a more realistic picture of the impact of the interaction on respect since no one scored 0 on the national solidarity worldview.

## Chapter Six

1. There is a large literature on corporate social responsibility (see, e.g., Crane et al. 2008; McWilliams, Siegel, and Wright 2006). The term *social responsibility* is used by social scientists to denote the idea that people have a responsibility to pursue the interests of the collective, not only their own self-interests (see, e.g., van Dijk and Wilke 1997; Molenmaker, de Kwaadsteniet, and van Dijk 2014) or the interests of those less fortunate in a society (see, e.g., Bobo 1991). Corporate social responsibility is about businesses having this responsibility.

2. The research on collective action problems, free riders, public goods dilemmas, and common resource dilemmas is extensive (see, e.g., Brewer and Kramer 1986; Dawes 1980; Fehr and Gächter 2000; Hardin 1968; Olson 1965; Orbell and Dawes 1981; Ostrom 1990; van Dijk and Wilke 1995).

3. Moral foundations theory has faced many criticisms (see, e.g., Gray and Keeney 2015; Hatemi, Crabtree, and Smith 2019; Kugler, Jost, and Noorbaloochi 2014; Smith et al. 2017; Suhler and Churchland 2011).

4. The model Janoff-Bulman and Carnes (2013) develop also includes two types of moral regulation system. Proscriptive moral regulation is avoidance oriented in the sense that people want to inhibit or protect something. It lets people know what they should not do and therefore inhibits people's actions and protects them from harm. Prescriptive moral regulation is approach oriented and involves people wanting to provide. It encourages people to do what they should do and therefore promotes helping behaviors and well-being. At the self-level, proscriptive morality leads to self-restraint and moderation, whereas prescriptive morality leads to industriousness. At the interpersonal level, proscriptive morality leads to harm avoidance, whereas prescriptive morality leads to helping and fairness. Liberals and conservatives hold both prescriptive and

proscriptive motivations at these two levels. Liberals and conservatives diverge at the group level, where liberals are more focused on prescriptive morality and conservatives on proscriptive morality.

5. Smith et al. (2011, 372) argue that people hold "bedrock principles" concerning how societies should be organized. The bedrock political issues include "leadership, defense, punishment of norm violators, devotion to traditional behavioral standards, and distribution of resources" and cover people's beliefs about how society works best. We focus specifically on social justice and national solidarity worldviews, but agree that people vary in how they think society ought to work.

6. Some of Young's early articles on the subject are Young (2004; 2006b; 2009); her penultimate argument on the topic is Young (2011).

7. Young does not deny individual responsibility in what she called the liability model of responsibility—if I rob a bank, I am responsible for that action. Structural injustice does not replace the idea of individual liability but is an additional kind of injustice that leads to an additional kind of responsibility.

8. While nationalism is now often associated with conservatism, its explosion in nineteenth-century Europe was associated with liberalism: the revolts against the monarchs and emperors were led by liberal nationalists looking to free their people. Today there are liberal and conservative defenders of nationalism and liberal and conservative critics of nationalism (though most of the conservative critics are libertarian). There are also other functionalist explanations of national identity that explain why the nation-state is so much part of the modern world (Anderson 1991; Gellner 1983). While there are similarities between liberal and conservative defenses of the nation, we focus here on the conservative defense (liberal defenses include Miller [1995] and Tamir [1993, 2019]).

9. See, for example, https://www.kff.org/coronavirus-covid-19/poll-finding/kff-covid-19-vaccine-monitor-july-2021/.

## Chapter Seven

1. Hobbes (1994 [1651]) says in chapter 13 of the *Leviathan*: "That which may perhaps make such equality incredible is but a vain conceit of one's own wisdom, which almost all men think they have in a greater degree than the vulgar; that is, than all men but themselves, and a few others, whom by fame, or for concurring with themselves, they approve. For such is the nature of men that howsoever they may acknowledge many others to be more witty, or more eloquent or more learned, yet they will hardly believe there be many so wise as themselves; for they see their own wit at hand, and other men's at a distance."

2. The rise of liberal egalitarianism, with Rawls at its center, is traced in Katrina Forrester's book, *In the Shadow of Justice*. What Rawls began, Forrester (2019) argues, is the placement of equality at the center of liberal discussions of justice. A few years later, the influential theorist Ronald Dworkin argued that equality was the "nerve of liberalism" (130). A few years after that, Amartya Sen (1980) began the "equality of what" debate (see also Forrester 2019, 208).

3. Rawls argues for the importance of mutual respect, and one can plausibly interpret the early Rawls as suggesting that we respect the rational, regardless of their views, to pursue their interests. For Rawls, the second principle is a matter of institutions, not an ethical principle guiding everyday behavior.

4. Relational egalitarians do not supply any evidence that income disparity leads to disrespect (Ryan and Spinner-Halev 2022).

5. Both Wolff (2010) and Cohen (2001) use the term *egalitarian ethos*, though our use of the term is modestly different.

6. George Crowder (2002) makes a similar argument about context and pluralism, though he does not privilege egalitarianism (or liberty).

7. We pass over responsiveness, one of Saffon and Urbinati's criteria, since it is not relevant to our argument about respect.

8. In her book on democracy, Urbinati's (2014, 53–58) discussion of wealth inequality focuses on limiting the effects of money on politics. The effects of money on politics is too far afield for us to comment on it.

9. We add the acceptance of losing, but we think that it is consistent with Saffon and Urbinati's argument. The importance of this criterion should be obvious in the aftermath of the 2020 American presidential election.

10. Thanks to Alex Kirshner and Barb Frank for suggesting this argument.

11. We have in mind here parties that are inspired by the Klu Klux Klan or the Nazis.

12. Maskivker use justice and the common good interchangeably, but because justice is associated with egalitarianism, we argue that citizens need only vote from their conception of the common good.

13. Both authors of this book have written about groups of all kinds.

14. There is evidence that status differences do translate into differences in how much people pay attention to one another, but those status differences do not directly track with income or wealth (Ryan and Spinner-Halev 2022).

## Chapter Eight

1. We repeat here what we said in chapter 2: it was quite hard to recruit conservative focus group participants, which means that our conservative focus group participants could be different in important ways from conservatives who refused to talk with us. Conservatives who distrust academics the most were not likely to want to spend an hour and a half talking with us. Taking ten minutes to answer survey questions anonymously is obviously more palatable.

## Appendix C

1. We use only the "Loving the United States (patriotism)" issue from this battery because the two excluded issues (defending religious freedom and gun rights) are liberty issues. We cover attitudes toward liberty with the three questions described above and we did not want to have this worldview measure too heavily focused on liberty. When we ran the results on respect using a worldview measure containing all three national solidarity issues and their moralization, the results are even stronger than those discussed in chapter 5.

# References

Abbey, Ruth, and Jeff Spinner-Halev. 2013. "Rawls, Mill and the Puzzle of Political Liberalism." *Journal of Politics* 75 (1): 124–36.

Abramowitz, Alan I., and Kyle L. Saunders. 2008. "Is Polarization a Myth?" *Journal of Politics* 70 (2): 542–55.

Abrams, Dominic, Margaret Wetherell, Sandra Cochrane, Michael A. Hogg, and John C. Turner. 1990. "Knowing What to Think By Knowing Who You Are: Self-Categorization and the Nature of Norm Formation, Conformity and Group Polarization." *British Journal of Social Psychology* 29 (2): 97–119.

Ackerly, Brooke A. 2018. *Just Responsibility*. Oxford: Oxford University Press.

Adelman, Levi, and Nilanjana Dasgupta. 2019. "Effect of Threat and Social Identity on Reactions to Ingroup Criticism: Defensiveness, Openness, and a Remedy." *Personality and Social Psychology Bulletin* 45 (5): 740–53.

Ahler, Douglas J. 2014. "Self-Fulfilling Misperceptions of Public Polarization." *Journal of Politics* 76 (3): 607–20.

Ahler, Douglas J., and Gaurav Sood. 2018. "The Parties in Our Heads: Misperceptions about Party Composition and Their Consequences." *Journal of Politics* 80 (3): 964–81.

———. 2022. "Typecast: A Routine Mental Shortcut Causes Party Stereotyping." *Political Behavior*. https://doi.org/10.1007/s11109-022-09780-8.

Alford, John R., Peter K. Hatemi, John R. Hibbing, Nicholas G. Martin, and Lindon J. Eaves. 2011. "The Politics of Mate Choice." *Journal of Politics* 73 (2): 362–79.

Anderson, Benedict. 1991. *Imagined Communities: Reflections on the Origins and Spread of Nationalism*. London: Verso.

Anderson, Elizabeth S. 1999. "What Is the Point of Equality?" *Ethics* 109 (2): 287–337.

———. 2008. "How Should Egalitarians Cope with Market Risks?" *Theoretical Inquiries in Law* 9 (1): 239–70.

———. 2012. "Equality: A Distributive Principle or an Ideal of Social Relations?" In *The Oxford Handbook of Political Philosophy*, edited by David Estlund, 40–56. Oxford: Oxford University Press.

Arnold, Samuel. 2012. "The Difference Principle at Work." *Journal of Political Philosophy* 20 (1): 94–118.

Ashton, Michael C., Henry A. Danso, Gregory R. Maio, Victoria M. Esses, Michael Harris Bond, and Doris Ka Yi Keung. 2005. "Two Dimensions of Political Attitudes and Their Individual Difference Correlates: A Cross-Culture Perspective." In *Culture and Social Behavior*, edited by Richard M. Sorrentino, Dov Cohen, James M. Olsen, and Mark P. Zanna, 1–30. New York: Psychology Press.

Atenasio, David. 2019. "Blameless Participation in Structural Injustice." *Social Theory and Practice* 45 (2): 149–77.

Attwell, Katie, David T. Smith, and Paul R. Ward. 2021. "'If Your Child's Vaccinated, Why Do You Care about Mine?' Rhetoric, Responsibility, Power and Vaccine Rejection." *Journal of Sociology* 57 (2): 268–85.

Avery, Patricia G. 2002. "Teaching Tolerance: What Research Tells Us." *Social Education* 66 (5): 270–75.

Avery, Patricia G., John L. Sullivan, and Sandra L. Wood. 1997. "Teaching for Tolerance of Diverse Beliefs." *Theory into Practice* 36 (1): 32–38.

Baatz, Christian. 2014. "Climate Change and Individual Duties to Reduce GHG Emissions." *Ethics, Policy & Environment* 17 (1): 1–19.

Bandura, Albert. 2015. *Moral Disengagement: How People Do Harm and Live with Themselves.* New York: Macmillan Higher Education.

———. 2017. "Moral Disengagement in the Perpetration of Inhumanities." In *Recent Developments in Criminological Theory*, 135–52. New York: Routledge.

Banks, Melany. 2013. "Individual Responsibility for Climate Change." *Southern Journal of Philosophy* 51 (1): 42–66.

Bastian, Brock, Simon M. Laham, Sam Wilson, Nick Haslam, and Peter Koval. 2011. "Blaming, Praising, and Protecting Our Humanity: The Implications of Everyday Dehumanization for Judgments of Moral Status." *British Journal of Social Psychology* 50 (3): 469–83.

Bejan, Teresa M. 2017. *Mere Civility.* Cambridge, MA: Harvard University Press.

Bellah, Robert N., Richard Madsen, William Sullivan, Ann Swidler, and Stephen M. Tipton. 1985. *Habits of the Heart: Individualism and Commitment in American Life.* Berkeley: University of California Press.

Berlin, Isaiah. 1969. *Four Essays on Liberty.* Oxford: Oxford University Press.

Björnsson, Gunnar. 2021. "On Individual and Shared Obligations: In Defense of the Activist's Perspective." In *Philosophy and Climate Change*, edited by Mark Budolfson, Tristram McPherson, and David Plunkett, 251–80, Oxford: Oxford University Press.

Blake, Michael. 2019. *Justice, Migration, and Mercy.* Oxford: Oxford University Press.

Bobo, Lawrence. 1991. "Social Responsibility, Individualism, and Redistributive Policies." *Sociological Forum* 6 (1): 71–92.

Bond, Robert M., Hillary C. Shulman, and Michael Gilbert. 2018. "Does Having a Political Discussion Help or Hurt Intergroup Perceptions? Drawing Guidance from Social Identity Theory and the Contact Hypothesis." *International Journal of Communication* 12:4332–52.

Bows-Larkin, Alice, Sarah L. Mander, Michael B. Traut, Kevin L. Anderson, and F. Ruth Wood. 2016. "Aviation and Climate Change—The Continuing Challenge." *Encyclopedia of Aerospace Engineering* (May): 1–11.

Brandt, Mark J., Christine Reyna, John R. Chambers, Jarret T. Crawford, and Geoffrey Wetherell. 2014. "The Ideological-Conflict Hypothesis: Intolerance among Both Liberals and Conservatives." *Current Directions in Psychological Science* 23 (1): 27–34.

Brandt, Mark J., Geoffrey Wetherell, and Jarret T. Crawford. 2016. "Moralization and Intolerance of Ideological Outgroups." In *The Social Psychology of Morality*, edited by Joseph P. Forgas, Lee J. Jussim, and Paul A. M. Van Lange, 239–56. New York: Psychology Press.

Brandt, Mark J., Daniel C. Wisneski, and Linda J. Skitka. 2015. "Moralization and the 2012 U.S. Presidential Election Campaign." *Journal of Social and Political Psychology* 3 (2): 211–37.

Branscombe, Nyla R., Naomi Ellemers, Russell Spears, and Bertjan Doosje. 1999. "The Context and Content of Social Identity Threat." In *Social Identity: Context, Commitment, Content*, edited by Naomi Ellemers, Russell Spears, and Bertjan Doosje, 36–58. Oxford: Blackwell.

Brettschneider, Corey. 2010. "A Transformative Theory of Religious Freedom: Promoting the Reasons for Rights." *Political Theory* 38 (2): 187–213.

Brewer, Marilynn B., and Roderick M. Kramer. 1986. "Choice Behavior in Social Dilemmas: Effects of Social Identity, Group Size, and Decision Framing." *Journal of Personality and Social Psychology* 50 (3): 543–49.

Brooks, Deborah Jordan, and John G. Geer. 2007. "Beyond Negativity: The Effects of Incivility on the Electorate." *American Journal of Political Science* 51 (1): 1–16.

Brown, Rupert. 2000. *Group Processes: Dynamics within and between Groups*. Oxford: Blackwell.

Burke, Thomas Patrick. 2011. *The Concept of Justice*. New York: Bloomsbury.

Bursztyn, Leonardo, and David Y. Yang. 2022. "Misperceptions about Others." *Annual Review of Economics* 14:425–52.

Butters, Ross, and Christopher Hare. 2020. "Polarized Networks? New Evidence on American Voters' Political Discussion Networks." *Political Behavior* 44 (3): 1079–103.

Carens, Joseph. 2013. *The Ethics of Immigration*. Oxford: Oxford University Press.

Carlin, Ryan E., and Gregory J. Love. 2018. "Political Competition, Partisanship and Interpersonal Trust in Electoral Democracies." *British Journal of Political Science* 48 (1): 115–39.

Carlson, Taylor N., and Jaime E. Settle. 2022. *What Goes without Saying: Navigating Political Discussion in America*. New York: Cambridge University Press.

Carnes, Nate, and Ronnie Janoff-Bulman. 2012. "Harm, Help, and the Nature of (Im)Moral (In) Action." *Psychological Inquiry* 23 (2): 127–42.

Cassese, Erin C. 2021. "Partisan Dehumanization in American Politics." *Political Behavior* 43:29–50.

Ceva, Emanuela. 2015. "Why Toleration Is Not the Appropriate Response to Dissenting Minorities' Claims." *European Journal of Philosophy* 23 (3): 633–51.

Ceva, Emanuela, and Federico Zuolo. 2013. "A Matter of Respect: On Majority-Minority Relations in a Liberal Democracy." *Journal of Applied Philosophy* 30 (3): 239–53.

Chambers, John R., Barry R. Schlenker, and Brian Collisson. 2013. "Ideology and Prejudice: The Role of Value Conflicts." *Psychological Science* 24 (2): 140–49.

Chen, M. Keith, and Ryne Rohla. 2018. "The Effect of Partisanship and Political Advertising on Close Family Ties." *Science* 360 (6392): 1020–24.

Cherniss, Joshua L. 2021. *Liberalism in Dark Times: The Liberal Ethos in the Twentieth Century*. Princeton, NJ: Princeton University Press.

Choi, Heesook. 2022. "How Partisan Cable News Mobilizes Viewers: Partisan Media, Discussion Networks and Political Participation." *Journal of Broadcasting & Electronic Media* 66 (1): 129–52.

Christiano, Thomas. 2008. *The Constitution of Equality: Democratic Authority and Its Limits*. Oxford: Oxford University Press.

Citrin, Jack, Cara Wong, and Brian Duff. 2001. "The Meaning of American National Identity: Patterns of Ethnic Conflict and Consensus." In *Social Identity, Intergroup Conflict, and Conflict*

*Reduction*, edited by Richard D. Ashmore, Lee J. Jussim, and David Wilder, 71–100. Oxford: Oxford University Press.

Clifford, Scott. 2017. "Individual Differences in Group Loyalty Predict Partisan Strength." *Political Behavior* 39: 531–52.

Cohen, Andrew Jason. 2014. *Toleration.* Cambridge: Polity.

Cohen, G. A. 2001. *If You're an Egalitarian, How Come You're So Rich?* Cambridge, MA: Harvard University Press.

Cramer, Katherine J. 2016. *The Politics of Resentment: Rural Consciousness in Wisconsin and the Rise of Scott Walker.* Chicago: University of Chicago Press.

Crane, Andrew, Dirk Matten, Abagail McWilliams, Jeremy Moon, and Donald S. Siegel, eds. 2008. *The Oxford Handbook of Corporate Social Responsibility.* Oxford: Oxford University Press.

Crick, Bernard. 1993. *In Defence of Politics.* Chicago: University of Chicago Press.

Crowder, George. 2002. *Liberalism and Value Pluralism.* New York: Bloomsbury.

Darwall, Stephen L. 1977. "Two Kinds of Respect." *Ethics* 88 (1): 36–49.

Dawes, Robyn M. 1980. "Social Dilemmas." *Annual Review of Psychology* 31:169–93.

Deveaux, Monique. 1998. "Toleration and Respect." *Public Affairs Quarterly* 12 (4): 407–27.

Dias, Nicholas C., Jacob Pearl, and Yphtach Lelkes. n.d. American Partisans Misperceive the Diversity, Not the Extremity, of Other Partisans' Attitudes." Unpublished manuscript.

Doosje, Bertjan, Nyla R. Branscombe, Russell Spears, and Antony S. R. Manstead. 1998. "Guilty by Association: When One's Group Has a Negative History." *Journal of Personality and Social Psychology* 75:872–86.

Doosje, Bertjan, Naomi Ellemers, and Russell Spears. 1999. "Commitment and Intergroup Behaviour." In *Social Identity: Context, Commitment, Content*, edited by Naomi Ellemers, Russell Spears, and Bertjan Doosje, 84–106. Oxford: Blackwell.

Druckman, James N., and Matthew S. Levendusky. 2019. "What Do We Measure When We Measure Affective Polarization?" *Public Opinion Quarterly* 83 (1): 114–22.

Dunn, Amina. 2020. "As the U.S. Copes with Multiple Crises, Partisans Disagree Sharply on Severity of Problems Facing the Nation." Pew Research Center (July 14), https://www.pew research.org/fact-tank/2020/07/14/as-the-u-s-copes-with-multiple-crises-partisans-dis agree-sharply-on-severity-of-problems-facing-the-nation/.

Dworkin, Ronald. 1981. "What Is Equality? Part 2: Equality of Resources." *Philosophy and Public Affairs* 10 (4): 283–345.

Economic Policy Institute. 2009. "Bipartisanship for Buy American." https://www.epi.org/publi cation/bipartisanship_for_buy_america/. Accessed January 31, 2023.

Edmondson, Catie. 2023. "Here Are the House Republicans to Watch if McCarthy's Bid for Speaker Falters." *New York Times.* January 2, 2023. https://www.nytimes.com/2023/01/02/us /politics/mccarthy-speaker-alternatives.html. Accessed January 3, 2023.

Eliasoph, Nina. 1998. *Avoiding Politics: How Americans Produce Apathy in Everyday Life.* Cambridge: Cambridge University Press.

Ellemers, Naomi, Bertjan Doosje, and Russell Spears. 2004. "Sources of Respect: The Effects of Being Liked by Ingroups and Outgroups." *European Journal of Social Psychology* 34 (2): 155–72.

Ellemers, Naomi, Stefano Pagliaro, and Manuela Barreto. 2013. "Morality and Behavioural Regulation in Groups: A Social Identity Approach." *European Review of Social Psychology* 24 (1): 160–93.

Ellemers, Naomi, Russell Spears, and Bertjan Doosje, eds. 1999. *Social Identity: Context, Commitment, Content.* Oxford: Blackwell.

Ellemers, Naomi, and Jojanneke Van der Toorn. 2015. "Groups as Moral Anchors." *Current Opinion in Psychology* 6:189–94.

Enders, Adam, Christina Farhart, Joanne Miller, Joseph Uscinski, Kyle Saunders, and Hugo Drochon. 2022. "Are Republicans and Conservatives More Likely to Believe Conspiracy Theories?" *Political Behavior,* https://doi.org/10.1007/s11109-022-09812-3.

Endres, Kyle, and Costas Panagopoulos. 2017. "Boycotts, Buycotts, and Political Consumerism in America." *Research & Politics* (October–December): 1–9.

Estlund, David. 2019. *Utopophobia.* Princeton, NJ: Princeton University Press.

Fahlquist, Jessica Nihlén. 2009. "Moral Responsibility for Environmental Problems—Individual or Institutional." *Journal of Agricultural and Environmental Ethics* 22 (2): 109–24.

Fehr, Ernst, and Simon Gächter. 2000. "Cooperation and Punishment in Public Goods Experiments." *American Economic Review* 90 (4): 980–94.

Feinberg, Matthew, Chloe Kovacheff, Rimma Teper, and Yoel Inbar. 2019. "Understanding the Process of Moralization: How Eating Meat Becomes a Moral Issue." *Journal of Personality and Social Psychology* 117 (1): 50–72.

Feldman, Stanley. 1988. "Structure and Consistency in Public Opinion: The Role of Core Beliefs and Values." *American Journal of Political Science* 32 (2): 416–40.

Feldman, Stanley, and John Zaller. 1992. "The Political Culture of Ambivalence: Ideological Responses to the Welfare State." *American Journal of Political Science* 36 (1): 268–307.

Fernandes, Daniel. 2020. "Politics at the Mall: The Moral Foundations of Boycotts." *Journal of Public Policy & Marketing* 39 (4): 494–513.

Finkel, Eli J., Christopher A. Bail, Mina Cikara, Peter H. Ditto, Shanto Iyengar, Samara Klar, Lilliana Mason, Mary C. McGrath, Brendan Nyhan, David G. Rand, Linda J. Skitka, Joshua A. Tucker, Jay J. Van Bavel, Cynthia S. Wang, and James N. Druckman. 2020. "Political Sectarianism in America." *Science* 370 (6516): 533–36.

Fiorina, Morris P. 1981. *Retrospective Voting in American National Elections.* New Haven, CT: Yale University Press.

Fitzgerald, Maggie. 2019. "Black and Hispanic Unemployment Is at a Record Low." CNBC (October 4), https://www.cnbc.com/2019/10/04/black-and-hispanic-unemployment-is-at-a-record-low.html.

Forrester, Katrina. 2019. *In the Shadow of Justice.* Princeton, NJ: Princeton University Press.

Forst, Rainer. 2018. "Toleration, Justice and Reason." In *The Culture of Toleration in Diverse Societies,* edited by Catriona McKinnon, and Dario Castiglione, 71–85. Manchester: Manchester University Press.

Foster-Frau, Silvia, and Sabrina Rodriguez. 2022. "Racial Breakdowns for Midterms Expose Shifting Electorate." *Washington Post.* https://www.washingtonpost.com/nation/2022/11/11/black-asian-latino-voter-turnout/. Accessed November 11, 2022.

Fourie, Carina. 2012. "What Is Social Equality? An Analysis of Status Equality as a Strongly Egalitarian Ideal." *Res Publica* 18 (2): 107–26.

Fourie, Carina, Fabian Schuppert, and Ivo Wallimann-Helmer. 2015. *Social Equality: On What It Means to be Equals.* Oxford: Oxford University Press.

Freeman, Samuel. 2009. *Justice and the Social Contract: Essays on Rawlsian Political Philosophy.* Oxford: Oxford University Press.

Gabrielson, Teena, Cheryl Hall, John M. Meyer, and David Schlosberg, eds. 2016. *Responsibility for Climate Change as a Structural Injustice*. Oxford: Oxford University Press.

Gaertner, Samuel L., John F. Dovidio, Phyllis A. Anastasio, Betty A. Bachman, and Mary C. Rust. 1993. "The Common Ingroup Identity Model: Recategorization and the Reduction of Intergroup Bias." *European Review of Social Psychology* 4 (1): 1–26.

Galeotti, Anna Elisabetta. 2015. "The Range of Toleration: From Toleration as Recognition Back to Disrespectful Tolerance." *Philosophy & Social Criticism* 41 (2): 93–110.

Galston, William. 1999. "Value Pluralism and Liberal Political Theory." *American Political Science Review* 93 (4): 769–78.

———. 2002. *Liberal Pluralism: The Implications of Value Pluralism for Political Theory and Practice*. Cambridge: Cambridge University Press.

———. 2009. "Moral Pluralism and Liberal Democracy: Isaiah Berlin's Heterodox Liberalism." *Review of Politics* 71 (1): 85–99.

Gellner, Ernest. 1983. *Nations and Nationalism*. Ithaca, NY: Cornell University Press.

Gibson, James L., and Richard D. Bingham. 1982. "On the Conceptualization and Measurement of Political Tolerance." *American Political Science Review* 76 (3): 603–20.

Giubilini, Alberto. 2021. "Vaccination Ethics." *British Medical Bulletin* 137 (1): 4–12.

Golebiowska, Ewa A. 2007. "The Contours and Etiology of Whites' Attitudes toward Black-White Interracial Marriage." *Journal of Black Studies* 38 (2): 268–87.

Gosepath, Stefan. 2021. "Equality." *Stanford Encyclopedia of Philosophy* (Summer Edition), Edward N. Zalta (ed.), https://plato.stanford.edu/archives/sum2021/entries/equality/. Accessed February 5, 2023.

Graham, Jesse, Jonathan Haidt, Sena Koleva, Matt Motyl, Ravi Iyer, Sean P. Wojcik, and Peter H. Ditto. 2013. "Moral Foundations Theory: The Pragmatic Validity of Moral Pluralism." In *Advances in Experimental Social Psychology*, Volume 47, edited by Patricia Devine and Ashby Plant, 55–130. San Diego, CA: Academic Press.

Graham, Jesse, Jonathan Haidt, and Brian A. Nosek. 2009. "Liberals and Conservatives Rely on Different Sets of Moral Foundations." *Journal of Personality and Social Psychology* 96 (5): 1029–46.

Graham, Jesse, Brian A. Nosek, and Jonathan Haidt. 2012. "The Moral Stereotypes of Liberals and Conservatives: Exaggeration of Differences across the Political Spectrum." *PLoS ONE* 7 (12), doi.org/10.1371/journal.pone.0050092.

Graham, Jesse, Brian A. Nosek, Jonathan Haidt, Ravi Iyer, Spassena Koleva, and Peter H. Ditto. 2011. "Mapping the Moral Domain." *Journal of Personal and Social Psychology* 101 (2): 366–85.

Gramlich, John. 2016. "It's Harder for Clinton Supporters to Respect Trump Backers Than Vice Versa." Pew Research Center, November 1, 2016. https://www.pewresearch.org/fact -tank/2016/11/01/its-harder-for-clinton-supporters-to-respect-trump-backers-than-vice -versa/. Accessed February 4, 2023.

Gray, John. 2020. *Isaiah Berlin: An Interpretation of His Thought*. Princeton, NJ: Princeton University Press.

Gray, Kurt, and Jonathan E. Keeney. 2015. "Disconfirming Moral Foundations Theory on Its Own Terms: Reply to Graham (2015)." *Social Psychological and Personality Science* 6 (8): 874–77.

Grossman, Matthew, Adam Anders, and Joseph Uscinski. 2021. "Conspiracy Beliefs Are Not Increasing Nor Exclusive to the Right." Niskanen Center, https://www.niskanencenter.org /conspiracy-beliefs-are-not-increasing-or-exclusive-to-the-right/. Accessed December 9, 2023.

Gutmann, Amy, and Dennis Thompson. 1996. *Democracy and Disagreement: Why Moral Conflict Cannot Be Avoided in Politics and What Should Be Done about It*. Cambridge, MA: Harvard University Press.

Haider-Markel, Donald P. 2005. "Morality Policy and Individual-Level Political Behavior: The Case of Legislative Voting on Lesbian and Gay Issues." *Policy Studies Journal* 27 (4): 735–49.

Haidt, Jonathan. 2001. "The Emotional Dog and Its Rational Tail: A Social Intuitionist Approach to Moral Judgment." *Psychological Review* 108 (4): 814–34.

———. 2012. *The Righteous Mind: Why Good People Are Divided by Politics and Religion*. New York: Pantheon.

Haidt, Jonathan, and Jesse Graham. 2007. "When Morality Opposes Justice: Conservatives Have Moral Intuitions That Liberals May Not Recognize." *Social Justice Research* 20 (1): 98–116.

Hardin, Garrett. 1968. "The Tragedy of the Commons: The Population Problem Has No Technical Solution; it Requires a Fundamental Extension in Morality." *Science* 162 (3859): 1243–48.

Hartman, Rachel, Will Blakey, Jake Womick, Chris Bail, Eli J. Finkel, Hahrie Han, John Sarrouf, Juliana Schroeder, Paschal Sheeran, Jay J. Van Bavel, Robb Willer, and Kurt Gray. 2022. "Interventions to Reduce Partisan Animosity." *Nature Human Behaviour* 6 (9): 1194–205.

Haslanger, Sally. 2012. *Resisting Reality*. Oxford: Oxford University Press.

Hatemi, Peter K., Charles Crabtree, and Kevin B. Smith. 2019. "Ideology Justifies Morality: Political Beliefs Predict Moral Foundations." *American Journal of Political Science* 63 (4): 788–806.

Hayek, Friedrich A. 1945. "The Use of Knowledge in Society." *American Economic Review* 35 (4): 519–30.

———. 1976. *Law, Liberty, and Legislation*. Vol. 2. Chicago: University of Chicago Press.

Hayward, Clarissa Rile. 2003. "The Difference States Make: Democracy, Identity, and the American City." *American Political Science Review* 4 (97): 501–14.

———. 2017. "Responsibility and Ignorance: On Dismantling Structural Injustice." *Journal of Politics* 79 (2): 396–408.

Hazony, Yoram. 2018. *The Virtue of Nationalism*. New York: Basic Books.

Heilinger, Jan-Christoph. 2019. *Cosmopolitan Responsibility: Global Injustice, Relational Equality, and Individual Agency*. Berlin: de Gruyter.

Herman, Melissa R., and Mary E. Campbell. 2012. "I Wouldn't, But You Can: Attitudes toward Interracial Relationships." *Social Science Research* 41 (2): 343–58.

Hetherington, Marc J., and Thomas J. Rudolph. 2015. *Why Washington Won't Work: Polarization, Political Trust, and the Governing Crisis*. Chicago: University of Chicago Press.

Hibbing, John R. 2020. *The Securitarian Personality: What Really Motivates Trump's Base and Why It Matters for the Post-Trump Era*. New York: Oxford University Press.

Hidalgo, Javier. 2015. "Resistance to Unjust Immigration Restrictions." *Journal of Political Philosophy* 23 (4): 450–70.

Hill, Thomas E., Jr. 1991. *Autonomy and Self-Respect*. Cambridge: Cambridge University Press.

Hiller, Avram. 2011. "Climate Change and Individual Responsibility." *Monist* 94 (3): 349–68.

Hjerm, Mikael, Maureen A. Eger, Andrea Bohman, and Filip Fors Connolly. 2020. "A New Approach to the Study of Tolerance: Conceptualizing and Measuring Acceptance, Respect, and Appreciation of Difference." *Social Indicators Research* 147:897–919.

Hobbes, Thomas. 1994 [1651]. *Leviathan*. Indianapolis, IN: Hackett.

Hochschild, Arlie Russell. 2016. *Strangers in Their Own Land*. New York: New Press.

Hogg, Michael A. 2001. "Social Identity and the Sovereignty of the Group: A Psychology of Belonging." In *Individual Self, Relational Self, Collective Self*, edited by Constantine Sedikides and Marilynn B. Brewer, 123–43. New York: Psychology Press.

Hogg, Michael A., and Dominic Abrams. 1988. *Social Identifications: A Social Psychology of Intergroup Relations and Group Processes*. New York: Routledge.

Horne, Will, James Adams, and Noam Gidron. 2022. "The Way We Were: How Histories of Co-Governance Alleviate Partisan Hostility." *Comparative Political Studies*, https://doi.org/10.1177/00104140221100197.

Hornsey, Matthew J. 2006. "Ingroup Critics and Their Influence on Groups." In *Individuality and the Group: Advances in Social Identity*, edited by Tom Postmes and Jolanda Jetten, 74–92. Thousand Oaks, CA: Sage.

Hornsey, Matthew J., Tim Grice, Jolanda Jetten, Neil Paulsen, and Victor Callan. 2007. "Group-Directed Criticisms and Recommendations for Change: Why Newcomers Arouse More Resistance Than Old-Timers." *Personality and Social Psychology Bulletin* 33 (7): 1036–48.

Hornsey, Matthew J., Tina Oppes, and Alicia Svensson. 2002. " 'It's OK if We Say It, But You Can't': Responses to Intergroup and Intragroup Criticism." *European Journal of Social Psychology* 32:293–307.

Horton, John. 2011. "Why the Traditional Conception of Toleration Still Matters." *Critical Review of International Social and Political Philosophy* 14 (3): 289–305.

Huber, Gregory A., and Neil Malhotra. 2017. "Political Homophily in Social Relationships: Evidence from Online Dating Behavior." *Journal of Politics* 79 (1): 269–83.

Huddy, Leonie. 2003. "Group Identity and Political Cohesion." In *Oxford Handbook of Political Psychology*, edited by David O. Sears, Leonie Huddy, and Robert Jervis, 511–58. Oxford: Oxford University Press.

Huddy, Leonie, and Nadia Khatib. 2007. "American Patriotism, National Identity, and Political Involvement." *American Journal of Political Science* 51 (1): 63–77.

Huntington, Samuel P. 2004. *Who Are We? The Challenges to America's National Identity*. New York: Simon & Schuster.

Igielnik, Ruth, Scott Keeter, and Hannah Hartig. 2021. "Behind Biden's 2020 Victory: An Examination of the 2020 Electorate, Based on Validated Voters." Pew Research Center (June 30), https://www.pewresearch.org/politics/2021/06/30/behind-bidens-2020-victory/. Accessed December 8, 2022.

Iyengar, Shanto, Yphtach Lelkes, Matthew Levendusky, Neil Malhotra, and Sean J. Westwood. 2019. "The Origins and Consequences of Affective Polarization in the United States." *Annual Review of Political Science* 22:129–46.

Iyengar, Shanto, Gaurav Sood, and Yphtach Lelkes. 2012. "Affect, Not Ideology: A Social Identity Perspective on Polarization." *Public Opinion Quarterly* 76 (3): 405–31.

Iyengar, Shanto, and Sean J. Westwood. 2015. "Fear and Loathing across Party Lines: New Evidence on Group Polarization." *American Journal of Political Science* 59 (3): 690–707.

Jackson, Chris, and Jocelyn Duran. 2021. "Americans Want the Government to Shop Domestically, No Matter the Price." Ipsos Survey. https://www.ipsos.com/en-us/news-polls/americans-want-government-shop-domestically-no-matter-price.

Jacoby, William G. 2006. "Value Choices and American Public Opinion." *American Journal of Political Science* 50 (3): 706–23.

Janoff-Bulman, Ronnie, and Nate C. Carnes. 2013. "Surveying the Moral Landscape: Moral Motives and Group-Based Moralities." *Personality and Social Psychology Review* 17 (3): 219–36.

———. 2016. "Social Justice and Social Order: Binding Moralities across the Political Spectrum." *PLoS ONE*, https://doi.org/10.1371/journal.pone.0152479.

Janoff-Bulman, Ronnie, and Amelie Werther. 2008. "The Social Psychology of Respect: Implications for Delegitimization and Reconciliation." In *The Social Psychology of Intergroup Reconciliation*, edited by Arie Nadler, Thomas Malloy, and Jeffrey Fisher, 145–70. Oxford: Oxford University Press.

Jennings, M. Kent, and Gregory B. Markus. 1984. "Partisan Orientations over the Long Haul: Results from the Three-Wave Political Socialization Panel Study." *American Political Science Review* 78 (4): 1000–18.

Jetten, Jolanda, Tom Postmes, and Brendan J. McAuliffe. 2002. "'We're All Individuals': Group Norms of Individualism and Collectivism, Levels of Identification and Identity Threat." *European Journal of Social Psychology* 32 (2): 189–207.

Johnson, Kathryn A., Eric D. Hill, and Adam B. Cohen. 2011. "Integrating the Study of Culture and Religion: Toward a Psychology of Worldview." *Social and Personality Psychology Compass* 5 (3): 137–52.

Jost, John T., Melanie Langer, and Vishal Singh. 2017. "The Politics of Buying, Boycotting, Complaining, and Disputing: An Extension of the Research Program by Jung, Garbarino, Briley, and Wynhausen." *Journal of Consumer Research* 44:503–10.

Kalla, Joshua L., and David E. Broockman. 2020. "Reducing Exclusionary Attitudes through Interpersonal Conversation: Evidence from Three Field Experiments." *American Political Science Review* 114 (2): 410–25.

Kalmoe, Nathan P., and Lilliana Mason. 2022. *Radical American Partisanship: Mapping Violent Hostility, Its Causes, and the Consequences for Democracy*. Chicago: University of Chicago Press.

Kane, John V. 2016. "Control, Accountability, and Constraints: Rethinking Perceptions of Presidential Responsibility for the Economy." *Presidential Studies Quarterly* 46 (2): 335–64.

Kendi, Ibram X. 2020. *Be Antiracist: A Journal for Awareness, Reflection, and Action*. New York: One World.

Kinder, Donald R. 1981. "Presidents, Prosperity, and Public Opinion." *Public Opinion Quarterly* 45 (1): 1–20.

Kingzette, Jon, James N. Druckman, Samara Klar, Yanna Krupnikov, Matthew Levendusky, and John Barry Ryan. 2021. "How Affective Polarization Undermines Support for Democratic Norms." *Public Opinion Quarterly* 85 (2): 663–77.

Koltko-Rivera, Mark E. 2004. "The Psychology of Worldviews." *Review of General Psychology* 8 (1): 3–58.

Kortetmäki, Teea. 2018. "Nobody's Fault? Structural Injustice, Food, and Climate Change." In *Food, Environment, and Climate Change: Justice at the Intersections*, edited by Erinn Gilson and Sarah Kenehan, 47–61. London: Rowman & Littlefield International.

Kubin, Emily, Curtis Puryear, Chelsea Schein, and Kurt Gray. 2021. "Personal Experiences Bridge Moral and Political Divides Better Than Facts." *PNAS* 118 (6).

Kugler, Matthew, John T. Jost, and Sharareh Noorbaloochi. 2014. "Another Look at Moral Foundations Theory: Do Authoritarianism and Social Dominance Orientation Explain Liberal-Conservative Differences in 'Moral' Intuitions?" *Social Justice Research* 27:413–31.

Kukathas, Chandran. 2003. *Liberal Archipelago: A Theory of Diversity and Freedom*. Oxford: Oxford University Press.

———. 2021. *Immigration and Freedom*. Princeton, NJ: Princeton University Press.

Kymlicka, Will. 2002. *Contemporary Political Philosophy: An Introduction*. Oxford: Oxford University Press.

Laham, Simon M., Sonavi Chopra, Mansur Lalljee, and Brian Parkinson. 2010. "Emotional and Behavioural Reactions to Moral Transgressions: Cross-Cultural and Individual Variations in India and Britain." *International Journal of Psychology* 45 (1): 64–71.

Laham, Simon M., Tania Tam, Mansur Lalljee, Miles Hewstone, and Alberto Voci. 2009. "Respect for Persons in the Intergroup Context: Self-Other Overlap and Intergroup Emotions as Mediators of the Impact of Respect on Action Tendencies." *Group Processes & Intergroup Relations* 13 (3): 301–17.

Lalljee, Mansur, Geoffrey Evans, Shreya Sarawgi, and Katrin Voltmer. 2013. "Respect Your Enemies: Orientations towards Political Opponents and Political Involvement in Britain." *International Journal of Public Opinion Research* 25 (1): 119–31.

Lalljee, Mansur, Simon M. Laham, and Tania Tam. 2007. "Unconditional Respect for Persons: A Social Psychological Analysis." *Gruppendynamik und Organisationsberatung* 38 (4): 451–64.

Lalljee, Mansur, Tania Tam, Miles Hewstone, Simon M. Laham, and Jessica Lee. 2009. "Unconditional Respect for Persons and the Prediction of Intergroup Action Tendencies." *European Journal of Social Psychology* 39:666–83.

Layman, Geoffrey C., Thomas M. Carsey, and Juliana Menasce Horowitz. 2006. "Party Polarization in American Politics." *Annual Review of Political Science* 9 (1): 83–110.

Leach, Colin Wayne, Naomi Ellemers, and Manuela Barreto. 2007. "Group Virtue: The Importance of Morality (vs. Competence and Sociability) in the Positive Evaluation of In-Groups." *Journal of Personality and Social Psychology* 93 (2): 234.

Lees, Jeffrey, and Mina Cikara. 2020. "Inaccurate Group Meta-Perceptions Drive Negative Out-Group Attributions in Competitive Contexts." *Nature Human Behaviour* 4 (March): 279–86.

———. 2021. "Understanding and Combating Misperceived Polarization." *Philosophical Transactions of the Royal Society B* 376 (1882), https://doi.org/10.1098/rstb.2020.0143.

Lelkes, Yphtach, and Sean J. Westwood. 2017. "The Limits of Partisan Prejudice." *Journal of Politics* 79 (2): 485–501.

Levendusky, Matthew S. 2009. *The Partisan Sort: How Liberals Became Democrats and Conservatives Became Republicans*. Chicago: University of Chicago Press.

———. 2018. "Americans, Not Partisans: Can Priming American National Identity Reduce Affective Polarization?" *Journal of Politics* 80 (1): 59–70.

Levendusky, Matthew S., and Neil Malhotra. 2016. "(Mis)perceptions of Partisan Polarization in the American Public." *Public Opinion Quarterly* 80 (S1): 378–91.

Levendusky, Matthew S., and Dominik A. Stecula. 2021. *We Need to Talk: How Cross-Party Dialogue Reduces Affective Polarization*. Cambridge: Cambridge University Press.

Lippert-Rasmussen, Kasper. 2018. *Relational Egalitarianism: Living as Equals*. Cambridge: Cambridge University Press.

Lowry, Rich. 2019. *The Case for Nationalism*. New York: HarperCollins.

Lukes, Steven. 1997. "Social Justice: The Hayekian Challenge." *Critical Review* 11 (1): 65–80.

Maboloc, Christopher Ryan. 2019. "What Is Structural Injustice?" *Philosophia* 47 (4): 1185–96.

Maltais, Aaron. 2013. "Radically Non-Ideal Climate Politics and the Obligation to at Least Vote Green." *Environmental Values* 22 (5): 589–608.

Mansbridge, Jane, James Bohman, Simone Chambers, Thomas Christiano, Archon Fung, John Parkinson, Dennis F. Thompson, and Mark E. Warren. 2012. "A Systemic Approach to Deliberative Democracy." In *Deliberative Systems*, edited by John Parkinson and Jane Mansbridge, 1–26. Cambridge: Cambridge University Press.

Marcus, George E., John L. Sullivan, Elizabeth Theiss-Morse, and Sandra L. Wood. 1995. *With Malice toward Some: How People Make Civil Liberties Judgments*. Cambridge: Cambridge University Press.

Marin, Mara. 2017. *Connected by Commitment*. Oxford: Oxford University Press.

Markus, Gregory B. 1979. "The Political Environment and the Dynamics of Public Attitudes: A Panel Study." *American Journal of Political Science* 23 (2): 338–59.

Markus, Hazel Rose, Carol D. Ryff, Alana L. Conner, Eden K. Pudberry, and Katherine L. Barnett. 2001. "Themes and Variations in American Understandings of Responsibility." In *Caring and Doing for Others: Social Responsibility in the Domains of Family, Work, and Community*, edited by Alice S. Rossi, 349–99. Chicago: University of Chicago Press.

Martherus, James L., Andres G. Martinez, Paul K. Piff, and Alexander G. Theodoridis. 2019. "Party Animals? Extreme Partisan Polarization and Dehumanization." *Political Behavior* 43: 517–40.

Maskivker, Julia. 2019. *The Duty to Vote*. Oxford: Oxford University Press.

Mason, Lilliana. 2013. "The Rise of Uncivil Agreement: Issue versus Behavioral Polarization in the American Electorate." *American Behavioral Scientist* 57 (1): 140–59.

———. 2018. "Ideologues without Issues: The Polarizing Consequences of Ideological Identities." *Public Opinion Quarterly* 82 (S1): 866–87.

Mason, Lilliana, and Julie Wronski. 2018. "One Tribe to Bind Them All: How Our Social Group Attachments Strengthen Partisanship." *Political Psychology* 39 (S1): 257–77.

McCann, Stewart J. H. 1997. "Threatening Times, 'Strong' Presidential Popular Vote Winners, and the Victory Margin, 1824–1964." *Journal of Personality and Social Psychology* 73 (1): 160–70.

McClosky, Herbert. 1964. "Consensus and Ideology in American Politics." *American Political Science Review* 58 (2): 361–82.

McClosky, Herbert, and John Zaller. 1984. *The American Ethos: Public Attitudes toward Capitalism and Democracy*. Cambridge, MA: Harvard University Press.

McCoy, Jennifer, and Murat Somer. 2019. "Toward a Theory of Pernicious Polarization and How It Harms Democracies: Comparative Evidence and Possible Remedies." *Annals of the American Academy of Political and Social Science* 681 (January): 234–71.

———. 2021. "Overcoming Polarization." *Journal of Democracy* 32 (1): 6–21.

McKeown, Maeve. 2018. "Iris Marion Young's 'Social Connection Model' of Responsibility: Clarifying the Meaning of Connection." *Journal of Social Philosophy* 49 (3): 484–502.

———. 2021. "Structural Injustice." *Philosophy Compass* 16 (7): http://dx.doi.org/10.1111/phc3.12757.

McKinnon, Catriona. 2003. "Basic Income, Self-Respect and Reciprocity." *Journal of Applied Philosophy* 20 (2): 143–58.

McTernan, Emily. 2013. "The Inegalitarian Ethos: Incentives, Respect, and Self-Respect." *Politics, Philosophy & Economics* 12 (1): 93–111.

McWilliams, Abagail, Donald S. Siegel, and Patrick M. Wright. 2006. "Corporate Social Responsibility: Strategic Implications." *Journal of Management Studies* 43 (1): 1–18.

Mill, John Stuart. 1882. *A System of Logic, Ratiocinative and Inductive*. New York: Harper and Brothers.

———. 1991 [1861]. "Considerations on Representative Government." In *On Liberty and Other Essays*, edited by John Gray. Oxford: Oxford University Press.

Miller, David. 1978. "Democracy and Social Justice." *British Journal of Political Science* 8 (1): 1–19.

———. 1995. *On Nationality*. Oxford: Oxford University Press.

Molenmaker, Welmer E., Erik W. de Kwaadsteniet, and Eric van Dijk. 2014. "On the Willingness to Costly Reward Cooperation and Punish Non-Cooperation: The Moderating Role of Type of Social Dilemma." *Organizational Behavior and Human Decision Processes* 125 (2): 175–83.

Mooney, Christopher Z. 1999. "The Politics of Morality Policy: Symposium Editor's Introduction." *Policy Studies Journal* 27 (4): 675–80.

Moore-Berg, Samantha L., Lee-Or Ankori-Karlinsky, Boaz Hameiri, and Emile Bruneau. 2020. "Exaggerated Meta-Perceptions Predict Intergroup Hostility between American Political Partisans." *PNAS* 117 (26): 14864–72.

Morgan, G. Scott, Linda J. Skitka, and Daniel C. Wisneski. 2010. "Moral and Religious Convictions and Intentions to Vote in the 2008 Presidential Election." *Analyses of Social Issues and Public Policy* 10 (1): 307–20.

Muravchik, Stephanie, and Jon A. Shields. 2020. *Trump's Democrats*. Washington, DC: Brookings Institution.

Mutz, Diana C. 2002. "Cross-Cutting Social Networks: Testing Democratic Theory in Practice." *American Political Science Review* 96 (1): 111–26.

———. 2006. *Hearing the Other Side: Deliberative versus Participatory Democracy*. Cambridge: Cambridge University Press.

———. 2007. "Effects of 'In-Your-Face' Television Discourse on Perceptions of a Legitimate Opposition." *American Political Science Review* 101 (4): 621–35.

Mutz, Diana C., and Byron Reeves. 2005. "The New Videomalaise: Effects of Televised Incivility on Political Trust." *American Political Science Review* 99 (1): 1–15.

Myers, Ella. 2010. "From Pluralism to Liberalism: Rereading Isaiah Berlin." *Review of Politics* 72 (4): 599–625.

Neuhäuser, Christian. 2014. "Structural Injustice and the Distribution of Forward-Looking Responsibility." *Midwest Studies in Philosophy* 38:232–51.

Niemi, Richard G., and M. Kent Jennings. 1991. "Issues and Inheritance in the Formation of Party Identification." *American Journal of Political Science* 35 (4):970–88.

Nussbaum, Martha C. 2011. *Creating Capabilities*. Cambridge, MA: Harvard University Press.

Okin, Susan Moller. 2002. "'Mistresses of Their Own Destiny': Group Rights, Gender, and Realistic Rights of Exit." *Ethics* 112 (2): 205–30.

Olson, Mancur. 1965. *The Logic of Collective Action: Public Goods and the Theory of Groups*. Cambridge, MA: Harvard University Press.

Oprea, Alex, Lucy Martin and Geoffrey Brennan. "Moving towards the Median: Compulsory Voting and Political Polarization." Unpublished manuscript.

Orbell, John M., and Robyn M. Dawes. 1981. "Social Dilemmas." In *Progress in Applied Social Psychology*, edited by G. M. Stephenson and James H. Davis, 37–65. New York: Wiley.

Ostrom, Elinor. 1990. *Governing the Commons: The Evolution of Institutions for Collective Action*. Cambridge: Cambridge University Press.

———. 2010. "Analyzing Collective Action." *Agricultural Economics* 41 (S1): 155–66.

Pagliaro, Stefano, Naomi Ellemers, and Manuela Barreto. 2011. "Sharing Moral Values: Anticipated Ingroup Respect as a Determinant of Adherence to Morality-Based (But Not Competence-Based) Group Norms." *Personality and Social Psychology Bulletin* 37 (8): 1117–29.

Parekh, Bhikhu. 2000. *Rethinking Multiculturalism: Cultural Diversity and Political Theory*. Cambridge, MA: Harvard University Press.

Pettigrew, Thomas F., and Linda R. Tropp. 2006. "A Meta-Analytic Test of Intergroup Contact Theory." *Journal of Personality and Social Psychology* 90 (5): 751–83.

Pettit, Philip. 2013. *On the People's Terms: A Republican Theory and Model of Democracy*. Cambridge: Cambridge University Press.

Pew Research Center. 2018. "The Public, the Political System and American Democracy." http://www.people-press.org/2018/04/26/the-public-the-political-system-and-american-democracy/. Accessed December 8, 2022.

Prothro, James W., and Charles M. Grigg. 1960. "Fundamental Principles of Democracy: Bases of Agreement and Disagreement." *Journal of Politics* 22 (2): 276–94.

Quong, Jonathan. 2022. "Public Reason." *Stanford Encyclopedia of Philosophy* (Summer Edition), Edward N. Zalta (ed.), https://plato.stanford.edu/archives/sum2022/entries/public-reason/.

Rabin, Roni Caryn. 2021. "As Virus Cases Rise, Another Contagion Spreads among the Vaccinated: Anger." *New York Times*. https://www.nytimes.com/2021/07/27/health/coronavirus-vaccination-hesitancy-delta.html. Accessed December 9, 2024.

Rauch, Jonathan. 2021. *The Constitution of Knowledge: A Defense of Truth*. Washington, DC: Brookings Institution.

Rawls, John. 1999 [1971]. *A Theory of Justice*. Rev. ed. Cambridge, MA: Harvard University Press.

———. 2001. *Justice as Fairness: A Restatement*. Cambridge, MA: Harvard University Press.

Redlawsk, David P. 2002. "Hot Cognition or Cool Consideration? Testing the Effects of Motivated Reasoning on Political Decision Making." *Journal of Politics* 64 (4): 1021–44.

Renger, Daniela, Alex Mommert, Sophus Renger, and Bernd Simon. 2016. "When Less Equal Is Less Human: Intragroup (Dis)respect and the Experience of Being Human." *Journal of Social Psychology* 156 (5): 553–63.

Renger, Daniela, Sophus Renger, Marcel Miché, and Bernd Simon. 2017. "A Social Recognition Approach to Autonomy: The Role of Equality-Based Respect." *Personality and Social Psychology Bulletin* 43 (4): 479–92.

Renger, Daniela, and Bernd Simon. 2011. "Social Recognition as an Equal: The Role of Equality-Based Respect in Group Life." *European Journal of Social Psychology* 41 (4): 501–7.

Riley, Jonathan. 2001. "Interpreting Berlin's Liberalism." *American Political Science Review* 95 (2): 283–95.

Ruggeri, Kai, Bojana Većkalov, Lana Bojanić, Thomas L. Andersen, Sarah Ashcroft-Jones, Nélida Ayacaxli, Paula Barea-Arroyo, Mari Louise Berge, Ludvig D. Bjørndal, and Aslı Bursalıoğlu. 2021. "The General Fault in Our Fault Lines." *Nature Human Behaviour* 5 (10): 1369–80.

Ryan, Timothy J. 2014. "Reconsidering Moral Issues in Politics." *Journal of Politics* 76 (2): 380–97.

———. 2017. "No Compromise: Political Consequences of Moralized Attitudes." *American Journal of Political Science* 61 (2): 409–23.

Ryan, Timothy J., and Jeff Spinner-Halev. 2022. "Who Gives Credence to Whom? Exploring Status and Relational Equality with Empirical Tests." *Journal of Politics* 84 (2): 1118–31.

Saffon, Maria Paula, and Nadia Urbinati. 2013. "Procedural Democracy, the Bulwark of Equal Liberty." *Political Theory* 41 (3): 441–81.

Sager, Alex. 2020. *Against Borders: Why the World Needs Free Movement of People*. New York: Rowman & Littlefield.

Sangiovanni, Andrea. 2018. "Structural Injustice and Individual Responsibility." *Journal of Social Philosophy* 49 (3): 461–83.

Santoro, Erik, and David E. Broockman. 2022. "The Promise and Pitfalls of Cross-Partisan Conversations for Reducing Affective Polarization: Evidence from Randomized Experiments." *Science Advances* 8 (25). https://doi.org/10.1126/sciadv.abn5515.

Sardo, Michael Christopher. 2020. "Responsibility for Climate Justice: Political Not Moral." *European Journal of Political Theory* 22 (1): 26–50.

Schatz, Robert T., Ervin Staub, and Howard Lavine. 1999. "On the Varieties of National Attachment: Blind versus Constructive Patriotism." *Political Psychology* 20 (1): 151–74.

Scheffler, Samuel. 2005. "What Is Egalitarianism?" *Philosophy & Public Affairs* 31 (1): 5–39.

———. 2015. "The Practice of Equality." In *Social Equality: On What It Means to be Equal*, edited by Carina Fourie, Fabian Schuppert, and Ivo Walliman-Helmer, 21–44. Oxford: Oxford University Press.

Schiff, Jade Larissa. 2014. *Burdens of Political Responsibility*. Cambridge: Cambridge University Press.

Schildkraut, Deborah J. 2005. *Press One for English: Language Policy, Public Opinion, and American Identity*. Princeton, NJ: Princeton University Press.

———. 2007. "Defining American Identity in the Twenty-First Century: How Much "There" Is There?" *Journal of Politics* 69 (3): 597–615.

———. 2014. "Boundaries of American Identity: Evolving Understandings of 'Us.'" *Annual Review of Political Science* 17:441–60.

Schirmer, Werner, Linda Weidenstedt, and Wendelin Reich. 2012. "From Tolerance to Respect in Inter-Ethnic Contexts." *Journal of Ethnic and Migration Studies* 38 (7): 1049–65.

Schlesinger, Arthur M. 1991. *The Disuniting of America*. Knoxville, TN: Whittle Direct Books.

Schultz, Katherine G., and James A. Swezey. 2013. "A Three-Dimensional Concept of Worldview." *Journal of Research on Christian Education* 22 (3): 227–43.

Schwartz, Shalom H., Gian Vittorio Caprara, and Michele Vecchione. 2010. "Basic Personal Values, Core Political Values, and Voting: A Longitudinal Analysis." *Political Psychology* 31 (3): 421–52.

Schwenkenbecher, Anne. 2021. "Structural Injustice and Massively Shared Obligations." *Journal of Applied Philosophy* 38 (1): 23–39.

Scruton, Roger. 2004. *The Need for Nations*. London: Civitas Institute for the Study of Civil Society.

Sears, David O., and Carolyn L. Funk. 1999. "Evidence of the Long-Term Persistence of Adults' Political Predispositions." *Journal of Politics* 61 (1): 1–28.

Sen, Amartya. 1980. "Equality of What?" In *Tanner Lectures on Human Values, Volume 1*, edited by S. McMurrin, 197–220. Cambridge: Cambridge University Press.

Shafranek, Richard M. 2021. "Political Considerations in Nonpolitical Decisions: A Conjoint Analysis of Roommate Choice." *Political Behavior* 43:271–300.

Simon, Bernd, and Hilmar Grabow. 2014. "To Be Respected and to Respect: The Challenge of Mutual Respect in Intergroup Relations." *British Journal of Social Psychology* 53 (1): 39–53.

Sinnott-Armstrong, Walter. 2005. "It's Not My Fault: Global Warming and Individual Moral Obligations." In *Perspectives on Climate Change: Science, Economics, Politics, Ethics*, edited by Walter Sinnott-Armstrong and Richard B. Howarth, 285–307. Bradford, UK: Emerald.

Sire, James W. 2015. *Naming the Elephant: Worldview as a Concept*. Downers Grove, IL: IVP Academic.

Skitka, Linda J. 2010. "The Psychology of Moral Conviction." *Social and Personality Psychology Compass* 4 (4): 267–81.

Skitka, Linda J., Christopher W. Bauman, and Edward G. Sargis. 2005. "Moral Conviction: Another Contributor to Attitude Strength or Something More?" *Journal of Personality and Social Psychology* 88 (6): 895–917.

Skitka, Linda J., Brittany E. Hanson, and Daniel C. Wisneski. 2017. "Utopian Hopes or Dystopian Fears? Exploring the Motivational Underpinnings of Moralized Political Engagement." *Personality and Social Psychology Bulletin* 43 (2): 177–90.

Skitka, Linda J., and G. Scott Morgan. 2014. "The Social and Political Implications of Moral Conviction." *Advances in Political Psychology* 35 (S1): 95–110.

Smith, Kevin B. 2002. "Typologies, Taxonomies, and the Benefits of Policy Classification." *Policy Studies Journal* 30 (3): 379–95.

Smith, Kevin B., John R. Alford, John R. Hibbing, Nicholas G. Martin, and Peter K. Hatemi. 2017. "Intuitive Ethics and Political Orientations: Testing Moral Foundations as a Theory of Political Ideology." *American Journal of Political Science* 61 (2): 424–37.

Smith, Kevin B., Douglas R. Oxley, Matthew V. Hibbing, John R. Alford, and John R. Hibbing. 2011. "Linking Genetics and Political Attitudes: Reconceptualizing Political Ideology." *Political Psychology* 32 (3): 369–97.

Smith, Kyle. 2017. "Why Colin Kaepernick's Protest Failed." *National Review Online.* https://www.nationalreview.com/2017/04/colin-kaepernick-protest-national-anthem-flag-patriotism-sports-football-politics-manners/. Accessed December 7, 2022.

Smith, Rogers M. 1988. "The 'American Creed' and American Identity: The Limits of Liberal Citizenship in the United States." *Western Political Quarterly* 41 (2): 225–51.

Spinner-Halev, Jeff, and Elizabeth Theiss-Morse. 2003. "National Identity and Self-Esteem." *Perspectives on Politics* 1 (3): 515–32.

Stenmark, Mikael. 2021. "Worldview Studies." *Religious Studies* 57:1–19.

Stone, Peter. 2022. "In the Shadow of Rawls: Egalitarianism Today." *Ethical Theory and Moral Practice* 25 (1): 157–68.

Strodtbeck, Fred L., Rita M. James, and Charles Hawkins. 1957. "Social Status in Jury Deliberations." *American Sociological Review* 22 (6): 713–19.

Stroud, Natalie J., and Jessica R. Collier. 2021. "Selective Exposure and Homophily during the 2016 Presidential Campaign." In *An Unprecedented Election: Media, Communication, and the Electorate in the 2016 Campaign*, edited by Benjamin R. Warner, Dianne G. Bystrom, Mitchell S. McKinney, and Mary C. Banwart, 21–39. Santa Barbara, CA: Praeger.

Suhler, Christopher L., and Patricia Churchland. 2011. "Can Innate, Modular 'Foundations' Explain Morality? Challenges for Haidt's Moral Foundations Theory." *Journal of Cognitive Neuroscience* 23 (9): 2103–16.

Sullivan, John L., George E. Marcus, Stanley Feldman, and James E. Piereson. 1981. "The Sources of Political Tolerance: A Multivariate Analysis." *American Political Science Review* 75 (1): 92–106.

Sullivan, John L., James E. Piereson, and George E. Marcus. 1982. *Political Tolerance and American Democracy.* Chicago: University of Chicago Press.

Tagar, Michal Reifen, G. Scott Morgan, Eran Halperin, and Linda J. Skitka. 2014. "When Ideology Matters: Moral Conviction and the Association between Ideology and Policy Preferences in the Israeli–Palestinian Conflict." *European Journal of Social Psychology* 44 (2): 117–25.

Tajfel, Henri. 1982. *Social Identity and Intergroup Relations.* Cambridge: Cambridge University Press.

Talisse, Robert B. 2019. *Overdoing Democracy.* Oxford: Oxford University Press.

Tamir, Yael. 1993. *Liberal Nationalism*. Princeton, NJ: Princeton University Press.

———. 2019. *Why Nationalism*. Princeton, NJ: Princeton University Press.

Taylor, Charles. 1992. "The Politics of Recognition." In *Multiculturalism and the Politics of Recognition*, edited by Amy Gutmann, 25–73. Princeton, NJ: Princeton University Press.

Tebble, Adam James. 2009. "Hayek and Social Justice: A Critique." *Critical Review of International Social and Political Philosophy* 12 (4): 581–604.

Testa, Paul F., Matthew V. Hibbing, and Melinda Ritchie. 2014. "Orientations toward Conflict and the Conditional Effects of Political Disagreement." *Journal of Politics* 76 (3): 770–85.

Theiss-Morse, Elizabeth. 2009. *Who Counts as an American? The Boundaries of National Identity*. New York: Cambridge University Press.

Tomasi, John. 2012. *Free Market Fairness*. Princeton, NJ: Princeton University Press.

Tuller, Hannah M., Christopher J. Bryan, Gail D. Heyman, and Nicholas J. S. Christenfeld. 2015. "Seeing the Other Side: Perspective Taking and the Moderation of Extremity." *Journal of Experimental Social Psychology* 59:18–23.

Turner, John C., Michael A. Hogg, Penelope J. Oakes, Stephen D. Reicher, and Margaret S. Wetherell. 1987. *Rediscovering the Social Group: A Self-Categorization Theory*. Oxford: Blackwell.

Tyler, Tom R. 1990. *Why People Obey the Law*. New Haven, CT: Yale University Press.

Tyler, Tom R., and Steven L. Blader. 2003. "The Group Engagement Model: Procedural Justice, Social Identity, and Cooperative Behavior." *Personality and Social Psychology Review* 7 (4): 349–61.

Tyler, Tom R., Robert J. Boeckmann, Heather J. Smith, and Yuen J. Huo. 1997. *Social Justice in a Diverse Society*. Boulder, CO: Westview.

Tyler, Tom R., and Heather J. Smith. 1999. "Justice, Social Identity, and Group Processes." In *The Psychology of the Social Self*, edited by Tom R. Tyler, Roderick M. Kramer, and Oliver P. John, 223–63. New York: Psychology Press.

Ulbig, Stacy G., and Carolyn L. Funk. 1999. "Conflict Avoidance and Political Participation." *Political Behavior* 21 (3): 265–82.

Urbinati, Nadia. 2014. *Democracy Disfigured*. Cambridge, MA: Harvard University Press.

Uscinski, Joseph E., Casey Klofstad, and Matthew D. Atkinson. 2016. "What Drives Conspiratorial Beliefs? The Role of Informational Cues and Predispositions." *Political Research Quarterly* 69 (1): 57–71.

Vance, J. D. 2016. *Hillbilly Elegy: A Memoir of a Family and Culture in Crisis*. New York: HarperCollins.

Van Dijk, Eric, and Henk Wilke. 1995. "Coordination Rules in Asymmetric Social Dilemmas: A Comparison between Public Good Dilemmas and Resource Dilemmas." *Journal of Experimental Social Psychology* 31 (1): 1–27.

———. 1997. "Is It Mine or Is It Ours? Framing Property Rights and Decision Making in Social Dilemmas." *Organizational Behavior and Human Decision Processes* 71 (2): 195–209.

Van Vugt, Mark, and Claire M. Hart. 2004. "Social Identity as Social Glue: The Origins of Group Loyalty." *Journal of Personality and Social Psychology* 86 (4): 585–98.

Voelkel, Jan G., James Chu, Michael Stagnaro, Joseph S. Mernyk, Chrystal Redekopp, Sophia L. Pink, James Druckman, David G. Rand, and Robb Willer. 2023. "Interventions Reducing Affective Polarization Do Not Necessarily Improve Anti-democratic Attitudes." *Human Nature Behavior* 7: 55–64.

Walzer, Michael. 1980. "The Moral Standing of States: A Response to Four Critics." *Philosophy & Public Affairs* 9 (3): 209–29.

———. 1983. *Spheres of Justice: A Defense of Pluralism and Equality*. New York: Basic Books.

Warner, Benjamin R., Colleen Warner Colaner, and Jihye Park. 2021. "Political Difference and Polarization in the Family: The Role of (Non)Accommodating Communication for Navigating Identity Differences." *Journal of Social and Personal Relationships* 38 (2): 564–85.

Warner, Benjamin R., Haley Kranstuber Horstman, and Cassandra C. Kearney. 2020. "Reducing Political Polarization through Narrative Writing." *Journal of Applied Communication Research* 48 (4): 459–77.

Warner, Benjamin R., and Astrid Villamil. 2017. "A Test of Imagined Contact as a Means to Improve Cross-Partisan Feelings and Reduce Attribution of Malevolence and Acceptance of Political Violence." *Communication Monographs* 84 (4): 447–65.

Webster, Steven W., and Alan I. Abramowitz. 2017. "The Ideological Foundations of Affective Polarization in the U.S. Electorate." *American Politics Research* 45 (4): 621–47.

Webster, Steven W., Elizabeth C. Connors, and Betsy Sinclair. 2022. "The Social Consequences of Political Anger." *Journal of Politics* 84 (3): 1292–305.

Wilson, James Lindley. 2019. *Democratic Equality*. Princeton, NJ: Princeton University Press.

Wojcieszak, Magdalena, and R. Kelly Garrett. 2018. "Social Identity, Selective Exposure, and Affective Polarization: How Priming National Identity Shapes Attitudes toward Immigrants via News Selection." *Human Communication Research* 44 (3): 247–73.

Wojcieszak, Magdalena, and Benjamin R. Warner. 2020. "Can Interparty Contact Reduce Affective Polarization? A Systematic Test of Different Forms of Intergroup Contact." *Political Communication* 37 (6): 789–811.

Wolak, Jennifer. 2020. *Compromise in an Age of Party Polarization*. New York: Oxford University Press.

Wolff, Jonathan. 1998. "Fairness, Respect, and the Egalitarian Ethos." *Philosophy & Public Affairs* 27 (2): 97–122.

———. 2007. "Equality: The Recent History of an Idea." *Journal of Moral Philosophy* 4 (1): 125–36.

———. 2010. "Fairness, Respect and the Egalitarian Ethos Revisited." *Journal of Ethics* 14 (3): 335.

Wrzus, Cornelia, Martha Hänel, Jenny Wagner, and Franz J. Neyer. 2013. "Social Network Changes and Life Events across the Life Span: A Meta-Analysis." *Psychological Bulletin* 139 (1): 53–80.

Young, Iris Marion. 1989. "Polity and Group Difference: A Critique of the Ideal of Universal Citizenship." *Ethics Young, 1989* 9 (2): 250–74.

———. 1990. *Justice and the Politics of Difference*. Princeton, NJ: Princeton University Press.

———. 2004. "Responsibility and Global Labor Justice." *Journal of Political Philosophy* 12 (4): 365–88.

———. 2006a. "Education in the Context of Structural Injustice: A Symposium Response." *Educational Philosophy and Theory* 38 (1): 93–103.

———. 2006b. "Responsibility and Global Justice: A Social Connection Model." *Social Philosophy and Policy* 23 (1): 102–30.

———. 2009. "Structural Injustice and the Politics of Difference." In *Contemporary Debates in Political Philosophy*, edited by Thomas Christiano and John Christman, 362–83. Wiley Online Library.

———. 2011. *Responsibility for Justice*. Oxford: Oxford University Press.

Ypi, Lea. 2017. "Structural Injustice and the Place of Attachment." *Journal of Practical Ethics* 5 (1): 1–21.

Zaino, Jeanne S. 1998. "Self-Respect and Rawlsian Justice." *Journal of Politics* 60 (3): 737–53.

Zakaras, Alex. 2004. "Isaiah Berlin's Cosmopolitan Ethics." *Political Theory* 32 (4): 495–518.

———. 2013. "A Liberal Pluralism: Isaiah Berlin and John Stuart Mill." *Review of Politics* 75 (1): 69–96.

Zdaniuk, Bozena, and John M. Levine. 2001. "Group Loyalty: Impact of Members' Identification and Contributions." *Journal of Experimental Social Psychology* 37 (6): 502–9.

Zheng, Robin. 2018. "What Is My Role in Changing the System? A New Model of Responsibility for Structural Injustice." *Ethical Theory and Moral Practice* 21 (4): 869–85.

Zink, James R. 2011. "Reconsidering the Role of Self-Respect in Rawls's *A Theory of Justice*." *Journal of Politics* 73 (2): 331–44.

# Index

10; egalitarian ethos and, 151, 228n5; egalitarian political theory and, xi, 4–5, 10, 12–13, 23, 148, 151–55, 162, 168–72, 227n2; equal opportunities versus outcomes and, 112–13; focus groups and, 30–31, 191–93, 195–96, 224nn6–7; government's role and, 113, 153; income inequality and, 12–13, 93–94, 227–4; individual versus structural solutions and, 86–87; justice and, 12, 14, 22, 153–55, 227n2; liberals versus conservatives and, 14, 22; moral, 15; neorepublicanism and, 223n23; pluralism and, 17, 151, 158–62, 228n6; procedural, 12–14, 31, 152; race and, 12–13; relational, 155, 171, 227n4; respect and, x–xi, 4, 10, 15, 26–33, 50, 53–54, 79, 102, 154–55, 169, 178–79; social justice worldview and, 79–80, 83, 101, 112, 156; substantive, 14, 17, 31, 33, 151–56, 161; surveys and, 29–30, 209, 213; Thomas Hobbes on, 227n1
Equality Attitudes Survey: administration of, 28; Bob vignette and, 40–44, 200–201, 210; characteristics of opposing partisans and, 38; heterogeneity of social networks and, 71–74; importance of respect and, 31–32; meaning of equality and, 29–30; party identification and ideology and, 21; political stereotyping and, 64, 73; research methods and, 199–200; respect for opposing partisans and, 34, 36, 42–46; survey questions and scales and, 208–9
ethnicity: COVID-19 and, 159; focus group demographics and, 190; immigration and, 114–15; national solidarity worldview and, 105–6; party affiliation and, 166–67; survey demographics and, 208; US history and, 110

Fahlquist, Jessica Nihlén, 131
Forrester, Katrina, 227n2
freedom and liberty: collective responsibility and, 147; equality and, 112–13, 156; individual and collective, 111; justice and, 111–12, 154, 156; LGBTQ identity and, 193, 194; loyalty and, 111; monism and, 156; national solidarity worldview and, 111–13, 118, 156; pluralism and, 158; procedural democracy and, 165; research methods and, 228AppCn1; social justice worldview and, 123; survey questions and scales and, 212–13; tribalism and, 111

Gates, Bill, 54
gender. See sex and gender
Grigg, Charles, 29
gun policy, 117–19, 121, 135, 212
Gutmann, Amy, 11, 53

Habitat for Humanity, 10
Haidt, Jonathan, 107, 127, 225n6
Hartman, Rachel, 179–80
Hayek, Friedrich, 83

Hazony, Yoram, 111, 132–33
Henry, Patrick, 10–11
Hobbes, Thomas, 153, 227n1
Hochschild, Arlie, ix, x
Horton, John, 9–10

immigration: American identity and, 180; citizenship status and, 121; Civic Respect Experiment and, 204; focus group protocols and, 192, 193; income inequality and, 192, 193; legal versus undocumented, 114, 115, 116–17, 167, 226ch5n4; libertarians and, 226ch534; Muslim ban and, 7; national solidarity worldview and, 113–15, 132; race and racism and, 167–68; refugees and, 116; rights and, 116–17; social justice worldview and, 113; xenophobia and, 167–68

Janoff-Bulman, Ronnie, 105, 127–28, 129, 132, 226–27n4
January 6, 2021, insurrection, 76, 152
Jefferson, Thomas, 110
justice: Democrats versus Republicans and, 85–92; distributive, 13–14; egalitarian, 154; equality and, 12, 14, 22, 155; focus group protocols and, 193, 194; immigration and, 113, 116–17; liberals versus conservatives and, 22, 154; liberty and, 111–12, 154, 156; moralization of issues and, 22–23; pluralism and, 5, 156; procedural democracy and, 165; race and, 6; respect and, 4–6, 8, 13, 50, 53, 96–100, 151, 153–56, 162; social justice as, 84; structural injustice and, 13–14. See also Social Justice and Solidarity Survey; social justice worldview

Kaepernick, Colin, 138
Kant, Immanuel, 15
Kendi, Ibram X., 129
Koltko-Rivera, Mark, 81

Latinos/Latinas, 19, 28, 68. See also ethnicity
legislative process, 10–11
Levine, John, 107
LGBTQ identity, 27, 81–82, 93, 108, 110, 193–94
liberal respect paradox: characteristics ascribed to opposing partisans and, 44–46; civic respect and, 8–9; collective responsibility, 126–27; equality and respect and, 29, 31, 102; general principle of respect and, 29, 33; intellect versus emotion and, 27; justice versus respect and, 8; loser effect and, 48–49; moralization of vote choice and, 41; national solidarity worldview and, 121; recognition respect and, 8–9, 15, 24; research methods and, x, xi; social justice worldview and, 79, 101; struggle to respect and, 37; testing of, 34; Trump effect and, 25, 36–37, 42–49, 50; vaccinations and, 147

# Chicago Studies in American Politics

A series edited by Susan Herbst, Lawrence R. Jacobs, Adam J. Berinsky, and Frances Lee; Benjamin I. Page, editor emeritus